AFGHANISTAN IN TRANSITION

Owing to its geo-strategic location and mineral wealth, Afghanistan has acquired significance in the inter-state politics of Asia as well as world politics during the past decades. This book discusses the Taliban's return which outlines the recent and current developments in contemporary Afghanistan.

The essays in this volume:

- Locate Afghanistan under globalisation and reflect on the state and nation-building efforts in Afghanistan by shedding light on the status of citizens, especially women.
- Analyse how the Taliban survived in all these years, and how it returned to power.
- Examine Afghanistan's relations with major powers like the USA, China, and India and explore the intricacies of ties between India, Pakistan, and Afghanistan within the Indian subcontinent.

Shedding light on a threshold moment in 21st Century world politics, this work will be useful to scholars and researchers in political science, international relations, sociology, area studies, and the interested general reader.

Rajen Harshé has taught Political Science and International Relations for more than four decades in places such as University of Hyderabad, Hyderabad, and South Asian University, New Delhi. He is a founding and the former Vice Chancellor of the Central University of Allahabad (2005–10), Prayagraj, India. He also worked as President of the G.B. Pant Social Science Institute (2014–20), Prayagraj. He has written extensively on African and International Affairs. His latest work is *Africa in World Affairs: Politics of Imperialism, the Cold War and Globalisation* (Oxon, New York, New Delhi, Routledge, 2019).

Dhananjay Tripathi is Associate Professor (Senior Grade) at the Department of International Relations, South Asian University (SAU), New Delhi, India. His recent publications are (ed) *Re-imagining Border Studies in South Asia* (2020, Routledge), co-edited *South Asia: Boundaries, Borders and Beyond* (2022, Routledge), *Afghanistan Post-2014: Power Configurations and Evolving Trajectories* (2016, Routledge). He has contributed several articles to reputed international academic journals.

AFGHANISTAN IN TRANSITION

From Taliban to Taliban

Second Edition

Edited by Rajen Harshé and Dhananjay Tripathi

Routledge
Taylor & Francis Group

LONDON AND NEW YORK

Designed cover image: Getty Images

First published 2025
by Routledge
4 Park Square, Milton Park, Abingdon, Oxon OX14 4RN

and by Routledge
605 Third Avenue, New York, NY 10158

Routledge is an imprint of the Taylor & Francis Group, an informa business

British Library Cataloguing-in-Publication Data
A catalogue record for this book is available from the British Library

ISBN: 978-0-367-22472-1 (hbk)
ISBN: 978-0-367-24313-5 (pbk)
ISBN: 978-0-429-28163-1 (ebk)

DOI: 10.4324/9780429281631

Typeset in Sabon
by Apex CoVantage, LLC

To the people of Afghanistan

CONTENTS

Preface and Acknowledgements   *ix*
Contributors   *xi*

PART I
Engaging With Afghanistan   1

1   Introduction   3
   Rajen Harshé and Dhananjay Tripathi

2   Situating Afghanistan in a Globalising World   11
   Rajen Harshé

3   'Pragmatism' Against 'Ideology' in Transnational
   Versus Regional Jihadist Groups: Situating the Taliban
   and Islamic State-Khorasan on a Conflict-Cooperation
   Continuum   28
   Mohit Sharma

PART II
What About the Taliban?   **45**

4   Through the Lens of Belief: The Taliban's Worldview
   and Its Influence   47
   Ahmed Sahal K.P.

5 Pieced Peace in Afghanistan: Evaluating the Peace
Processes for Ending the Conflict in Afghanistan
Post-2014 64
Chayanika Saxena

6 State Building in Talibanized Afghanistan: Lessons
From History 81
Arezou Nooristani

PART III
Afghanistan and Major Powers **107**

7 The US Role in Afghanistan: A Critical Overview 109
Dhananjay Tripathi

8 China's Engagement With Afghanistan: Quest for
Security, Stability and Strategy 124
Sankalp Gurjar

9 Is the Past a Prologue? Deciphering India's
North-West Engagement 145
Raghav Sharma

Index *156*

PREFACE AND ACKNOWLEDGEMENTS

Afghanistan has captured the attention of scholars and policymakers in South Asian and international affairs for several decades. Certain dramatic developments that occurred in two distinct phases abundantly highlight this proposition. Out of these, the first phase began with the commencement of the Second Cold War due to the Soviet military intervention in Afghanistan in 1979. Subsequently, the Soviet troops from Afghanistan had to withdraw in 1989, which gradually paved the way for the emergence of the Taliban regime in 1996. The second phase began with the ouster of the Taliban regime owing to the United States of America (USA)-led military intervention in Afghanistan in the aftermath of 9/11. Consequently, Afghanistan went through the experiment of building democracy from 2002 to 2021 with the help of the USA and its western allies. The second phase ended with the unceremonious exit of the USA's forces from Afghanistan and the advent of the Taliban to power in August 2021. Indeed, such dynamic and significant developments inspired us to take a critical look at the evolution of Afghanistan's politics, economy, society, and foreign policy in the context of contemporary international relations through the present volume. Incidentally, this is our second volume on Afghanistan.

This volume could be conceived and completed because of the unwavering support and invaluable contributions of our esteemed contributors. We are delighted and proud to present a collection of mostly new chapters in this volume that offer a fresh perspective on this subject. We extend our heartfelt thanks to each and every one of our contributors for their sincere and significant participation in this project.

This volume is an outcome of a well-attended conference on Afghanistan organised by the Department of International Relations of the South Asian

University (SAU) and supported by the Indian Council of World Affairs (ICWA). We are glad that we could reach the stage of publication after inviting, gathering, and revising the relevant papers on different themes.

We would be failing in our duty if we did not thank Ambassador Vijay Thakur Singh, the Director General (DG) of the ICWA, for generously supporting this conference.

We would also like to take this opportunity to record our thanks to the SAU administration for extending all possible support for successfully organising this conference.

Furthermore, we would like to express our gratitude to the new President of the SAU, Prof. K K Aggarwal, for his support and ongoing efforts to engage the university community with regional themes pertaining to South Asia. This is one small step in that direction.

We would like to express our thanks to Prof. Senthil Venugopal (Acting Vice President) and Prof. Muhammad Abulaish (Acting Registrar) for providing all necessary official clearances to organise this conference. Besides, we would like to acknowledge the constant help rendered by Prof. Sanjay Chaturvedi, Dean, Faculty of Social Sciences, South Asian University, to execute this project. Evidently, this was the first major offline event of the SAU after the COVID lockdown, and we are thankful for every possible help that came from different departments of the university, like the IT department, faculty assistant, and public relations officer (PRO).

We especially thank our keynote speakers, Dr. C Raja Mohan and Ambassador TCA Raghavan, for their stimulating ideas and thoughts, and Prof. Gulshan Sachdeva for chairing the first session and providing valuable suggestions.

Editing such a volume requires a lot of time and intellectual encouragement. Thanks to the Department of International Relations of the SAU for always being with us.

We would also like to express our gratitude to our publisher, Routledge, for accepting our edited volume and giving us enough time to complete this project.

Last but not least, thank you to our families for their tremendous emotional support and immense cooperation throughout all these years.

Rajen Harshé and Dhananjay Tripathi

CONTRIBUTORS

Sankalp Gurjar is an assistant professor (Geopolitics and Geo-economics), Gokhale Institute of Politics and Economics, Pune, India. He is the author of *The Superpowers' Playground: Djibouti and Geopolitics in the Indo-Pacific in the 21st Century* (Routledge, 2023). He works on geopolitics of the Indo-Pacific, South Asian geopolitics and India's national security.

Arezou Nooristani is a human rights activist, and before the takeover of the Taliban she was a diplomat at the Ministry of Foreign Affairs of Afghanistan; she was head of STOORAY magazine which was one of two publications of the ministry. At the same time, she was a university lecturer as well. Currently, she is a Ph.D. candidate in international relations at the South Asian University of New Delhi.

Ahmed Sahal K.P. is currently pursuing a doctorate in international relations at the South Asian University in New Delhi. He holds a bachelor's degree in electrical and electronics engineering and a master's degree in political science. Before beginning his Ph.D. program, he worked for two years as an electrical engineer in the oil and gas industry in Abu Dhabi, United Arab Emirates. Subsequently, he served as a project coordinator in an IT company based in Dubai for an additional two years. Following that, he dedicated two years to working in the Calicut chapter of the Institute of Objective Studies, New Delhi, where he played a crucial role in coordinating various research projects and organizing public programs.

Chayanika Saxena, Ph.D., is President's Graduate Fellow from the National University of Singapore. She holds a bachelor's (honours) degree in political science from the University of Delhi (New Delhi) and double master's in international relations from the South Asian University (New Delhi) and the S. Rajaratnam School of International Studies (Singapore). Her current doctoral research looks at the displacement experiences of the Afghan migrants and refugees in the Indian cities of New Delhi and Kolkata. Her works, peer-reviewed and opinion pieces, have appeared regularly in Indian and international journals, think-tanks and news outlets. She has also presented extensively on issues related to Afghanistan refugee and migration crises at different national and international forums. She is fluent in Hindi, English and Urdu, and has working knowledge of Dari-Persian and beginner's linguistic proficiency in Arabic.

Mohit Sharma is a doctoral candidate at the Department of International Relations, South Asian University, New Delhi. His research project delves into the 'cultural turn' in counterinsurgency strategies, with a specific focus on the Human Terrain System in Afghanistan. Previously, he worked as a research associate at the Centre for Air Power Studies, New Delhi, where he researched on the administrative structure of Afghan Taliban and tracked development of insurgent groups operating in the Afghanistan-Pakistan region. He has a post-graduate degree in international relations and area studies from the School of International Studies, Jawaharlal Nehru University, New Delhi.

Raghav Sharma is an associate professor and director at the Centre for Afghanistan Studies at the School of International Affairs, O.P. Jindal Global University. Prior to this he taught at the Good Governance Afghanistan Program at the Willy Brandt School of Public Policy, University of Erfurt, Germany and has worked in the humanitarian sector in Afghanistan. He is the author of *Nation, Ethnicity and the Conflict in Afghanistan: Political Islam and the Rise of Ethno-Politics (1992–1996)* (Routledge, 2017). Dr. Raghav Sharma has published with peer-reviewed journals; he occasionally contributes to media commentaries and has worked as a consultant with international non-governmental organizations in Afghanistan.

PART I
Engaging With Afghanistan

1

INTRODUCTION

Rajen Harshé and Dhananjay Tripathi

Who would have thought that within two decades there would be a day when the Taliban, who were ousted out of power in Afghanistan in 2001, would walk back into the corridors of power in August 2021? The tenacity with which the Taliban successfully resisted the United States of America (USA) and its allied powers was indeed remarkable. Consequently, the USA virtually had to flee from Afghanistan. Although, the Taliban is back with more flexible agenda towards state, society, religion and foreign policy, it has not shown signs of any substantial change. Especially, its attitude towards emancipation of women continues to remain the same. Such attitudes relegate women to secondary status and throw them into background. In spite of this similar attitude towards women, there is still something different from the past in the *modus operandi* of the Taliban. The post-2021 Taliban is more confident and willing to engage with the world. This booming confidence can be safely attributed to the fact that they are considered as victors forcing the military super-power of the post-Cold War world like the USA to retreat from Afghanistan for all practical purposes. In that case, did the USA, along with its allied powers, succeed in achieving its objective in Afghanistan? Going by the statement of the Biden administration, the USA had completed its mission. According to the White House statement,

As he laid out to the American people, after twenty years, the United States had accomplished its mission in Afghanistan: to remove from the battlefield the terrorists who attacked the United States on 9/11, including Osama bin Laden, and degrade the terrorist threat to the United States. Over two decades, the United States had also – along with our NATO allies and partners – spent hundreds of billions of dollars training and

DOI: 10.4324/9780429281631-2

equipping the Afghan National Defense and Security Forces (ANDSF) and supporting successive Afghan governments. At the outset, America's goal was never to nation-build. But, over time, this is what America drifted into doing.

(The White House, 2023)

While it is true that the USA did not intend to stay in Afghanistan for nation-building, it remained involved in Afghanistan's internal affairs. At one stage, the USA had put its full weight behind Hamid Karzai (2002–2014) by giving (tacit) support to him as the head of the interim government after the ouster of the Taliban out of Kabul in 2001. Ironically, at the Bonn conference of December 2001, around 80 per cent of the delegates had voted in favour of Abdul Sattar Sirat, who was from the Uzbek ethnic minority. Western media published his name as the likely head of the interim government (McCarthy and MacAskill, 2001). The idea behind backing Karzai so far as the USA is concerned was that he belonged to the majority ethnic community of Pashtuns. In substance, the USA was keenly involved in the internal affairs of Afghan which subsumed sustaining Afghanistan in its attempt at the project of 'nation-building' (Whitlock, 2021).

From 2001, the USA remained on grounds in Afghanistan on some pretext or the other and kept supporting the government and the Afghan Army. Its exit in 2021 was, in a way, not sudden but a well-thought strategy. Moreover, the USA had not estimated the chaos it might create in the aftermath its exit from Afghanistan. Unsurprisingly, the pictures of people making desperate attempts to leave Afghanistan in the media shook the world. Such visuals of how ordinary Afghans stormed into the Kabul airport, risking their lives to flee the country, are still fresh in our minds. The decision to leave Afghanistan by the USA was made in February 2020 after it signed a peace deal agreement with the Taliban at Doha. However, the process of negotiations was not truly intra-Afghan and inclusive. Strangely, the then Afghan President Ashraf Ghani regime (2014–2021), was not a part of the process since the Taliban refused to accept the Ghani regime as a *de jure* entity. Eventually, the Taliban toppled the Ghani regime in Kabul on 15 August 2021, seized Kabul and took control of the government without making prior legal arrangements towards transfer of power with the previous regime headed by Ashraf Ghani.

Generally, the presence of a foreign force in a country often draws the ire of citizens, but Afghanistan has been used to such interventions due to its inherent political instability. In fact, the Soviet military intervention in Afghanistan had started the phase of the second Cold War in the world politics in 1979. Apparently, the Soviet military intervened in Afghanistan at the behest of the then Afghan government to support the latter on ideological grounds. In the process, the USA decided to support Afghan Mujahedeen with arms against the Soviet army. Besides, Pakistan as a frontline state accommodated the Mujahedeen on its soil, Saudi Arabia provided financial assistance in the war and the USA surreptitiously supplied arms to anti-Soviet holy warriors in a conjoint operation against the Red army. It was also argued in certain quarters that the USA resisted the Soviets because the former wanted take revenge against the latter for its defeat in Vietnam (Haqqani, 2013).

After the process of the withdrawal of the Soviet troops in 1989, the USA ceased to play an active role in Afghanistan. This created a power vacuum that resulted in civil war and political chaos in Afghanistan. The Taliban was formed during that phase of turmoil which promised order and peace to the people (Zaeef, 2010). However, the Taliban soon realised that it was not easy for them to control the whole of Afghanistan since the country was divided on ethnic lines and the powerful warlords were not going to accept the diktat of one organisation. The Taliban faced stiff resistance while countering their enemies. Consequently, they started networking with Islamic radicals from other countries, gave refuge to Osama bin Laden and relied on the Pakistan intelligence agency, the Inter-Services Intelligence (ISI).

Both bin Laden and the ISI supported the Taliban but had their own objectives in the politics of the region and the world. Osama bin Laden had already expanded his terrorist outfit, namely Al Qaeda, by using Afghanistan as the base for its operations. He successfully established links with the Islamic radical groups in other parts of the world and promoted the idea of global Jihad. It was from the soil of Afghanistan that Osama bin Laden efficiently planned and executed terror attacks on the USA that led to the fall of the World Trade Center (WTC), known colloquially as 'the twin towers', on 11 September 2001, or '9/11'. Moreover, Afghanistan and the ISI also began to dabble in fellow South Asian countries such as India. Evidently, the ISI used the Taliban to extend support to the terror groups operating in the states of Jammu and Kashmir of India (Shahzad, 2011). However, it was the Taliban's association with Al Qaeda and the fall of the twin towers that pushed the USA into action.

As a result, the USA decided to dislodge the Taliban from Kabul and eliminate Osama bin Laden. It succeeded in both. While the Taliban regime was overthrown in 2001, Osama bin Laden was killed in an astonishing military operation in Abbottabad, Pakistan in May 2011. However, the cost of twenty-year protracted military and economic engagement in the Afghanistan imbroglio for the USA was roughly $2.3 trillion. Despite such a heavy cost, it failed to defeat the Taliban emphatically. Apart from the material costs, owing to the post-9/11 war with the Taliban, the USA lost more than 700 personnel in Iraq and Afghanistan and many war veterans committed suicide (Watson Institute International and Public Affairs, 2021). However, the loss of Kabul in 2001 and the death of bin Laden and had not impacted the morale of the Taliban. They continued to combat against the foreign forces, including what they believed to be puppet regimes and not the valid Afghan government. As in the earlier days, the Taliban had unambiguous support from Pakistan. Having been exhausted in Afghanistan, the USA, since the days of the Obama administration, thought of leaving Afghanistan.

After the eventual withdrawal, Afghanistan once again went in the hands of the Taliban. This time, the Taliban agreed not to support any anti-USA terror group. The Taliban also committed that it would not allow anyone to use the Afghan territory to wage war on another country. Such assurances gave the impression that it is a new Taliban or what is described as the Taliban 2.0. It would be futile, however, to reach hasty conclusions about the nature of the Taliban 2.0 at this stage. In the 1990s, apart from the Taliban's closeness with various terrorist groups, it was also condemned for severely violating the human rights, particularly those of women. During the reign of the Taliban from 1996 to 2001, Afghan women faced unprecedented repression and virtually had no civil rights once a girl child entered into the adulthood. Thus, the Taliban, in its second innings, will not merely be evaluated on what is promised on the issue of terrorism but also on how it protects the civil rights of the ordinary Afghan citizens. And the signs emerging out of Afghanistan since 2021 do not appear encouraging.

Unfortunately, as far as the emancipatory project for women is concerned, even today, there is no sign of change in the ideology of the Taliban, and Afghan women once again are facing harsh diktats that curtail even the fundamental right to education of women. As of now, the Taliban has suspended girls' education above the sixth standard. Women are barred from employment, and recently, even beauty salons are closed in Afghanistan. Indeed, these ever-shrinking political and social spaces for women in Afghanistan are viewed with grimness in the rest of the world. This time, the Taliban has come back to power not through armed insurrection but by signing a deal with the USA. Although the USA is still a military super-power, it appears drained out in the context of Afghanistan.

The re-entry of the Taliban in Kabul is being treated like a victory over the forces of USA-led imperialism. So, while the Taliban is willing to give assurances to the world about snapping ties with international terror groups, it is hesitant to change itself politically and socially. They follow Sharia law and defend its rigorous implementation, citing examples of other Islamic countries. More often, scholars and activists contend that the Taliban is harsher and more rudimentary in its interpretation of Sharia (Vohra, 2021). The Taliban has shown no remorse or rethinking on social issues, leaving us to draw our own conclusions.

The confident Taliban 2.0 is indeed keeping itself closed to the outer world on political issues, although economically they are eager to integrate with the world economy. But the Western countries, at this juncture, are invested in dealing with Russia and its ongoing war in the Ukraine, with little energy left to pay attention to the other regions. Moreover, after exiting Afghanistan, it is hard to assume that the West will show much interest in the country. However, it is not easy for countries in the region to ignore Afghanistan.

Afghanistan will keep drawing the attention of academics, activists and the general public across the world. In short, the behaviour of the Taliban as a governing power will remain under scrutiny and this edited volume is precisely meant to discuss recent and current developments in contemporary Afghanistan. The book is divided into three sections and ten chapters including the Introduction. The three sections are thematically organized in the following manner. The first section locates Afghanistan under globalisation and reflects on the state and nation-building efforts in Afghanistan by shedding light on the status of citizens, especially women. The second section of the book is an analysis of the Taliban. Today no discussion of Afghanistan is comprehensive without a proper examination of how the Taliban survives in all these years, and how it returned to power. The last section examines Afghanistan's relations with major powers like the USA, China and India, and explores the intricacies of ties between India, Pakistan and Afghanistan within the Indian subcontinent.

Before dealing with the substance of individual chapters, at this stage, we would like to note that two chapters in this work, such as those written by Rajen Harshé and Dhananjay Tripathi, are revised and updated versions of their earlier chapters that appeared in their earlier co-edited work with a title *Afghanistan Post-2014: Power Configurations and Evolving Trajectories* (Routledge, 2016). Keeping this in view, the sequence of this work could be stated as follows.

After the Introduction, the first section begins with Rajen Harshé's comprehensive chapter that locates Afghanistan in a globalising world. By taking historical and geo-strategic factors into account, it situates contemporary Afghanistan in the context of interventionist/imperialist powers like the former Soviet Union and the USA. After briefly touching upon the democratic experiment (2001–21), it explores the nature of the structure of terrorism in Afghanistan and its wider impact. Subsequently, the chapter proceeds to highlight the role and the stakes of external powers in Afghanistan to appraise the nature of regime transformation and global realignments in Afghanistan. The second chapter is by Mohit Sharma, who has taken us to the more substantial theme of the conflict-cooperation continuum between the Taliban and the Islamic State – Khorasan (IS-K). The relationship between the two is critical for the future of Afghanistan. Any contemporary understanding of Afghanistan is incomplete without deeply analysing Taliban as a militant organisation. Taliban was chased out of Kabul in 2001, struggled for twenty years and returned to Kabul again in 2021. Today, major stakeholders have accepted (if not openly) that without the Taliban, we cannot discuss Afghanistan.

The second section of the book, therefore, is focused on the Taliban, examining various aspect of its organisation. There are three chapters in this section. The first chapter in this section is by Ahmad Sahal K.P., who has explained how the Taliban views the world and how their interpretation shapes its policies and engagement with the world. There is a lot of debate on the Taliban 2.0, and this chapter is quite useful in giving us a perspective on this theme. How the Taliban did overcome challenges posed by the USA remains a difficult question to answer. The popular perception of the Taliban is that it is a militant organisation that excels in guerrilla warfare. However, contrary to this perception, the Taliban successfully exhibited diplomatic skills and successfully concluded a peace deal with the USA in February 2020. The second chapter in this section is on the peace process written by Chayanika Saxena. This well-researched chapter gives us a required insight to better understand the Taliban. Chayanika Saxena has analysed three peace processes – *Murree Process* (2015), Quadrilateral Coordination Group on Afghanistan (QCG, 2017), and the Moscow-Format (2016–18). It is essential to study how these peace processes have evolved and their major outcomes. Since the Taliban is back in power in Afghanistan, they are facing difficult questions about the governance in a war-torn country. They must be realising that governing is more complicated than waging and fighting a war with an outside power. With no formidable internal resistance to the Taliban and with absolute control over the country, it is expected that the Taliban will deliver something on account of governance. Arezou Nooristani's chapter covers the history of state-building in Afghanistan in different periods. The author has underscored the difficulties of state-building in the Taliban-controlled Afghanistan. Especially, she has unravelled how the Taliban's notion of the state and orthodox Islam are intricately intertwined. Overall, this section examines the Taliban from a different lens and gives us valuable details about the organisation.

Coming to the book's third and last section, we have three articles examining the engagement of the USA, China, India and Pakistan with Afghanistan. Historically, these countries have maintained close links with Afghanistan. They have demonstrated an interest, strategic or otherwise, with different regimes of Afghanistan. At the same time, owing to their varying interests, they lack a common approach towards Afghanistan. Nevertheless, they would like to ensure stability and peace in Afghanistan. In this section, the first chapter by Dhananjay Tripathi is about the USA's policy towards Afghanistan. The chapter raises pertinent questions regarding the success of the USA's policy in Afghanistan. Tripathi analyses how the USA's presence in Afghanistan post-9/11 cannot be termed in simple and straightforward terms. There were apparent lacunas right from the beginning, and despite the initial successes, the USA had to struggle in Afghanistan.

The next chapter by Sankalp Gurjar is about China's policy toward Afghanistan. After Britain, Soviet Russia and the US, China is the fourth major power that is taking an active interest in Afghan affairs. China is willing to expand its political, economic and commercial presence in the country. Domestic insecurities and strategic interests play a role in China's engagement with Afghanistan. The chapter sheds light on China's continued engagement with Afghanistan irrespective of the regime type. Sankalp Gurjar offers a critical perspective on the evolving Sino-Afghan ties. The third chapter is by Raghav Sharma that discusses the complex and triangular association between India, Pakistan and Afghanistan. Without overlooking the complicated trajectories of Afghan history that were essentially situated in the context of the history of the Indian subcontinent with the advent of British imperialism, Raghav Sharma presents a nuanced and balanced view of the interrelationships between the three countries. His succinct presentation of the events of the past allows us to look at the contemporary Afghanistan more critically.

Having summarised the essence of this edited work, as the editors we would like to express our heartfelt gratitude towards the Indian Council of World Affairs (ICWA), New Delhi, for generously supporting us in this project. The book is an outcome of a seminar organised by the Department of International Relations of the South Asian University in September 2022. We would like to take this opportunity to thank all our contributors. Although some of them did not participate in the conference physically, they accepted our request for joining us in this endeavour. This is the second book on Afghanistan by the editors, a country where politics keep changing at a pace which sometimes makes us rethink our ideas, repeatedly. Thus, it may appear that some of the relevant themes related to contemporary Afghanistan are not covered in the book. We acknowledge it most humbly with an assurance that our academic engagement with Afghanistan will continue. Consequently, we will certainly address critical gaps in this volume in our forthcoming endeavours on Afghanistan.

References

Haqqani, H. (2013). *Magnificent Delusions Pakistan, the United States, and an Epic History of Misunderstanding.* New Delhi: Thomson Press India Lt.

McCarthy, R., and MacAskill, E. (2001, December 3). *King's Aide Is Favourite to be Next Leader.* Retrieved July 2023, from The Guardian: www.theguardian.com/world/2001/dec/03/afghanistan.ewenmacaskill1

Shahzad, S. S. (2011). *Inside Al – Qaeda and the Taliban: Beyond Bin Laden and 9/11.* London: Pluto Press.

Vohra, A. (2021, 21 October). *The Taliban's Sharia Is the Most Brutal of All.* Retrieved July 2023, from Foreign Affairs: https://foreignpolicy.com/2021/10/13/the-talibans-sharia-is-the-most-brutal-of-all/

Watson Institute International and Public Affairs. (2021, July). *Costs of War*. Brown University. Retrieved July 2023, from Watson Institute International and Public Affairs.

The White House. (2023, April 6). *The US Withdrawal from Afghanistan*. Retrieved July 2023, from The White House: www.whitehouse.gov/briefing-room/statements-releases/2023/04/06/the-u-s-withdrawal-from-afghanistan/

Whitlock, C. (2021). *The Afghanistan Papers a Secret History of the War*. New York: Simon and Schuster.

Zaeef, A. S. (2010). *My Life With the Taliban*. London: C Hurst and Co.

2

SITUATING AFGHANISTAN IN A GLOBALISING WORLD

Rajen Harshé

I: Introduction

Afghanistan, a geo-strategically significant landlocked state that essentially links Asia's major regions such as south, central and west Asia through its territory, has inevitably been a focal site of struggles between diverse contending world powers and forces. For the past two centuries some of the major imperialist powers such as the Great Britain, the former Soviet Union and the United States of America (US), during different phases of history, have ventured to consolidate their hold over Afghanistan with a long-term strategy to shape politics and political economy of Asia.

Admittedly, Afghanistan also functioned as a buffer state between the British imperialism in India and the Czarist imperialism in Central Asia in the late nineteenth and the early twentieth centuries. Besides, the Soviet military intervention in Afghanistan in 1979 triggered a phase of the new Cold War between the US and what was then the Soviet Union. This period also threw up several new actors including the US, Pakistan, Saudi Arabia and the Mujahideen that were committed to ousting the atheist communists from Afghanistan. In the process, the seeds of terror emanating from radicalisation of Islam were sown in southwest Asia. The rise of terrorism, in its turn, was linked with the production of drugs, poppy cultivation and the sale of arms. Unsurprisingly, in their bid to oust the Soviet troops, as will be argued later, the ground was prepared for factional as well as intra- and inter-state violence in southwest Asia.

Such violence eventually reached its intolerable limits, as far as the US was concerned, when the twin towers of the World Trade Center were brought down on 11 September 2001 (9/11) in the city of New York. From 1996 to 2001 the Taliban regime apart from striking cordial ties with a multinational

DOI: 10.4324/9780429281631-3

terrorist outfit such as Al Qaeda and its leader, Osama bin Laden, had become notorious for violation of human rights and gender discrimination. It was the rise of radical Islam through the advent of the Taliban that gave alarming signals. Thus, the devastating impact of the terrorist violence was brought into sharp focus under the Bush administration (2001–2009) when the US declared war on terror after 2001 and intervened militarily, along with its North Atlantic Treaty Organization (NATO) allies in Afghanistan to combat terrorism and restore peace, order, and democracy. Although the democratic experiment lasted for almost twenty years, eventually the Taliban was able to seize power from the Ashraf Ghani regime on the 15 August 2021 and the US forces had to retreat from Afghanistan quite unceremoniously.

This article sheds light on the developments in Afghanistan in a broader context of globalisation that witnessed alliances and counter alliances between the forces that were at once transnational and local. By examining interconnections between national, regional, and global dimensions of the Afghan problem since the 1970s, the article demonstrates how through speedy and unusual transition from transnational to global, Afghanistan has become an important nerve centre of world politics under globalisation. Before tracing the evolution of developments in Afghanistan it would be worth reflecting on the processes that characterise globalisation.

II: Substance of Globalisation and Its Relevance to Afghanistan

The term globalisation essentially denotes multiple economic, political, social, and cultural processes that are simultaneously at work between states and societies across the world. In fact, globalisation, especially after the disintegration of the Soviet Union in 1991, has opened up new forms of cooperation, through networks of regional organisations, as well as conflicts, including those between the state and non-state actors. Ostensibly, globalisation has been facilitating free movement of goods, capital, services, technology, knowledge, finance, terror, diseases, information, and people, leading to the compression of time and space where ideally the notion of a global village could be perceived. However, this description of globalisation may not be accurate because it hides underlying forces that are stimulating such varied movements leading to definite shrinkage in time and space. To put it tersely, globalisation has inextricable links with diverse forms of capitalism. Capitalism signifies organisation of production whereby means of production are owned privately or by corporate bodies with shareholders. As a mode of production and the world system, it has constantly destroyed and recreated itself according to circumstances by accumulating capital through surplus accrued owing to profits, rents, and dividends on the world scale. Admittedly, apart from conventional capitalist countries of North America, Western European countries, and other countries such as Japan, China, Brazil,

India, Indonesia, Malaysia, South Africa, etc., are in the process of evolving their own variety of capitalist state, society, and culture. At the same time the phase of globalisation need not be reduced to only capitalism. There are movements of resistance locally and transnationally that are constantly agitating against capitalism at different levels allowing capitalism to be reformed. Even die-hard capitalists have offered sharp critique of unbridled exploitation that capitalism had brought in its wake after the Cold War to ensure that capitalism functions smoothly by observing minimum standards of justice (Soros 1997).

Unprecedented movement of capital and dynamism in currency mobilisation has made the current phase of globalisation unique by spreading new forms of inequalities, migrations, and unemployment in different parts of the world. For instance, in the erstwhile Third World one comes across exclusive localities in urban centres where people lead lives like those in the First World. In contrast, thanks to migrations or innate socio-economic inequalities there are localities in the urban centres of the First World where people lead impoverished lives like the people in the poorer countries. Besides, imperialism as a phenomenon signifying asymmetric forms of interdependence between materially advanced and backward societies is alive under globalisation as a by-product of capitalism (Harshé 1997: 10). One can also construe imperialism in its multilateral forms by analysing the dominance of the global North in the world political economy.

What is more, as Negri and Hardt have argued that as against imperialism there is rise of empire, under globalisation. The notion of empire denotes decentred and deterritorialising apparatus of rule that incorporates the entire globe within its expanding frontiers (Negri and Hardt 2001: XII). They have elaborated at length flexible hierarchies, hybrid identities, and a variety of actors as also networks that constitute an Empire. This Empire, which is a product of the free flow of factors of production such as money, technology, goods, and people across the frontiers, is in search of theorisation.

It needs to be underscored that terrorism as a phenomenon which happens to be relevant in the Afghan context has acquired global dimensions through multinational terrorist outfits like Al-Qaeda and Al Shabaab. Apparently, the world under globalisation is becoming borderless with the gradual erosion of the primacy of the nation states. However, this could be a fairly superficial assertion. For, even though the phase of globalisation has witnessed the rise of transnational regimes such as the World Trade Organization (WTO) or supranational organisations from the European Union (EU) and diverse regional organisations including the South Asian Association for Regional Cooperation (SAARC), the state is the primary and indispensable unit in their making. Similarly, the so-called borderless world could also be a myth. Indeed, new borders are being drawn all over the world. The rise of Central Asian Republics after the fall of the Soviet Union or the resurgence of ethno-nationalism in Eastern Europe abundantly demonstrates how the transition is taking place in different parts of the world from empire to nation. Moreover, the functioning of the developed regional organisation like the EU is characterised by Germany's capacity to assert the German pre-eminence in the realm of finance. Such assertion is accompanied by protest from weaker nationalities such as Spain, Portugal, and Greece which aspire to become appropriately accommodated within the EU in spite of their worsening economic conditions due to global financial crisis. Furthermore, after the Brexit of 2016, the EU also has lost its erstwhile pre-eminence in Europe. Besides, Germany and France are unable to manage their multi-cultural societies that are becoming plagued by anti-immigrant sentiments as well as Islamophobia.

In fact, the processes of globalisation were unleashed by President George H. W. Bush after the Cold War ended in 1991. Paradoxically, under President Donald Trump (2017–21) the US ushered in the era of 'America First'. It walked out of Iran nuclear deal signed in 2015 and the Paris accord on climate change signed in 2015, restrained from shouldering the responsibility of the NATO alliance, and became indifferent to the idea of Trans-Pacific Partnership. Domestically, the US rigorously began to follow anti-immigration policy, opposed free trade, and turned protectionist and aggravated discriminations against races other than white races within the US. In light of the US example it can be asserted that the processes of globalisation have no single leader. As a multi-dimensional and multi-layered reality, the processes of globalisation are volatile and constantly in a state of flux.

Indeed, Afghanistan has to be located in the complex context mentioned earlier. Evidently, the issues related to ethnicity, nationality, tribalism, and borders are alive in the context of most of the developing countries of the erstwhile Third World or for that matter even in any other parts of the world despite globalisation. In Afghanistan the powerful landlords too have had their say in determining the course of political events. Most of these issues are influenced by globalisation on one hand and they are also shaping the processes of globalisation, on the other. Afghanistan is a case in point (Jalalzai and Jefferess 2011). Afghanistan and its predicament need to be placed in a context within which porous borders coupled with ethnic-tribal strife has been co-existing along with umpteen modes of transnational realities that include the manoeuvrings of imperialist powers such the former Soviet Union as well as the US. Especially, in the case of US the presence of international troops mustered through transnational coalition of forces, the flow of arms and drugs, and general global interest in registering presence in Afghanistan of the major powers seems evident. In essence even under globalisation any discussion regarding borders, ethnic or national, is legitimate. Among the borders in Afghanistan, the significance of the Durand Line could be placed in perspective as follows.

III: Durand Line

Afghanistan is a multi-ethnic and multilingual country. Among the ethnic groups, Pashtuns are roughly forty-two per cent, followed by other groups such as Tajiks, Hazaras, Uzbeks, Aimaks, Turkmen, and Baloch. Moreover, Pashto and Dari are both official languages of Afghanistan. Considering Afghanistan's geopolitical location, its ethno-cultural diversities, and porous borders, the geographical space of Afghanistan has been vulnerable to invasions for a long time. For instance, in the fifth century BC, Cyrus the Great, who was founder of the Persian Empire, had invaded present-day Afghanistan on his way to Hindu Kush. Likewise, over the last 1,500 years, Alexander the Great, the Scythians, the Parthians, the White Huns, the Arabs, the Turks, and the Mongols also invaded Afghanistan from the northwest. During the entire nineteenth century the rivalry between Britain and Russia to control central Asia/Afghanistan was vividly described as the Great Game. The British, in their own ways, chose to draw a map of Afghanistan with an idea of developing Afghanistan as a buffer zone between the British Empire in India and the Czarist Empire in Central Asia. In the process Mortimer Durand, the then British Secretary based in British India, drew the border between Afghanistan and India (currently Pakistan) that is known as the Durand Line.

After two Anglo-Afghan wars (1838 and 1878) the Durand Line came into existence as a result of an agreement between Amir Abdur Rehaman Khan of Afghanistan and British India in 1893. It is 2,640 kilometres long. By signing this agreement with Britain, Afghanistan relinquished a few districts, including Swat, Chitral, and Chagel, and had gained elsewhere in Nuristan or Asmar in northeastern Afghanistan, areas which it had not controlled traditionally. The Durand Line cuts across Pashtun tribal areas to farther south of the Baluchistan region. It politically divides Pashtuns, Baluch, and other ethnic groups. It also demarcates Khyber Pakhtunkhwa, the Federally Administered Areas, Baluchistan, and Pakistan-controlled Kashmir/Gilgit Baltistan of northern and western Pakistan from the northeastern and southern provinces of Afghanistan. Geopolitically, it is considered among the most dangerous borders in contemporary international relations (Rahi 2014). Subsequently, the Rawalpindi Treaty of 1919 only slightly modified the earlier agreement of 1893 that had drawn the Durand Line. Thus, even though globalisation theoretically is supposed to eliminate symbolic borders, the notion of borders, continues to be a burning issue.

In fact, the Durand Line is not recognised by the Pashtuns on either side of the divide. Nevertheless, the Nadir Shah regime in Afghanistan (1929–1933) had recognised the Durand Line as an international border (Saikal 2004: 102). Ironically, Pakistan, in the eastern part, has had to deal with India so far as the Kashmir issue is concerned, and in the western part with Afghanistan as far as the Durand Line, and also the aspirations of Pakistani Pashtuns, are concerned. Since Pakistan, during the Cold War phase (1945–90), chose to seek US military assistance and aid in 1953, Afghanistan turned to the then Soviet Union. From 1953 to 1973 the Soviets supported regimes in Kabul with aid and military assistance and trained civilian and military personnel from Afghanistan in Soviet Russia. However, the current situation in Afghanistan could be placed in a proper perspective after analysing a few significant developments that commenced Afghanistan's prolonged search for political stability.

IV: Afghanistan in Search of Political Stability

Afghanistan witnessed speedy political transition with the ouster of King Mohammad Zahir Shah who was replaced by Mohammad Daoud in July 1973. Daoud chose to establish a more progressive regime by proclaiming Afghanistan as a republic. He also wanted to modernise Afghanistan and reduce corruption and inefficiency under his regime. Since the primary source of aid to Afghanistan was the Soviet Union, Daoud allowed the quasi-Marxist People's Democratic Party of Afghanistan (PDPA) to develop and play a significant role in politics at the risk of being targeted by it in the future (Lowther 2007: 127). The Daoud regime was overthrown on 28 April 1978 after a bloody military coup, aided by the PDPA. Nur Mahammad Taraki emerged as the President of the Revolutionary Council and the Prime Minister of the new Democratic Republic of Afghanistan (DRC) after the coup. Taraki's manner of functioning, especially his brutal course of reforms, fuelled insurgency in Nuristan. Subsequently, a former Prime Minister and Defence Minister, namely Hafizullah Amin, replaced Taraki through a palace coup. In a word, by the time Red army paratroopers began landing in Kabul on 24 December 1979, the political conditions in Afghanistan were chaotic and almost unmanageable.

V: The Soviet Intervention in Afghanistan and the New Cold War

There are a few developments which had a lasting impact after the Soviet intervention that warrant closer scrutiny. Firstly, the decade-long (1979–89) Soviet military presence in Afghanistan led to realignment of forces in politics of southwest and west Asia due to the US's interest in repealing the Soviet advances in the region. The US, especially after the Islamic revolution and the fall of Shah regime in Iran in 1979, had already waged the so called New Cold War against the "evil empire" of the Soviet Union. In every other part of the globe, the Reagan administration in the early Eighties was containing the possible advances of the Soviet Union and its allies. It tried to regroup America's west European allies along with Japan. It went to the extent of supporting dictatorial regimes, e.g. Pinochet (Chile), Mobutu (Zaire), Zia ul-Haq (Pakistan),

Marcos (the Philippines), etc., and apartheid regimes in South Africa and the Zionist state of Israel to achieve this objective. In southwest and west Asia, the US aimed at withdrawal of the Soviet troops from Afghanistan. In its bid to contest and eventually eliminate Soviet military presence in Afghanistan, the US used Pakistan as a frontline state and poured and funnelled arms to combat the Soviet forces through Pakistan. In fact, the Zia regime (1978–1986) in Pakistan could perceive the Soviet intervention in Afghanistan as an opportunity to exploit the US and its economic and military support. Pakistan took full advantage of its location and offered a ready base to forces that were going to fight for the withdrawal of the Soviet troops.

The US went as far as to seek support from the holy warriors or diverse Mujahideen groups who were prepared to declare *Jihad* against the communist presence in Afghanistan. Obviously, all such groups landed on the soil of Pakistan. They were financed by Saudi Arabia and armed by the US through the Inter-Services Intelligence (ISI) of Pakistan. The alignment of Pakistan, Saudi Arabia, the US, and Mujahideen groups represented an unusual coalition that eventually proved potent enough to put sufficient pressure on the Soviet Union to withdraw its troops. In any case, in view of the overall rising military expenditure due to external military commitments in east Europe and Afghanistan and the declining performance of the Soviet economy, the Soviet Union too required breathing space which it earned by withdrawing almost 100,000 Soviet military personnel from Afghanistan in 1989. By then the Soviet Union was in the twilight of transition, owing to ideas associated with *glasnost* and *perestroika* which in effect were leading towards liberalisation of the Soviet system and economy.

VI: The Advent of Global Terror

Thanks to such withdrawal, the radical Islamic groups which constituted Mujahideen forces emerged victorious. Unsurprisingly, Osama bin Laden who fought against the Soviet intervention emerged as a hero among the radical Islamic groupings in west Asia (Mockaitis 2011). After 1989, emboldened by his Afghan adventure, Osama bin Laden went as far as to challenge the Saudi king for allowing the US to station its troops in Saudi Arabia during the first US-Iraq war of 1991 over the latter's occupation of Kuwait. Eventually he had to flee Saudi Arabia and he left for Sudan where at Khartoum he could train terrorist groups from different parts of the Muslim world until 1995. The rise of the Taliban regime in Afghanistan in 1996 gave Osama bin Laden and his organisation, Al-Qaeda, a territorial base and proper state support to function. The Taliban regime and Al-Qaeda could see eye to eye in terms of promoting Islamic radicalism and playing a key role in the Arab Muslim world. As far as Al-Qaeda is concerned, Israel, the US, and even India, due to the Kashmir question, were its enemies owing to the way they were treating Muslims. In a word, terrorism was now being housed in Afghanistan with state patronage. Paradoxically, even though Al-Qaeda was anti-US, it was the latter's policy of embracing and supporting Mujahedeen groups against the Soviets that had proved counterproductive enough to bring into existence the antithesis of the US in the form of Al-Qaeda and even the Taliban.

In fact, Al-Qaeda, as an antithesis of the US-led imperialism, also began to operate on a global scale (Harshé 2008). It continuously expanded its activities in more than eighty countries of the world. Osama bin Laden formed the World Islamic Front in 1998 and struck alliances with the other radical Islamic groupings. It needs to be underscored that Jaish-e Mohammed (JeM) and Lashkar e-Taiba (LeT) or Jamad-Ul Dawa (JuD), two significant terrorist outfits associated with terrorist assaults in different Indian cities, almost functioned like affiliates of Al-Qaeda (Harshé 2003). To put it briefly, the phase of globalisation offered the anti-communist coalition of forces, built under the leadership of the US, and the multinational terrorist outfits such as Al-Qaeda a far wider geographical space where states as well as societies from different parts of the world could be induced to carry their respective crusades.

What is more, Pakistan from 1996–2001 had not merely recognised and supported the Taliban regime in Afghanistan but also had chosen to covertly resolve some of its outstanding issues through promoting terrorist outfits. Actually, America's Afghan war had flooded Pakistan with innumerable problems. On its western front Pakistan had to tackle and resolve the problem of refugees which were more than five million people.[1] The war with the Soviets had allowed an arms bazaar to flourish in Pakistan. Arms acquired by the ISI were freely floating in the black markets of that bazaar. This had endangered internal security. To add fuel to the fire, poppy cultivation had become a regular feature on the Afghanistan-Pakistan border. In fact, Afghanistan virtually ceased the production of consumable agrarian products in the 1990s and turned arable land into poppy fields for the production and consumption of heroin which apparently increased farmers' annual income from $600 to $6,500 (Lowther 2007: 129). In the process, drugs were being sold for arms. Pakistan was also adding to its military strength by purchasing arms through transacting drugs. In spite of Pakistan's support for the Taliban regime, General Musharraf-led Pakistan chose to join the US-led war on terror declared by President George W. Bush after the twin towers were brought down by Al-Qaeda in the terrorist attack in New York on 9/11.

VII: Afghanistan After 9/11

After the fall of the twin towers in 2001, the Bush administration was determined to carry the war against terror to its logical conclusion. It swiftly moved into action to install a democratic regime in Afghanistan by toppling the Taliban regime in 2001. Further, no stone was left unturned in the search for Osama bin Laden in the Af-Pak region. What is more, the domestic politics of Afghanistan as well as the politics in the west Asian region was globalised as the International Security Assistance Forces (ISAF) were established under the auspices of the United Nations Security Council Resolution No. 1386 of December 2001 to aid the Afghan interim administration. The ISAF primarily was constituted by the US and its allies from the NATO and it was designed to train up Afghan National Security Forces (ANSF) to handle the transition of Afghanistan towards democracy and counter any threats posed by the Al-Qaeda-Taliban alliance.

Ensuring security, stabilising democratic polity, and promoting steady development processes posed daunting tasks for the Karzai regime that assumed power after the overthrow of the Taliban regime in Afghanistan. In essence, Afghanistan was undergoing a major phase of transition (D'Souza 2012). At one level, the participation of the ISAF forces and training of the ANSF have had their share in contributing to societal and individual security in Afghanistan. Besides, in their long-term strategic interests in the region, the US contributed the largest number of troops throughout the first decade of this century, out of the total troops estimated around 130,000. Consequently, the US suffered the largest number of casualties. While upholding the flag of democracy and consolidating transnational forces of the coalition against terrorism, the NATO members, in their respective ways, were drawing their mileage in the process of globalising Afghan war in terms of adding to their prestige, domestically as well as internationally. At one level, the US has been committed to spreading democracy in different parts of the world. After the defeat of the Taliban, it opted to promote a coalition constituted by the Northern Alliance under Karzai's leadership to give stability and legitimacy to political order in Afghanistan. In the process, it sought the support to build a coalition of transnational forces which became a unique experiment in contemporary international relations. This experiment stands in sharp contrast to the US-led intervention in Iraq.

In Iraq, the US along with some of its NATO allies such as Britain intervened militarily to topple Saddam Hussein's regime under the false pretext that it was manufacturing weapons of mass destruction in 2003. In addition, the Hussein regime was also guilty of gross human rights violation. The US did not get support from France and Russia which are permanent members of the United Nations Security Council (UNSC) in its Iraq misadventure. In any case, democracy as a form of governance can neither be exported nor superimposed. Unlike Iraq, however, there was agreement across the spectrum of countries over war on terror declared by the US in Afghanistan. However, did the ouster of the Taliban regime signify the end of terror? For, since the last two decades of the twentieth century, terrorism and terrorist outfits that have gathered roots are being sustained by socio-economic structures in Afghanistan.

VIII: Structures of Terrorism

With the advent of the Taliban regime under Mullah Omar even any minor trace of a representative form of government was wiped out as the regime relied on its fanatic commitment to spread jihadist ideas and rested on the institutionalised gender inequalities whereby women were kept indoors and oppressed. Such institutionalised inequalities indeed are medieval in modern times but one need not assail only Afghanistan for practicing them. Until 1994, apartheid South Africa had been practicing racial inequalities on the basis of its constitution. The constitution allowed only the white minorities to enjoy all the constitutional rights, and the disenfranchised black races that constituted three fourths of the South African population were subjected to all forms of violence, including poverty as a form of structural violence. What is more, the US, which is parading to be a citadel of modern democracy, had treated its Afro-American populations, from the sixteenth century until almost the middle of the last century, in a manner that left much to be desired.

With the replacement of the Taliban rule by a democratic regime and sub-sequent efforts to promote gender equalities there was a perceptible change in state-society ties in Afghanistan. It certainly enhanced human security and overall state security. Irrespective of the advent of the democratic regimes led by Karzai and Ghani (2014–21), the threat from the Taliban and their resurgence persisted in Afghanistan. Taliban's presence in certain pockets including on the Afghan border regions with Turkmenistan, Uzbekistan, Pakistan, etc. had remained a source of threat to the democratic regime.[2] In fact, through their dogged workmanship and urge to recapture power in Kabul, by 2017 almost sixty per cent of the area in Afghanistan had come under the control of the Taliban. Due to the significant presence of the Taliban there was always a lurking fear that the withdrawal of the NATO forces could as well draw Afghanistan into fresh modes of civic conflicts.

Furthermore, in order to launch developmental projects, Afghanistan needs to generate its own resources. The economy of Afghanistan is enveloped in poppies or red gold (Gibson 2011: 32). Afghanistan has become the opium capital of the world and a cheap source of heroin. Immediately after Karzai assumed power, he asserted, "Either Afghanistan destroys opium or opium destroys Afghanistan" (Gibson 2011). The opium industry employs over three million people in Afghanistan. If poppy cultivation is stopped what could be alternative sources of employment in the region? Earlier the so-called warlords used drug money to pay for weapons in Afghanistan. Although a relatively unexplored area there are thorough reports on the nature of drug industry in Afghanistan (Buddenburg and Byrd 2006). Obviously, for the want of alternative sources to manage development requirements, even the democratic regimes in Afghanistan, plausibly, could not have found immediate alternative sources to replace the drug money.

In the aftermath of the accelerated pace of globalisation, especially after the disintegration of the Soviet Union, Afghanistan has been integrated in the globalising world as a centre of narcotic networks that underlines important aspects of world politics including the sale of drugs, transactions of weapons through drugs, and money laundering. To put it simply, any agenda of development in Afghanistan would obviously warrant very drastic transformation in its current state of political economy. Besides, practically all the major powers such as the US and its NATO allies, Russia, China, India, Pakistan, and Iran, have had their vested interests in Afghanistan. That is why international aid in the form of development assistance began to pour in the project of reconstruction in post-9/11 Afghanistan as a peaceful democratic polity. By 2014, the US had already decided to withdraw its forces from Afghanistan, whose number was reduced to 8,900.

However, the Ghani regime in Afghanistan failed to handle the resurgent Taliban which steadily succeeded in controlling two thirds of the land in rural areas in Afghanistan. If the Taliban had become among the major actors to reckon with the major external powers like the US, Russia and China were willing to accommodate the Taliban in the processes of dialogue and negotiations while promoting the project of peace in Afghanistan. President Trump's participation in a dialogue in Doha in February 2020 paved the way for the eventual withdrawal of the American troops and process of possible sharing of power in Afghanistan among the contending parties (Maizland 2020). The agreement was necessitated by the fact that in eighteen years of war in Afghanistan more than 157,000 people were killed and the US had lost US $2 trillion (Ibid). However, the aggressive and sustained assault of the Taliban on the Ghani regime catapulted the former into corridors of power on 15 August 2021 which was, of course, followed by withdrawal of the US troops from the Afghan soil. We can proceed to assess the stakes and the role of external powers in the Afghan imbroglio.

IX: Afghanistan and External Powers

Thanks to its estimated mineral resources such as coal, copper, lithium, gold, rare earths, and substantial reserves of natural gas worth roughly $1 trillion, the external powers cannot lose their stakes in Afghanistan. For instance, having battled with the terrorist forces and seen Afghanistan through until the democratic presidential election in April 2014, the US had already invested substantially to the tune of over $100 billion in non-military assistance to Afghanistan since 2002 (Brinkley 2013). Besides, its military expenditure was to the tune of roughly $300 billion (Rais 2012: 147). In view of its military requirements and growing dependence on the minerals in the region, the US carved out its own space in the region by signing the Bilateral Security Agreement (BSA) with Afghanistan in September 2014. The BSA not merely allowed the US to maintain its 9,800 troops but also permitted additional 2,000 troops from the NATO countries to be stationed on Afghan soil even after the end of international combat mission on 31 December 2014 (Evans 2014) The BSA was supposed to come in force from 1 January 2015 and remain in force until January 2024 unless terminated by either party (Recknagel 2014). However, the developments towards the ascent of the Taliban virtually forced the Trump administration to negotiate with them. It eventually led to the exit of the US from Afghanistan. However, the US has not cut off the ties with the Taliban completely. It has offered $1.1 billion as an aid package to the Taliban regime (Maizland 2023).

The Chinese have always been averse to American presence in the region. At the same time, they are aware that the Taliban militancy cannot be contained only through military might. Indeed, the Taliban have the capacity to fuel insurgencies in diverse parts of the world by striking alliances with radical Islamic terrorist organisations including Al-Qaeda. For instance, a section of Uyghurs of Xinjiang region has connections with radical Islamic elements of Pakistan, Afghanistan, and the Taliban. In view of this, China construes negotiations as a viable strategy to win over the Taliban (Jacob 2014). In the past, the Chinese have directly indulged in negotiations and deals with right wing parties from Pakistan such as Jamat-e Islami or Jamat-ul-Dawa in 2012.

Besides, China continues to perceive a threat in the autonomous area of Xinjiang where the Uyghur separatists have launched the East Turkestan Independence Movement (ETIM). In fact, the completion of the projects such as the China Pakistan Economic Corridor (CPEC) and Belt Road Initiative (BRI) in the southwest Asian region warrants peace and cooperation from Afghanistan. China is rightly apprehensive of the outfits like the Islamic State of Iraq and Syria (Khorasan) that are targeting the former to avenge the way China has been treating people of Uyghur ethnicity. Plausibly, Pakistan is likely to be a bridge between Afghanistan and China because it provides one axis of connection from China to Afghanistan via the Karakoram Highway in addition to the central Asian route. However, the Wakhan corridor that connects China to Afghanistan is poor in terms of road and infrastructure facilities. To put it simply China may have to coordinate its efforts with Pakistan to reach out to Afghanistan.

More than development assistance, the Chinese presence in the mining/ extracting sector in Afghanistan has become conspicuous. China, on 6 January 2023, signed a twenty-five-year-long multi-billion-dollar contract with Afghanistan to extract oil. In fact, the Taliban signed contract with the Xinjiang Central Asia Petroleum and Gas Company (CAPEIC), a subsidiary of the state owned Chinese National Petroleum Company (CNPC), to extract oil from Amu Darya Basin which stretches from Central Asian countries and Afghanistan (Kumar and Noori 2023). Similarly, China is planning to exploit rich copper deposits of Mes Aynak mines in Afghanistan. Among the handful of states China and Russia have accredited selected diplomats to the Islamic Emirate of Afghanistan and opened up diplomatic relations with the Taliban regime.

Likewise, Afghanistan continues to be a strategically significant area for Pakistan in view of its hostile ties with India. Pakistan has had to handle problems related to Afghan refugees on its soil and protect strategically important areas like Khyber Pakhtunkhwa, federally administered areas, and Baluchistan from terrorist insurgencies. Pakistan, in order to enhance its security in the region, would like to control Afghanistan or at least ensure the existence of a friendly regime in that country. Both of these are not easy tasks to achieve. Besides, Pakistan is apprehensive of India's role in Afghanistan and perceives India's policies as means to destabilise it from the rear.

India initially entered Afghanistan through its massive investments in the form of development assistance to the tune of US $2.6 billion (Mullen 2013) which steadily grew up to US $3 billion. Prior to the fall of the Ghani regime in Kabul, India was executing over 400 development related projects (Harshé 2021: 8). India is taking a keen interest in overall development cooperation in Afghanistan in the areas of infrastructure, communication, education, food, health, training, and capacity building (Norfolk 2012). The projects such as the Indira Gandhi Institute of Child Health and funding the building of the parliament in Kabul are cases in point. It has also helped in building the Salma hydro-electric dam at Herat. Besides, India is admitting Afghan students in Indian universities as a part of capacity building. What is more, public-private cooperation among Indian companies is promoting Indo-Afghan cooperation. India actually believes in containing the spectre of terror by sustaining initiatives in development cooperation.

Moreover, India needs to have access to Afghanistan and central Asian markets as resources to bolster its energy security. Since India is unable to gain such access through Pakistan, it has turned towards Iran to get access. India has assisted Iran in building the Chabahar port in Iranian Baluchistan as an alternative to the Gwadar port in Pakistan constructed by China. Unfortunately, when the US applied sanctions against Iran in mid-2019, India ceased buying oil from the latter and waited until the US lifted its sanctions. In fact, the Iranian oil had brought a number of benefits including longer cycle credit as well as low freight cost (Harshé 2021: 8). By clearly leaning towards the US, India alienated Iran for a while. India also has helped connect the Iranian Chabahar port to the Afghan ring road by constructing the strategic Zaraj-Delaram Highway (Mir 2012: 140). Irrespective of these developments India has been legitimately concerned about its security interest in the region because of Pakistan's role as the hub of terrorism. Also, the Pulwama attack of February 2019 in the state of Jammu and Kashmir by the JEM was planned from the Helmand province of Afghanistan. Incontestably, the rise of the Taliban in 2021 has given Pakistan and its terrorist outfits a wider ground to operate.

India has always refused to distinguish between good terrorist and bad terrorist. It condemns any act of terrorism and has often refused to negotiate with the terrorist outfits. When Russia, the US, China, and Pakistan met in Moscow in March 2021 to discuss the prospects of dialogue between the Taliban and the then Afghan government led by President Ghani, India was not even invited to the conference. Although it was difficult to normalise relationship with Afghanistan, India gradually chose to engage with the Taliban in various formats without necessarily endorsing the Taliban regime. Evidently, India's long-term plan to get oil from Iran through a pipeline via Afghanistan and Pakistan or the projects of obtaining natural gas through Turkmenistan, Afghanistan, Pakistan, and India (TAPI) now appear like distant dreams.

Russia's interest in Afghanistan stems from its immediate concern for the countries in central Asia. It has alliance responsibilities under the Collective Security Treaty Organisation (CSTO), a Moscow-led military alliance in the Eurasia of Russia and six post-Soviet states. Political instability and violence in Afghanistan can affect central Asian states in terms of the spread of terrorism, radicalisation of Islam, drug trafficking, and flow of refugees. Likewise, Turkey is equally concerned about political stability in Afghanistan. Thanks to its geo-strategic location, Turkey considers Afghanistan to be at the centre of Asia. Turkey has demonstrated concern for stability in Afghanistan through a regional initiative on Afghanistan known as the 'Heart of Asia – Istanbul Process'. Turkey has advised the Taliban to run an inclusive government and ensure girls' education under its rule. It already has roughly 5 million refugees, mostly from Syria and other neighbouring countries, and it will not be able to absorb immigrants from Afghanistan.

Similarly, since Afghanistan is a part of Muslim world, countries like Iran and Saudi Arabia would also influence development in Afghanistan. Indeed, without taking cognisance of the involvement of such an impressive array of countries, transnational companies, and troops as well as civil society organisations in the context of globalisation, it may be difficult to get even a tentative idea of how the developments in Afghanistan are likely to shape in the future.

X: Concluding Remarks

Afghanistan, owing to its strategic location and resources, has always been and continues to be vulnerable to the aggressive/expansionist designs of the major external powers and forces. Shrinkage of spaces with the onset of globalisation have certainly trans-nationalised the areas of conflict and cooperation between different actors that are already existing in Afghanistan. In the recent past, the territory of Afghanistan has been hostage to imperial ambitions of both the Soviet Union and the US and its NATO allies. Besides major powers such as the former Soviet Russia, Russia, China, Pakistan, Turkey, Iran, and Saudi Arabia; terrorist outfits such as Al-Qaeda and the Taliban; and ISIS have had their notable presence on the political landscape of Afghanistan.

In fact, during the past few decades Afghanistan has been among the most devastated countries in the south and southwest Asian regions. Owing to the protracted civil strife among the warlords and ethnic groups, the economy of the country has been virtually destroyed. The internal wars have already undermined the agrarian base of Afghanistan, despite its meagre but fertile arable soil. Social evils including inefficiency, physical insecurity, gender oppression, and corruption literally have plagued Afghanistan. One of the worst impacts of these evils could be perceived in gradual devastation of the political institutions and legitimate order. The democratic experiment has proved short-lived with the advent of the Taliban in August 2021.

Further, Afghanistan's increasing dependence on poppy cultivation for revenue generation, in the long run, may not allow it to build a more viable cluster of institutions capable of restoring a semblance of order. After the withdrawal of the NATO troops, whether the major powers continue to serve their vested interests by fishing in domestically troubled waters or whether Afghanistan witnesses an advent of stable polity under the Taliban remains to be seen. Most of the major powers are still reluctant to offer *de jure* recognition to the Taliban-led regime.

The new regime has to seek the support of external powers in technology, capacity building, and development cooperation to enhance the stature of Afghanistan as a communication hub. Indeed, if infrastructure and communication facilities are made more up to date, Afghanistan has the potential to become such a hub. Through such a hub, even serious problems of energy security of countries like India can be resolved if the SAARC countries like Afghanistan and Pakistan choose to work together. What is more, with education and development cooperation, it will be possible to dilute the impact of terrorist outfits in the politics of the entire region. This language of 'ifs' and 'buts', however, has to take more concrete shape with the political will of the power elite in Afghanistan and other major external powers in the globalising world that are engaged in Afghanistan during the forthcoming decade. However, the Taliban-led regime is still acting as a stumbling block while promoting all these positive plans.

Notes

1 The number of refugees is estimated variously. However, according to one United Nations High Commissions for Refugees report, over five million refugees from Afghanistan were repatriated after 2002 from Pakistan. See http://en.wikipedia.org/wiki/Afghans_in_Pakistan, accessed on April7, 2014. For more thorough and scholarly expose to refugee question see Margesson, Rhoda (2007) "Afghan Refugees: Current Status and Future Prospects" order code RL 33851 CRS Report for Congress, Congressional Research Service www.fas.org/sgp/crs/row/RL33851.pdf, accessed on April 7, 2014.

2 For details see BBC, Asia News: 2013 URL: www.bbc.com/news/world-asia-21338263

References

Brinkley, Joel. 2013. 'Money Pit: The Monstrous Failure of U.S. Aid to Afghanistan' World Affairs, www.worldaffairsjournal.org/article/money-pit-monstrous-failure-us-aid-afghanistan (accessed on 18 April 2014).

Buddenburg, Borris and Byrd William A. (eds.). 2006. 'Afghanistan's Drug Industry Structure, Functioning, Dynamics and Implications for Counter Narcotics Policy' The United Nations Office on Drug and Crime chrome-extension://efaidnbmnnnibpcajpcglclefindmkaj/www.unodc.org/pdf/afg/publications/afghanistan_drug_industry.pdf (accessed on 7 March 2023).

D'Souza, Shantie Mariet (ed.). 2012. *Afghanistan in Transition, Beyond 2014?* New Delhi: Pantagon Press.

Evans, John R. 2014. 'Bilaterla Security Agreement: A New Era of Afghan-US Cooperation' www.brookings.edu/blog/up-front/2014/09/30/bilateral-security-agreement-a-new-era-of-afghan-u-s-cooperation/September 31 (accessed on 13 March 2023).

Gibson, Nigel C. 2011. 'It's Opium Stupid' in Zubeda Jalalzai and David Jefferess (eds), *Globalizing Afghanistan: Terrorism, War and the Rhetoric of Nation Building*, pp. 31–49. Durham: Duke University Press.

Harshé, Rajen. 1997. *Twentieth Century Imperialism Shifting Contours and Changing Conceptions*. New Delhi: Sage.

Harshé, Rajen. 2003. 'Cross- Border Terrorism: Road Block to Peace Initiatives', *Economic and Political Weekly*, 38 (35): 3621–3625.

Harshé, Rajen. 2008. 'Unveiling the Ties between US Imperialism and Al Qaida', *Economic and Political Weekly*, 43 (51): 67–72.

Harshé, Rajen. 2021. 'India's Afghan Policy: Challenges and Anxieties', *Economic and Political Weekly*, 56 (35) August 28.

Jacob, Jabin T. 2014. 'India, China and the Coming US Drawdown in Afghanistan: A Choice of Dilemmas', *Economic and Political Weekly*, 49 (14): 24–27.

Jalalzai, Zubeda and David Jefferess (eds.). 2011. *Globalizing Afghanistan: Terrorism, War and the Rhetoric of Nation Building*. Durham: Duke University Press.

Kumar, Ruchi and Noori Hikmat. 2023. 'Why China's Latest Investment in Afghanistan Actually Work', https://www.aljazeera.com/economy/2023/2/27/will-chinas-latest-investment-in-afghanistan-actually-work Feb 27 (accessed on 20 August 2024).

Lowther, Adam. B. 2007. *Americans and Asymmetric Conflict: Lebanon, Somalia and Afghanistan*. New Delhi: Pentagon Press.

Maizland, Land say. 2023. 'The Taliban in Afghanistan', www.cfr.org/backgrounder/taliban-afghanistan Jan 19 (accessed on 13 March 2023).

Maizland, Lindsay. 2020. 'U.S.-Taliban Peace Deal: What to Know', www.cfr.org/backgrounder/us-taliban-peace-deal-agreement-afghanistan-war, March 2 (accessed on 9 March 2023).

Mir, Haroun. 2012. 'Is Regional Consensus on Afghanistan Possible?' in D'Souza Shantie Mariet (ed), *Afghanistan in Transition, Beyond 2014?*, pp. 133–144. New Delhi: Pentagon Press.

Mockaitis, Thomas R. 2011. *Osama Bin Laden: A Biography*. New Delhi: Pentagon Press.

Mullen, Rani. D. 2013. 'The India-Afghanistan Partnership', *The Centre for Policy Research*, May 16, http://idcr.cprindia.org/p/afghanpartnership.html (accessed on 20 April 2014).

Negri, Antonio and Machel Hardt. 2001. *Empire*. Harvard: Harvard University Press.

Norfolk, Daniel. 2012. 'India's Engagement with Afghanistan: Developing a Durable Policy Architecture' in Shantie Mariet D'Souza (ed), *Afghanistan in Transition, Beyond 2014?*, pp. 161–183. New Delhi: Pantagon Press.

Rahi, Arwin. 2014. 'Why the Durand Line Matters: It Is Time for Kabul to Accept the Legality of Border', *The Diplomat*, http://thediplomat.com/2014/02/why-the-durand-line-matters/(accessed on 3 April 2014).

Rais, Rasuk Bakhsh. 2012. 'Pakistan's Perspective on Afghanistan Transition' in Shantie Mariet D'Souza (ed), *Afghanistan in Transition, Beyond 2014?*, pp. 145–160. New Delhi: Pantagon Press.

Recknagel, Charles. 2014. 'Explainer: Key Points in US-Afghan Bilateral Security', 30 September,www.rferl.org/a/explainer-bsa-afghan-us-security-agreement-bsa/26613884.html (accessed on 5 March 2023).

Saikal, Amin.2004. *Modern Afghanistan: A History of Struggle and Survival*. London: I.B Tauris.

Soros, George. 1997. *'The Capitalist Threat'* The Atlantic Online, www.theatlantic.com/past/docs/issues/97feb/capital/capital.htm (accessed on 7 March 2014).

3

'PRAGMATISM' AGAINST 'IDEOLOGY' IN TRANSNATIONAL VERSUS REGIONAL JIHADIST GROUPS

Situating the Taliban and Islamic State-Khorasan on a Conflict-Cooperation Continuum

Mohit Sharma

In regions where violence has historically functioned as a mechanism for establishing order, Afghanistan being a pertinent example, the conventional binaries of peace and violence not only oversimplify the intricate dynamics at play but also obscure and impede the broader advancement of ideals of 'peace.' Various strands of political thought have enabled the conceptualization of peace to be approached subjectively and within a relative context. For the purpose of this study, 'peace' can be said to possess an objective basis for all its subjective associations wherein its ontological reality incorporates within itself various epistemological relativisms in a Kantian sense of knowledge production. Pursuing a holistic and enduring peace, particularly within the Afghan landscape, requires an understanding of 'peace' that may be localized, temporary, and transactional, involving practical and tactical decisions made within the context of ongoing conflict. This sharply contrasts the liberal peace theory employed in Afghanistan by the United States and its allies. The manner and circumstances of the US's withdrawal from Afghanistan underscore the inadequacy of liberal peace, which aims to be realized through a security-development nexus, a Western model wherein counterinsurgency would provide the security environment (Walter, 2016). At the same time, development was to be pursued through neo-liberal market-oriented programs and the construction of infrastructural projects (ibid.). The Provincial Reconstruction Teams (PRT) in the country needed to understand that their effectiveness lay not in the performance of fulfilling basic functions of the government but in the perception of their governance in the eyes of the people (Egnell, 2010). The Taliban, former insurgents turned state actor, could turn their tactical losses into victories of perception. Focusing on the outcome of achieving peace, it is vital to jettison the reductionist

DOI: 10.4324/9780429281631-4

understanding of Jihadist groups as irrational and ideologically determined. Given that Afghanistan remains a battleground for various jihadist groups, all roads to peace necessitate understanding of these groups and the intricacies of their interrelationships.

This chapter aims to examine the nuanced relationship between the Taliban and Islamic State-Khorasan (IS-K) by delving into the factors of cooperation and conflict between these two jihadist organizations, which are ideologically different. The rationale for selecting these two groups is to explore the underlying factor driving conflict at the micro-level where the influence of 'state' predominantly lacks (see Gunning, 2007). It is hypothesized that both groups adapt their strategies, oscillating between cooperation and conflict, based on their situational needs and priorities. Given the landscape of Afghanistan, where various powerbrokers pursue different politico-economic agendas, a dilemma arises concerning identifying those to be excluded and those to be embraced. In this milieu, where different social forces compete for social control, it is important to understand the hybridized nature of politics involving formal and informal structures (Carter, 2013). By highlighting the interplay of pragmatism and rationalism, this research challenges literature that portrays terrorist groups as irrational and ideologically rigid, instead emphasizing the triumph of pragmatic decision-making over entrenched ideological frameworks. The study engages with the literature about cooperation theories between rebel groups, followed by detailing a conceptual framework that helps to situate the Taliban and IS-K in a broad jihadist landscape. Subsequently, the conflict-cooperation continuum between the two organizations is assessed from 2014 to 2021, followed by an analysis of their relationship.

Why Do Militant Groups Cooperate?

The relationship between the Taliban and Islamic State-Khorasan is central to the broader debate on the dynamics of conflict and cooperation between various jihadist groups. On one end of the spectrum, we see rivalries and conflicts between groups that eventually lead to intense radicalization of people, creating conditions for competitive bidding and a propensity to outdo the other group for accessing limited resources (Ibrahimi and Akbarzadeh 2019, p. 2). Conversely, we see cooperation and alliances between jihadist groups in pursuit of shared ideological goals (Bacon, 2018). A thorough examination of the motivations underlying inter-group alliances, with a particular emphasis on the drivers and implications of cooperative interactions, has been undertaken by scholars like Bond (2010) and Karmon (2005), who emphasize the importance of survival as a fundamental motivator for group collaboration. Furthermore, the concept of security cooperation is examined, emphasizing allied organizations' mutual expectation of future facilitation.

The concept of 'sense of empowerment' developed by Moghadam (2017, as cited in Jadoon, 2022) throws light on how transnational coalitions might strengthen smaller regional groupings. He recognizes that certain alliances form due to a perceived danger created by variables such as internal conflicts, limited civilian support and resources, and state actors' counterterrorism and counterinsurgency activities. Moghadam (2015) fixes the undertheorized and understudied explorations of cooperation between the militant organizations. He distinguishes between high-end relationships that include mergers and strategic partnerships and low-end relationships that include tactical and transactional cooperations. In a merger, the involved groups become entirely interdependent, while the weaker partner usually loses its autonomy involving a formal pledge of allegiance. It is predicated upon a high degree of ideological affinities and susceptible to leadership splits. In a transactional one, the groups' autonomy and independence remain intact. Low-end cooperation manifests the triumph of pragmatism over ideological affinities since it can happen between ideologically opposed groups, exemplified by the case of the Taliban and Islamic State-Khorasan. Horowitz and Potter (2014) emphasize the importance of inter-group ties in increasing group capability, often leading to more devastating attacks on the state apparatus. Bacon (2018), in her remarkable scholarship, has delved into why terrorist groups form alliances. She proposes three joint conditions as prerequisites: "organizational needs, shared identity characteristics, and trust." Alliances are formed despite being seen as suspicious and clandestine, and face existential threats because they increase the risk of leaks and infiltration. She sees groupings as gravitating towards the most formidable entities in their surroundings, resulting in a core-periphery structure within alliances, also known as 'alliance hubs' (Bacon, 2018). Forming coalitions with groups in the core of such networks may produce higher benefits than forming several agreements with weaker parties (ibid.). Scholars have recognized the importance of this dynamic, emphasizing the subtle significance of inter-group connections in defining the trajectory of violent behavior.

On the other end, Phillips (2015) conceptualizes violent rivalries in how they relate to the inter-organizational dynamics of various rebel groups. According to him, violent rivalries extend a group's longevity as against the conventional belief that two violent groups diminish and neutralize each other. He describes four mechanisms by which this happens: "encouraging civilians to pick a side to support, fomenting innovation in order to survive, providing additional incentives to group members, and spoiling peace talks" (Phillips, 2015, p. 63). Inter-organizational collaboration can also affect the capabilities, strategy, and tactics of the cooperation parties (Karmon, 2005, as cited in Moghadam, 2015). However, it is Jadoon's (2022) distinction between official local affiliates of a transnational group and a local group that cooperates with a transnational group for tactical or strategic purposes that holds considerable significance within the context of my study. She examines an understudied topic: how the existence of transnational affiliates affects the militancy and the associated violence in the region, by examining the relationship of the Islamic State affiliate in the Afghanistan-Pakistan region, i.e., Islamic State-Khorasan (IS-K) with the local regional groups of Lashkar-e-Jhangvi (LeJ) and Jamaat-ul-Ahrar (JuA) in Pakistan. Using data analysis, she explains how operational linkages with transnational jihadist organizations affect the lethality, tactics, targets, and geography of local militants' operations.

Conceptual Framework

Building on Jadoon's (2022) distinction of *affiliates of global transnational group* and *local regional groups*, this chapter attempts to situate the Islamic State-Khorasan (which is an affiliate of a transnational group, i.e., Islamic State) and the Afghan Taliban (a local national group turned state actor) on a continuum of cooperation and conflict wherein both repeatedly swing towards either side. For this study, I equate cooperation with low-end cooperation, in which tactical alliances shift and end abruptly as the interests of the groups diverge (Moghadam, 2015). Ibrahimi and Akbarzadeh (2019) conceived the Taliban and IS-K as part of a broader jihadist scenario that emphasizes the significance of resource availability and aggregation in the emergence of social movements. In this context, resources are not limited to economic determinants but also encompass non-material resources such as moral, cultural, and social legitimacy in symbolic forms (Edwards and McCarthy, 2004, as cited in Ibrahimi and Akbarzadeh, 2019). On the aspect of unity, the two groups can be defined by an underlying ideological affinity, a common religious identity, and a sense of group cohesion. These elements contribute to a sense of shared purpose and cooperation among them. Conversely, on the conflict side, the groups might be characterized by ideological differences, operational discrepancies, and divergent agendas. These elements could exacerbate tensions and conflicts between the two groups. The interaction of the IS-K and the Taliban is shaped by the interplay of unity and conflict dynamics, revealing the complexities of their cooperation. Hence, the two groups in our object of study show parallel dynamics of convergence and divergence.

The literature discussed earlier underscores the factors essential for conflict and cooperation, which can be observed in the interactions between the Taliban and IS-K. Though the proliferation of jihadist groups has intensified inter-competition, they can leverage their shared history and ideological affinity to navigate and circumvent tactical and ideological differences. The transition of the Taliban into a state actor in August 2021 marks a significant development that should not overshadow the historical relationship between the Taliban and IS-K, since both have claimed the same territory. Before delving into our case study, i.e., the period of conflict and cooperation between the Taliban and IS-K from 2014–2021, we shall explore a brief history of the 'Khorasan' movement, IS-K's relationship with IS-Central (transnational group with its affiliate), and IS-K's divergences with the Taliban.

Behind the Word 'Khorasan'

Scholars trace the origin of the word Khorasan in Islamic theology. In one saying of the hadith, as narrated by Abu Hurairah,

> If you see the black banners coming from Khurasan, join that army, even if you have to crawl over ice; no power will be able to stop them. And they will finally reach Baitul Maqdis (Jerusalem), where they will erect their flags.
>
> *(Crowley, 2014)*

Some scholars, however, share doubts about the authenticity of the hadith. Al-Tirmizi, the author of Sunan Al-Tirmizi ('Collection of Hadith by Al-Tirmizi'), rules this narration as weak because the actual chain of narrators is doubtful (Bahari and Hassan, 2014). It is interesting to note that six weeks after the 9/11 attacks, the al-Qaeda operative and confidant of bin Laden, Abu Jandal, quoted the same hadith while he was being interrogated by the FBI (Crowley, 2014). The term 'Khorasan' refers to a historic belt spanning Afghanistan, Iran, Turkmenistan, Tajikistan, Uzbekistan, and Pakistan. Going by the hadith, the term sheds light on the grandiose and apocalyptic Caliphatic vision that drives Sunni extremists to terrorism. As in the prophecy, the great victory amounts to the 'Islamic version of the Armageddon' (Soufan and Freedman, 2011). Jihadists tend to deny the legitimacy of modern nations, and hence, they prefer to use historical terms that were in vogue during the time of the great Caliphates (Taylor, 2014), providing them with the Islamist pedigree required to attract young jihadists from various parts of the globe. With the inception of the Islamic State in Iraq and Syria (ISIS)[1] around 2014, the group quickly found a receptive audience among Pashtuns in Afghanistan and Pakistan's frontier region. Reports began to circulate about the distribution of Daesh[2] fliers in Peshawar, Pakistan and the adjoining Afghan provinces to Khyber Pakhtunkhwa (ISIS, 2014), where militant outfits started to pledge allegiance to the Islamic State and its caliph, Abu Bakr al-Baghdadi (Six Pakistan, 2014). A prominent Afghan Taliban leader, Abdul Rauf Khadim, went to Syria in late 2014 to give allegiance to the Islamic State and bring Daesh to Afghanistan (Azamy, 2016). With incoming pledges of Tehreek-e-Taliban Pakistan (TTP) and Afghan Taliban leaders, IS-Central[3] declared the Afghanistan-Pakistan region as part of the Khorasan branch of IS. The central leadership appointed a former TTP leader, Hafiz Saeed Khan, as the head of Islamic State-Khorasan (IS-K) and Khadim as the deputy (Roggio, 2015). The arrival of Daesh in Afghanistan intensified the maze of military landscapes, which saw rapid alliances between different militant organizations, both local and foreign. This was seen as a platform that would give refuge to disgruntled elements in the Afghan Taliban. The divisions between pro- and anti-Daesh groups continued to grow as the disenfranchised members of the Afghan Taliban and the Pak Taliban grouped with Islamic State to counterbalance the hegemony of the Taliban in the region (Azamy, 2016). Several groups who had pledged their allegiance to the nascent organization started to coalesce around some prominent leaders to form organizations affiliated with IS-K. Several coagulation points emerged, reflecting the segmentary character of the already existing insurgent groups like Taliban. These fronts that then established a distinct relationship with IS-K, each having different origins, were Tehreek-e-Khilafat Khorasan (TKK), Khilafat Afghan and Muslim Dost group, Azizullah Haqqani group, and Tehreek-e-Khilafat Pakistan (TKP) (Guistozzi, 2018, p. 27).

Relationship Between IS-Central (Transnational Group) and IS-K (Regional Affiliate)

Initially, the IS-K was deemed a franchise of the parent organization. For some, the group wanted to "draw weaker local players under its brand and into a loosely constituted network of radical actors" (Rani, 2016). However, gradually, it became known that the structure would move beyond a franchise. According to Jadoon, Sayed, and Mines (2022), the IS-K was authorized to make autonomous decisions about operations in the military domain, procurement and salaries, and recruitment without consulting the IS-Central. However, the Central leadership would supervise and monitor the new group via their advisors and inspection teams. This suggests that even during the formation days, the structure was more than franchised and indicated a shift towards a hierarchical one. The IS-K had to report the figures on membership, groups that pledged allegiance to the IS, leadership appointments, the outcomes of clashes with the Taliban, and operations in Pakistan. The relationship between them gets complex when the ideological variable is brought in. Despite the ideological difference, the members of the IS-K, who originally were Deobandis, adopted a new ideology that was largely alien to the region. But did the members of the IS-Khorasan really take the aspect of ideology seriously? Were they fixated upon the establishment of the Caliphate as early as possible? The answers to these questions would lead us to discover the pragmatism employed by the IS-K when it was planting its foothold in the region.

Case Study IS-K vs. Taliban (Regional Affiliate of Transnational Group vs. Regional Group)

Before delving into the relationship between the Taliban and IS-K at the ground and operational level, it is important to discuss their differences in terms of ideology and state conception.

Nationalism vs. Salafism

Ideologically, the two groups are separated, contributing to the causes of conflict. The Islamic State-Khorasan follows the Salafi-jihadist interpretation of Islam, which is extremely literal in its interpretation of the scripture, disregards the development of Islamic thought over centuries, and is critical of mainstream Sunni Muslims (Kidwai, 2022). However, Hanafis (the Taliban) adhere to Abu Hanifa's[4] lessons and rely on teachings from the Prophet Mohammed's everyday life. They use their own judgment when dealing with issues like the treatment of non-Muslims and individual freedom, and oppose takfiri or the ex-communication of fellow Muslims (Kidwai, 2022). With the majority of Muslims adhering to this belief, it enjoys a sizable following among the Taliban. They have a more nationalistic goal of building an Islamic Emirate confined to Afghanistan and do not consider Shias to be heretics, unlike the sectarian Salafist ideology. This is the primary explanation for why al-Qaeda, despite its Salafist approach, was close to the Taliban, which possessed a more pan-Islamist vision. The IS built its ideological foundation on the extreme interpretation of the concept of 'asabiyya,' which refers to 'kinship within the realm of political organization' in Islamic thought (Kadercan, 2019). By its interpretation, it includes only the Sunnis who explicitly obey the group's interpretation as full members (ibid.)

Fluid vs. Fixed Borders

Kadercan (2019) describes the Islamic State's conception of territoriality which places it in the category of the revolutionary state. The IS demands fluid frontiers as opposed to fixed and rigid borders. Its territorial vision is based upon the principle of destroying the 'gray zone,' i.e., regions where Sunnis and non-Sunnis share the same physical environment in a common social context. It tends to underscore the Manichean division of 'us vs. them' simultaneously attacking the Westphalian ideal. The Islamic State detests the Taliban's provincial and nationalistic tendencies. Kadercan (2019) places the IS in the category of 'virulent territoriality,' in which fluid frontiers are combined to achieve socio-spatial homogeneity. States seeking to consolidate control over the link between space and society are motivated to reterritorialize specific areas they regard as targets. This reterritorialization entails a drastic alteration of these places to coincide with the desired image and ideology of the state, a process through which the spatial organization and characteristics of a particular territory are remade or reconstructed in accordance with a specific agenda or vision.

Taliban Retreat in 2015 – As the IS-K was being annihilated in Helmand in 2014–15, it was simultaneously gaining strength in Nangarhar. In 2015, the IS began to fly its black flags in the Mohmand area of the Achin district, bordering the Tirah Valley (Adeel, 2015). They shed their façade of a benign organization and started directly clashing with the Taliban and tribal communities. It spread to the neighbouring Logar province and attacked Sufi shrines (Ibid.). The IS-K was allowed to take root at the village level and establish cross-border sanctuaries in Pakistan unhindered (Johnson, 2016, p. 10). Osman (2016) investigates the Islamic State's journey at length in Afghanistan. The IS-K went on an offensive and built a strong enough base of support. The Taliban, then, had to retreat from the Kot, Achin, Nazyan, and Deh Bala districts to the westward district of Khogiani, where they would regroup. The IS-K did not target the Afghan security forces, who maintained a static regional presence. This tactic mirrors the IS-Central's playbook, in that the Jabhat al-Nusra front was initially the only target and restrained from attacking Bashar al-Assad's forces. The Taliban had to wait until December 2015 to launch a counter-offensive against the Islamic State forces.

Taliban Counteroffensive – According to Johnson (2016), the local perceptions about the IS-K had changed by the end of 2015. They resorted to executing tribal elders and imposed a ban on poppy cultivation, which was an essential source of livelihood in Nangarhar. The social and religious strictures of life enforced by the Islamic State were not well received by the communities. The Taliban started to send fighters and materials to Khogiani, which was used as a base to launch counteroffensives into the Chaparhar and Kot districts. The large-scale Taliban offensives, community uprisings, and US drone strikes halted its territorial expansion. Many commanders and their families started to retreat back to Orakzai agencies in Pakistan. Some, however, shifted to the northern mountainous province of Kunar, which was expected to be a new front of the IS-K. Groups like Shamali Khilafat, which enjoyed better relations with the Taliban, did not fight.

Cooperation in 2017 – Since the membership of both the Taliban and IS-K overlapped in many areas of respective influence, cooperation between the two was not surprising. It is also noteworthy that when the Taliban issued a fatwa against them permitting their men to fight, the war was framed as a 'Defensive Jihad' restricted to self-defense (Osman, 2015). Though the Taliban was keen to preserve its dominance in the jihad landscape in Afghanistan, many Taliban leaders with transnational ties, like the Haqqani Network, wanted to avoid confrontations with the IS-K (Ibrahimi and Akbarzadeh, 2019). Haqqanis are said to have negotiated with them in 2016–17 when they launched attacks on the then government of Afghanistan under the name of Daesh (Amiry, 2018). Cooperation with the IS-K in organizing attacks gave the Taliban a potent tool of plausible deniability. The Islamic State's attacks on Shia Hazaras and other civilians provided the Taliban with benefits whereby they did not have to bear the legal, political, or moral cost of claiming responsibility for such attacks (Ibrahimi and Akbarzadeh, 2019). It also made the Taliban look more moderate and less threatening than their adversaries. During this period, the Taliban's political machinery was grappled with internal schisms. When Mansur Dadullah (a prominent Taliban leader) formed his own Shura called the High Council of Islamic Emirate as an alternative to Quetta Shura or the central Taliban council, both the Taliban and IS-K cooperated against him for a brief period (Guistozzi, 2018, p. 184). Ishaqzais (a sub-tribe of Pashtuns) negotiated co-existence with the IS-K, allowing groups to re-establish a presence in western and southwestern Afghanistan. In some places, like the districts of Sangin and Musa Qala, the Obeidullah faction of the Taliban and IS-K also shared narcotics revenue (Ibid. p. 188). Atiqullah Mahaz, the front associated with Peshawar Shura of the Taliban, also entertained friendly relations with the IS-K for a period (Ibid.).

Resurgent IS-K – From 2020 onwards, the IS-K started to resurge, around the same time when peace negotiations between the Taliban and the United States were ongoing. The IS-K saw an opportunity to establish itself as the only guardian of jihad in Afghanistan. The growth of its attacks was exponential, as could be gauged from the numbers, which rose from 3 attacks in June 2020 to 41 attacks in June 2021 (Jadoon, Sayed and Mines, 2022). They started appealing to a sectarian agenda and continued to attack the Hazara community, including a devastating attack at a Hazara girls' school in Kabul that killed and wounded over 200 girls and teachers (Ochab, 2021). Just after the Taliban takeover, the IS-K attacked Kabul airport, killing Afghan civilians along with the American service members (Sayed, 2021). The sudden increase in attacks carried out by them mirrors what the Taliban did to discredit the previous Afghan regime, i.e., to strike at what their adversaries promise to the local people – governance and authority (Jadoon, Sayed and Mines, 2022).

Kabul Cell – The IS-K, for some years now, has an operational presence in Kabul, which carries out fatal attacks on an occasional basis. Running such a cell in the capital, far from the strong belts of Nangarhar and Kunar, requires a coordinated and efficient logistical apparatus. As Osman (2020) describes, most of the recruits come from an urban background and do not belong to the stereotypical Salafi-jihadist circle. They were raised in comfortable Kabul neighborhoods without any history of support for violent groups. Another distinct feature of Kabul recruits is their remarkable educational background. State-funded dormitories attached to public universities in many provinces have acted as a fertile recruitment pool for extremist groups (Osman, 2020). The ethnic background is another unusual distinction. Though the middle-class Pashtuns fill the ranks, many Kabul cell members and supporters are ethnically Tajiks from the areas north of Kabul, namely Parwan, Panjsher, and Kapisa (Ibid.). Since Panjsher and Parwan are known for their anti-Taliban resistance, youth from these areas have occupied ranks in the Kabul cell. The greatest strength of the Islamic State has been its ability to repeatedly enlist new recruits even after facing setbacks (Steinberg and Albrecht, 2022).

The strategy of IS-K attacks shifted after the United States' peace negotiations with the Taliban. It started to organize more complex attacks, like the one witnessed in the Jalalabad prison break in 2020 (Ghazi and Mashal, 2020). In a report by Jadoon, Sayed, and Mines (2022), the shift is seen from suicide bombings in mosques to targeting electricity pylons and oil tankers. This signals a strategy of economic warfare that directly challenges the authority of the Taliban as a state actor. With the absence of the United States and any other external counterterrorism efforts, the IS-K will tend to exploit the Taliban's limited resources and fragile control in some parts of the country. As a countermeasure, the Taliban have resorted to crackdowns and reprisals against the civilians who are seen as supportive of the Islamic State. The heavy-handed approach will further tend to alienate the local population that goes well with the IS-K's plan.

Analysis

The IS-K's Survivability – The Islamic State appealed to "broader supporters of jihadist movements as it carved itself as an authentic, transnational, and ideologically non-comprising group" (Ibrahimi and Akbarzadeh, 2019, p. 8). Compared to other transnational groups, the Islamic State aspires to capture physical territories through its affiliates, impose Sharia rule within these territories, and engage in sectarian warfare. It is reasonable to anticipate the Islamic State to encourage or even compel its allies to align with their puritanical stance. According to Jadoon (2022), the Islamic State-Khorasan can be viewed as the primary entity within an alliance hub, providing significant benefits to cooperating organizations. Due to increased operational capabilities, linked groups may expand their geographical reach, increase the frequency of their attacks, and carry out more severe acts of violence by establishing operational links with the IS-K. Furthermore, militant groups engaged in operational collaboration can participate in inter-group learning and innovation. Transnational organizations rely on local militant infrastructure to adapt their jihad to new places, while local groups can learn about new strategies and tactics. As a result, the interconnection of groups enables information flow and the creation of militant techniques. With the degradation of the Islamic State-Central and al-Qaeda, the local affiliates of these organizations have gained traction for power projection. These affiliates have access to a pool of funds to attract allies in the region.

On the ground, however, as we study the IS-K's conflict with the Taliban, the sense of pragmatism can be clearly observed. Guistozzi (2018) brilliantly captures the projection of the 'State' dimension of the Islamic State to be more directed towards the foreign fighters and the international ummah. Regionally, the IS downplayed the 'Caliphate' in its indoctrination operations in Khorasan and tried not to import extreme features of Salafism like 'Takfir.'[5] The commanders were not very interested in the state dimension of Islamic State. Also, the donors who helped the IS-K financially (mostly from the Gulf) had other aims than just ideological and were more concerned about countering Iranian[6] and Russian interests in the region. Still, the IS-K tried to implement alien principles in areas more suited for foreign ideology – Kunar and Nangarhar. It pursues an approach in territorial practices whereby it adapts to each region's specific social and political dynamics and behaves in an ad-hoc manner by selectively invoking Islamic texts and practices (Hamdan, 2016, as cited in Kadercan, 2019). The Islamic State-Central knew that global jihadism and Salafism were insufficient factors to lay a strong base on which a cohesive organization could be formed, so they decided to upgrade the IS-K organizationally (Guistozzi, 2018, p. 82). They increased the numerical strength of advisors and trainers, which were deployed to Khorasan. This coincided with the time when central leadership was facing immense pressure in Syria and Iraq, and hence, they started to view Khorasan as a strategic theatre of operations (Basit, 2017). The IS-K's utilization of the historicity of Hijrah, when the Prophet Mohammad left Mecca for Medina when faced with an overwhelming threat and pressures from enemies, enables the group to justify its strategic retreats in the face of Taliban advances without contradicting its claim to Islamic statehood (Kadercan, 2019). By framing its retreats as tactical moves aligned with historical Islamic precedents, the IS-K seeks to maintain its Islamic legitimacy and convey a sense of pragmatism while adapting to changing circumstances on the ground.

Guistozzi (2018), however, also accounts for language barriers, cultural differences, and educational gaps that hindered the flow of skills from the IS-Central to the IS-Khorasan. Despite all efforts at cohesion, the local conditions, the geography,[7] and resistance of constituent group leaders limited the impact of IS-Central efforts to instill a stronger sense of institutional belonging than the Taliban. In contrast to the IS-K, which exported a strict chain of command to its members in Khorasan, the Taliban structure was polycentric, wherein fighters could take orders from multiple commanders (Guistozzi, 2019).

Taliban's Primacy of the 'Political' – To align with the shifting counterinsurgency strategies during the 'War on Terror,' a transition from enemy-centric focus to population-centric, the United States endeavored again to harness cultural anthropology in Afghanistan where they employed Human Terrain Teams to carry out intelligence for non-kinetic operations to 'win hearts and minds.' In a policy blunder, the cultural turn transformed into a tribal turn in which 'tribe' was seen as a straightjacket worn by all and served as a guide to practice (see Manchanda, 2018). Counterinsurgency practitioners failed to link the cultural understanding to the political, in which insurgent networks were conceptualized as depoliticized, ideological, and transnational (Belcher, 2013, p. 59). The Taliban, when operating as insurgents, had a number of feuds amongst themselves, but the group maintained cohesion because the political leaders of each faction of Taliban had a better understanding of what constitutes 'political' in Afghanistan. The ascent of Haqqanis within the Taliban highlights their conduct as rational actors. They were seen through a tribal lens and as a proxy for the ISI,[8] which now operates from such a place of strength that they tend to undermine even the Pakistani leadership (Abbas, 2014, p. 211). The Taliban's dealing with Iran and the Shiite Islamic Revolutionary Guard Corps (IRGC) underscores the pragmatism involved at the operational level. The IRGC reportedly is believed to have sponsored the Mashhad front, the most sophisticated Taiban offshoot since 2010 (Guistozzi, 2019). These elements add to a complicated dynamic that calls into question long-held ideas about power dynamics and external support behind the Taliban resurgence. The ban on women's education in Taliban-controlled Afghanistan has been explained from an ideological and cultural perspective. However, it is equally possible that it is a political tussle and not just ideological between different groups in the Taliban. It was reported that the de-facto ruling trinity of Mullah Yaqoob, Mullah Baradar, and Sirajuddin Haqqani were initially on board with the resumption of education for women (Jackson, 2022). The higher ulema council, who felt sidelined in the functioning of the governance, took the Emir Haibatullah Akhundzada on their side and reversed the decision on the ban, which was lifted in March 2022 (ibid.). The Islamic State criticizes the Taliban for having cooperated with the Pakistani military and sees it as an instrument of Pakistan's Inter-Services Intelligence. However, the recent clashes between the Pakistani and Afghan military along the border tell a different story. The evolving perspective suggests that the Taliban may not be directly controlled by the Pakistani military but rather exercises influence over it.

Prospect for Peace

Is 'pragmatic peace' possible in a place that has endured decades of war, and is governed by a medley of state and non-state actors/non-state turned state actor? Pragmatic approaches to peacebuilding have challenges and dilemmas regarding its conceptualization and accountability. Stepputat (2018) came up with the notion of 'emerging governscapes' which did not take nation-state as the default norm for societal and political organization, and by which he understood "landscapes with different constellations of authority and governance that form and spread unevenly within and beyond national boundaries." It can fit in its spatial, perspectival, and dynamic characteristics within the context of Afghanistan where the geographical reach of authority and governance is irregular, and the perceptions of ruling actors vary timely (Stepputat, 2018). The shift from liberal peace to pragmatic peace, however, has entailed a 'local turn' which runs the risk of reifying and romanticizing the local, reminiscent of the discourse about 'tribal turn' discussed earlier in the study. The advocacy of a pragmatic peace here avoids any totalizing tendencies and sees pragmatism, in its philosophical sense, as the construction of a web of beliefs and assumptions that enables to organize experiences (Smith, 1996) to embrace uncertainty. Podder (2013) has accounted for the potential of non-state armed groups for stability by turning their violent domination into political power. In her context, the Taliban, though seemingly, might have just begun on the path to peacebuilding after transforming into a state actor. Though she would exclude groups like the IS-K from any consideration of state-building and legitimacy, the pragmatic approach does not rule out any potentially constructive effects of rebel groups cooperating with one another, irrespective of their enjoying legitimacy among the subjects. De Conning terms an approach that "embraces uncertainty, focuses on processes rather than end-states, and invests in the resilience of local institutions" as an 'adaptive peace' (De Coning, 2018, p. 317). Now, these approaches can hardly be described as near to state-building, but they might emerge as the only 'best amongst a number of bad options' during the darkest hours (Raeymaekers et al., 2008, as cited in, Stepputat, 2018). With their ascension to power in 2021, the Taliban's ideological disagreements with groups like the IS-K look to intensify, especially in their commitment to safeguard ethnic minorities like the Hazaras. Having that said, the Taliban are caught in a difficult situation in which they need to balance internal and external demands. The international community urges the Taliban to take a more moderate and inclusive stance within Afghanistan to gain international recognition and support, contributing to the new regime's stability. However, embracing a more moderate stance may alienate Islamist insurgents who have aligned themselves with the Taliban in their pursuit of power. These militant factions may view a move towards moderation as a betrayal of their shared radical ideology, potentially leading to their dissociation from them. The journey ahead for the Taliban is far from easy as they transition from a polycentric command structure to a centralized one. Ultimately, any peace that produces winners and losers would be undesirable, whether liberal or pragmatic.

Notes

1 Also known as the Islamic State (IS).
2 Daesh is the Arabic acronym for Islamic State in Iraq and Syria (ISIS) which stands for 'al-Dawla al-Islamiya fil Iraq wa al-Sham'.
3 IS-Central in this chapter refers to the leadership of the Islamic State in Iraq and Syria (IS).
4 Imam Abu Hanifa was an influential Islamic jurist and scholar. He is considered one of the founders of the Hanafi school of Islamic jurisprudence. He developed a systematic approach to legal reasoning and the formulation of legal opinions (fatwas). His legal methodology emphasized rationality, independent reasoning, and flexibility in adapting Islamic law to new contexts.
5 Takfir is the process of excommunicating a Muslim from his religious fold.
6 'Anti-Iran' was one of the major attractions for defected members from the Taliban to the IS. This was also the time when Taliban-Iran relations were growing popular. The groups with sectarian tendencies found it easier to go to the IS fold. Also, with the requirement of donors, anti-Shia and anti-Iran proclivities helped the IS carve out its own path.
7 Much of the wartime tactics that the IS employed in Iraq and Syria could not be employed in Afghanistan due to dense mountainous regions.
8 Inter-Services Intelligence (ISI) is the intelligence agency of Pakistan.

References

Abbas, H. (2014). *The Taliban Revival: Violence and Extremism on the Pakistan-Afghanistan Frontier*. London, UK: Yale University Press.
Adeel, M. (2015, April 29). ISIS Promotes Training Camp in Logar Province of Afghanistan, *Khaama Press*, www.khaama.com/isis-promotes-training-camp-in-logar-province-of-afghanistan-9403/.

Amiry, S. (2018, January 8). Haqqani Network Behind Big Attacks, Not Daesh: MoD, *Tolo News*, https://tolonews.com/afghanistan/haqqani-network-behind-big-attacks-not-daesh-mod.

Azamy, H. (2016). Challenges and Prospects for Daesh in Afghanistan and Its Relations with the Taliban, Singapore: *Panorama-Insights into Asian and European Affairs Journal*, www.kas.de/de/politikdialogasien/en/publications/46739/.

Bacon, T. (2018). Is the Enemy of My Enemy My Friend?, *Security Studies*, https://doi.org/10.1080/09636412.2017.1416813

Bahari, M. and Hassan, M.H. (2014). The Black Flag Myth: An Analysis from Hadith Studies, *Counter Terrorist Trend and Analysis*, 6(3), 15–20, www.jstor.org/stable/26351277.

Basit, A. (2017). IS Penetration in Afghanistan-Pakistan: Assessment, Impact, and Implications, *Perspectives on Terrorism*, 11(3), 19–39, www.jstor.org/stable/26297839?seq=1.

Belcher, O.C. (2013). The Afterlives of Counterinsurgency: Postcolonialism, Military Social Science, and Afghanistan 2006–2012 [Doctoral thesis, The University of British Columbia].

Bond, K.D. (2010). *Power, Identity, Credibility & Cooperation: Examining the Development of Cooperative Arrangements Among Violent Non-State Actors* [Doctoral thesis, The Pennsylvania State University].

Carter, W.R. (2013). War, Peace, and Stabilisation: Critically Reconceptualising Stability in Southern Afghanistan. *Stability: International Journal of Security and Development*, 2(1): 15, 1–20, https://dx.doi.org/10.5334/sta.bi

Crowley, M. (2014, September 25). Khorasan: Behind the Name of the Newest Terrorist Threat, *TIME*, https://time.com/3430960/obama-isis-khorasan-terrorism/.

De Coning, C. (2018). Adaptive peacebuilding. *International Affairs*, 94(2), 301–317. https://doi.org/10.1093/ia/iix251

Edwards, B. and McCarthy, J. D. (2004). Resources and Social Movement Mobilization. In D. A. Snow, S. A. Soule and H. Kriesi (Eds.), *The Blackwell Companion to Social Movements* (pp. 116–152). Malden, MA: Blackwell Publishing.

Egnell, R. (2010). Winning 'Hearts and Minds'? A Critical Analysis of Counterinsurgency Operations in Afghanistan. *Civil Wars*, 12(3), 282–303. https://doi.org/10.1080/13698249.2010.509562.

Ghazi, Z. and Mashal, M. (2020, August 3). 29 Dead after ISIS Attack on Afghan Prison, *The New York Times*, www.nytimes.com/2020/08/03/world/asia/afghanistan-prison-isis-taliban.html.

Guistozzi, A. (2018). *The Islamic State in Khorasan: Afghanistan, Pakistan and the New Central Asian Jihad*. London: C. Hurst & Co.

Guistozzi, A. (2019). *The Taliban at War: 2001–2018*. Oxford University Press.

Gunning, J. (2007). A Case for Critical Terrorism Studies? *Government and Opposition*, 42(3), 363–393, https://doi.org/10.1111/j.1477-7053.2007.00228.x

Hamdan, A.N. (2016). Breaker of Barriers? Notes on the Geopolitics of the Islamic State in Iraq and Sham. *Geopolitics*, 21(3), 605–627, https://doi.org/10.1080/14650045.2016.1138940

Horowitz, M.C. and Potter, B.K. (2014). Allying to Kill: Terrorist Intergroup Cooperation and the Consequences for Lethality, *Journal of Conflict Resolution*, 58(2), 199–225, https://doi.org/10.1177/0022002712468726.

Ibrahimi, N. and Akbarzadeh, S. (2019). Intra-jihadist Conflict and Cooperation: Islamic State-Khorasan Province and the Taliban in Afghanistan. *Studies in Conflict & Terrorism*, 43(12), 1086–1107, https://doi.org/10.1080/1057610X.2018.1529367

ISIS Trying to Expand Its Influence in Pakistan, Distributes Pamphlets. *The Times of India*, September 3, 2014, https://timesofindia.indiatimes.com/world/pakistan/isis-trying-to-expand-its-influence-in-pakistan-distributes-pamphlets/articleshow/41618755.cms.

Jackson, A. (2022, March 29). The Ban on Older Girls' Education: Taleban Conservatives Ascendant and a Leadership in Disarray. *Afghanistan Analysts Network*. www.afghanistan-analysts.org/en/reports/rights-freedom/the-ban-on-older-girls-education-taleban-conservatives-ascendant-and-a-leadership-in-disarray/.

Jadoon, A. (2022). Operational Convergence or Divergence? Exploring the Influence of Islamic State on Militant Groups in Pakistan, *Studies in Conflict and Terrorism*, https://doi.org/10.1080/1057610X.2022.2058374.

Jadoon, A., Sayed, A. and Mines, A. (2022). The Islamic State Threat in Taliban Afghanistan: Tracing the Resurgence of Islamic State Khorasan, *Combating Terrorism Centre at West Point*, 15(1), 33–45, https://ctc.westpoint.edu/the-islamic-state-threat-in-taliban-afghanistan-tracing-the-resurgence-of-islamic-state-khorasan/.

Johnson, C.G. (2016, November). The Rise and Stall of the Islamic State in Afghanistan, *USIP Special Report*, www.usip.org/sites/default/files/SR395-The-Rise-and-Stall-of-the-Islamic-State-in-Afghanistan.pdf.

Kadercan, B. (2019). Territorial Logic of the Islamic State: An Interdisciplinary Approach, *Territory, Politics, Governance*, https://doi.org/10.1080/21622671.2019.1589563.

Karmon, E. (2005). *Coalitions between Terrorist Organizations: Revolutionaries, Nationalists and Islamists*. Brill.

Kidwai, S.A. (2022). Rivalry between Taliban and ISKP: The Collision of Terror, *India Quarterly*, 78(4), 544–557, https://doi.org/10.1177/09749284221127791.

Manchanda, N. (2018). The Imperial Sociology of the 'Tribe' in Afghanistan. *Millennium: Journal of International Studies*, 46(2), 165–189. http://doi.org/10.1177/0305829817741267

Moghadam, A. (2015). Terrorist Affiliations in Context: A Typology of Terrorist Inter-Group Cooperation, *CTC Sentinel*, 8(3), 22–25, https://ctc.westpoint.edu/pledging-baya-a-benefit-or-burden-to-the-islamic-state/.

Moghadam, A. (2017). *Nexus of Global Jihad: Understanding Cooperation among Terrorist Actors*. Columbia University Press.

Ochab, E. U. (2021, May 9). Bombings Outside a School in Afghanistan Kill Over 68 People, Mostly Children, *Forbes*, www.forbes.com/sites/ewelinaochab/2021/05/09/bombings-outside-a-school-in-afghanistan-kill-over-68-people-mostly-children/?sh=57db70b61f3a.

Osman, B. (2015, February 12). The Shadows on Islamic State in Afghanistan: What Threat Does It Hold? *Afghanistan Analysts Network*, www.afghanistan-analysts.org/en/reports/war-and-peace/the-shadows-of-islamic-state-in-afghanistan-what-threat-does-it-hold/.

Osman, B. (2016, July 27). The Islamic State in Khorasan: How It Began and Where It Stands Now in Nangarhar, *Afghanistan Analysts Network*, www.afghanistananalysts.org/the-islamic-state-in-khorasan-how-it-began-and-where-it-stands-now-innangarhar.

Osman, B. (2020, June 1). Bourgeois Jihad: Why Young, Middle-Class Afghans Join the Islamic State, *United States Institute of Peace*, www.usip.org/publications/2020/06/bourgeois-jihad-why-young-middle-class-afghans-join-islamic-state.

Phillips, B.J. (2015). Enemies with Benefits? Violent Rivalry and Terrorist Group Longevity, *Journal of Peace Research*, 52(1), 62–75. https://doi.org/10.1177/0022343314550538

Podder, S. (2013). Non-State Armed Groups and Stability: Reconsidering Legitimacy and Inclusion, *Contemporary Security Policy*, 34(1), 16–39. https://doi.org/10.1080/13523260.2013.771029

Raeymaekers, T., Menkhaus, K. and Vlassenroot, K. (2008). State and Non-State Regulation in African Protracted Crises: Governance without Government?, *Afrika focus*, 21(2), 7–21. https://doi.org/10.1163/2031356X-02102003.

Rani, M. (2016, August 31). The Marketplace of Terrorist Ideas: Is ISIS Beating the Competition in Pakistan?, *Foreign Affairs*, www.foreignaffairs.com/articles/pakistan/2016-08-31/marketplace-terrorist-ideas.

Roggio. (2015, February 2). Pakistani Taliban Emir for Bajaur Joins Islamic State, *Long War Journal*. Pakistani Taliban emir for Bajaur joins Islamic State | FDD's Long War Journal.

Sayed, A. (2021, August 29). ISIS-K Is Ready to Fight the Taliban. Here's How the Group Became a Major Threat in Afghanistan, *The Washington Post*, www.washington-post.com/opinions/2021/08/29/abdul-sayed-isis-k-taliban-afghanistan-threat/.

Six Pakistan Taliban Leaders Swear Allegiance to ISIS: Spokesman, *NBC News*, October 14, 2014, www.nbcnews.com/storyline/isis-terror/six-pakistan-taliban-leaders-swear-allegiance-isis-spokesman-n225386.

Smith, S. (1996). Positivism and Beyond. In S. Smith, K. Booth and M. Zalewski (Eds.), *International Theory: Positivism and Beyond* (pp. 11–44). Cambridge: Cambridge University Press.

Soufan, A. and Freedman, D. (2011). *The Black Banners: The Inside Story of 9/11 and War against al-Qaeda*. New York: W.W Norton. & Co.

Steinberg, G. and Albrecht, A. (2022). *Terror against the Taliban: Islamic State Shows New Strength in Afghanistan*. (SWP Comment, 12/2022). Berlin: Stiftung Wissenschaft und Politik -SWP- Deutsches Institut für Internationale Politik und Sicherheit. https://doi.org/10.18449/2022C12

Stepputat, F. (2018). Pragmatic Peace in Emerging Governscapes, *International Affairs*, 94(2), 399–416. https://doi.org/10.1093/ia/iix233.

Taylor, A. (2014, September 25). The Strange Story Behind the 'Khorasan' Group's Name, *The Washington Post*, www.washingtonpost.com/news/worldviews/wp/2014/09/25/the-strange-story-behind-the-khorasan-groups-name/.

Walter, B. (2016). Interpreting the "Human Terrain" of Afghanistan with Enlightenment Philosophy. *International Studies Perspective*, 18, 409–424, http://doi.org/10.1093/isp/ekw009

PART II

What About the Taliban?

4

THROUGH THE LENS OF BELIEF

The Taliban's Worldview and Its Influence

Ahmed Sahal K.P.

Introduction

In the discipline of International Relations, which mainly centers on nation-states, the significance of religion is frequently overlooked. Violent actors, deeply rooted in their unique religious beliefs, have diverse world views with respect to contemporary nation-states and other non-state actors. The Taliban, a prime example, recently transitioned from a militant group into a fully established government, reinstating the Islamic Emirate of Afghanistan in August 2021. While many of the Emirate's practices align with those of contemporary nation-states, they are predominantly influenced by the aspects of their religious worldview.

Existing literature offers a mix of perspectives on the motivational forces steering the Taliban's actions. Amidst these diverse viewpoints, limited attention has been given to the religious worldview of the Taliban, a critical aspect in understanding their conduct. By looking through the lens of the nation-state, the Taliban or the Islamic Emirate of Afghanistan (IEA) is commonly viewed as evil and lacking an evident and significant standpoint. However, the adoption of this type of approach could lead to missing many insights regarding distinct or alternative perspectives the Taliban has of the world.

To understand this better, epistemic worldview analysis, drawing from Mark Juergensmeyer and Mona Kanwal Sheikh's socio-theological approach, is deployed, which combines the religious reasoning of actors with their social context. By using this approach, this chapter attempts to focus primarily on the Taliban's religious worldview on the aspects of the state.

Examining the speeches and writings of the Taliban leaders reveals that they interpret events in accordance with their religious beliefs, which departs from the secular and liberal paradigms, and they utilize a particular religious

DOI: 10.4324/9780429281631-6

perspective of social reality to justify their activities. Because the epistemic worldview analysis aims at the insider-oriented approach to understanding the perspectives of religiously driven actors, the chapter analyses the important Taliban documents such as statements, decrees, orders, and instructions of the Supreme Leader, works of the current Chief Justice Abdul Hakim Haqqani, Layhas (intermittently released codes of conduct), official correspondences, and other data taken from their websites and social media profiles. Analysis of recurrent narratives and themes in these texts helps identify key components of the Taliban's worldview and how they rationalise their rule and policies. This study brings forth alternative worldviews of state and governance, diverging from the established Westphalian nation-state paradigm. Understanding this is essential not only to comprehend the rationale behind the actions of the Emirate of the Taliban but also to make sense of a new world that is emerging in which state and government framework may not be the same as in the past centuries. The religious armed groups, such as Al Shabaab in Somalia and JNIM in the Sahel region, are gaining strength, which is a testament to the evolving geopolitical milieu. So, understanding the worldview of these actors is significant since they would play increasingly consequential roles in future interactions with nation-states.

Religion and International Relations

Traditionally, within the field of international relations, which has historically focused on the nation-state, religious perspectives have often been marginalised to the periphery. Fox (2001) invites our attention to the major reason by saying, "[P]erhaps the most influential explanation of why the role of religion in international politics is overlooked is that the social sciences, including international relations, have their origin in the rejection of religion" (p. 54).

The classical liberal principles nurtured by Western scholars call for a clear demarcation of religion from political affairs. Furthermore, it is hard to measure religion as a variable in the context of quantitative studies. These are some of the prominent explanations for why religion does not receive the attention it deserves in the domain of international relations. However, while examining it properly, we come to know that religion has an impact on world politics through its influence on foreign policies, serving as a justification for or against government actions, and by making regional religious issues transcend borders and become global concerns (Fox, 2001, pp. 55–59).

However, in critiquing Fox, Sheikh (2012) asserts that he was unable to construct a comprehensive understanding of the connection between religion and international relations. She argues that Fox's work lacks a framework for addressing the three aspects he previously outlined (p. 374).

Furthermore, the September 11 attacks of 2001 brought about a heightened emphasis to religious ideas within the field of international relations, such as the consideration of 'the West' and 'Islam' as fundamentally distinct global communities. This transformation has reshaped the study of both political science and international relations, elevating religion to a central area of focus. This shift particularly underscores the roles and impacts of non-state actors alongside state actors. In this regard, the ideologies of violent non-state religious actors, such as Al Qaeda and the Taliban, received significant attention, particularly after 2001. The interaction between international society, representing the alliance of sovereign states united by shared interests, values, and norms, and globally influential non-state religious actors, became a significant area of interest (Haynes, 2021, p. 7).

In mainstream international relations theories, there is a tendency to overlook the religious motivations of political actors, argues Philpott (2009). He suggests that, unlike other political subjects, religions are primarily concerned with existential beliefs rather than the structure or policies of political orders, making them challenging to confine within national boundaries. He claims that while most religious groups and leaders recognize the authority of governments, they often advocate for specific types of governments and policies that align with their beliefs and values (Philpott, 2009, pp. 187–193). However, there are numerous religious actors today who firmly believe in rejecting all forms of modern democratic principles and advocate for a completely different governance system and political order.

In international relations, religion is often marginalized due to the reluctance of IR theory scholars to incorporate it, rather than it being an inherent characteristic of the field itself (Sandal and James, 2011, p. 4). They advocate for a comprehensive approach by utilizing classical realism, neorealism, and neoliberalism – three established IR traditions – to illustrate how religion can enhance our understanding of international affairs. This approach underscores the necessity of exploring how various strands of thought within IR theory can accommodate the study of religion (Sandal and James, 2011, pp. 18–19).

But, contrary to this idea, while discussing the reintroduction of religion into international relations, posited that international relations theory should go beyond simply integrating religion into current theories, concepts, and frameworks, or recognizing religion as a form of soft power or a contributing factor. Instead, it should acknowledge the pivotal role of religion in shaping the identities of politically influential social movements and, to a significant extent, even in shaping the international system itself. He claims that a comprehensive understanding of religion's impact on politics can only be achieved when it is acknowledged as a distinct narrative, different from the Enlightenment and other secular worldviews that form the foundation of contemporary social science (Thomas et al., 2005, p. 235).

However, the approach of Thomas lacked a detailed method to understand the connection between changing religious beliefs and ideas and how they affect actions and policies (Sheikh, 2012, p. 374). Shiekh further explores three distinct analytical ideas about religion, each with significant aspects: religion as a belief community, religion as power, and religion as a speech act. Studying religion's important elements, like its teachings and moral values, becomes meaningful in international relations when it can be related to how they affect people's behaviour and society, connecting inner beliefs to real-life actions. She highlights that, for a deeper understanding of the actions of religious individuals, it is crucial to examine the authoritative religious texts they rely on for validation. This proves particularly valuable in the analysis of conflicts involving religious actors, encompassing an exploration of religious laws, the guidance of influential religious figures, and accepted interpretations of just wars, acceptable methods in warfare, and rules governing battle. Furthermore, in the realm of state strategies and policies regarding religious actors, Sheikh points out the importance of recognizing religion as a competitor with the state in delivering order, justice, security, and the rightful use of force. This competition necessitates a re-evaluation of traditional approaches to issues of authority, regulations, and legitimacy in wartime (Sheikh, 2012).

As we explore various perspectives on the link between religious beliefs and actions in international relations, it is crucial to highlight Lynch's (2014) Neo-Weberian approach, which offers a fresh viewpoint on religion and violence. She emphasizes that one cannot assume that religion inherently leads to violence or peace because it all depends on how people interpret their religious teachings in real-life situations. Her approach considers the broader social, economic, and political contexts in which religious beliefs are practiced. Central to Lynch's framework is the concept of casuistry, a method of ethical decision-making that takes into account religious doctrine, historical precedents, and the specific situation at hand. Casuistry serves as a tool for religious adherents to discern right from wrong and align their actions with the common good. Lynch emphasizes the importance of understanding how individuals employ casuistry to justify their stance on various actions, including violence, whether they advocate for or oppose them. This approach acknowledges the dynamic nature of religious beliefs and practices, recognizing that they can evolve, leading to diverse interpretations and actions, even within religious groups (p. 280–290).

Juergensmeyer (2013) brings our attention to the noteworthy shift in the way social sciences engage with religion, marking what could be described as a "sociotheological turn". This transformation, led by a group of dedicated scholars, reflects a departure from the quantitative and reductionist approaches to religious phenomena. It embodies a commitment to explore religion not only as a facet of social identity but as an important element shaping social worldviews. The idea of the "sociotheological turn" isn't entirely new. However, it gained significant momentum in the latter half of the twentieth century. Scholars like Peter Berger and Robert Bellah began to take religion's impact on social reality seriously, investigating not just religious things but also the way social reality is perceived through a religious lens. In recent years, this trend has gained even more traction (Juergensmeyer, 2013, p. 940).

The world stage has further highlighted the necessity of integrating religious perspectives into social analysis. Militant movements employ religious language and myth to legitimize their actions, necessitating a comprehensive understanding of their motivations. These movements blur the lines between religious spirituality and communal aspiration for a redemptive social order, challenging the secularism that separates religion from the public realm. The sociotheological concept embraces the insider's perspective, understanding worldviews from within and acknowledging the interplay between religion and other aspects of society. It is an alternative to the traditional positivist approaches and recognizes the significance of religious thinking in social analysis (Juergensmeyer, 2013, p. 944).

Why Religion Matters in World Politics

Building upon the preceding ideas, Juergensmeyer and Sheikh (2013) introduces sociotheological approach aimed at understanding the worldview of actors. This approach combines religious reasoning with the social context. The authors propose the epistemic worldview as a "framework for thinking about reality and acting appropriately within a perceived understanding of the world. The idea of an epistemic worldview has much in common with the notion of religion (and other ways of thinking about the world, such as science and poetry) as being an awareness of an alternative view of reality" (p. 739). The sociotheological approach, as argued by Juergensmeyer and Sheikh, encompasses two key elements: an analysis of internal epistemic worldviews and a study of the social setting. It supports understanding different worldviews in their specific social contexts and how those who share these worldviews interact with broader social and power systems. At its core, this approach champions the idea of understanding the world as seen through the eyes of others. The authors advocate for empathetic immersion, a process involving stepping into their shoes, understanding their perspectives, and deciphering their points of reference. Frequently recurring themes within the religious framework furnish valuable insights into a group's outlook on the world. To gain insight into a group's worldview, it is essential to unravel its central motives, encompassing images, narratives, and other fundamental ideas it values greatly. By examining the complex interaction of social power dynamics within a group's perspective, factors contributing to what they consider successful in their actions can be understood. When viewed through alternative worldviews, an armed group may appear irrational and their actions reprehensible. However, by exploring their religious worldview and justifications, a rational thread emerges, revealing the logic behind their actions. The authors also aptly observe that epistemic worldviews are fluid entities, evolving over time.

For worldview analysis to be a valuable tool in the social sciences, especially regarding conflicts, it should shift its focus away from simple cause-and-effect questions that link worldviews directly to violence. Instead, it should concentrate on constructivist inquiries, like understanding how individuals with certain worldviews perceive the world in a way that leads to violent actions. The objective is to grasp how people think about reality and behave based on their perceived understanding of the world. To conduct an effective worldview analysis, three critical traps should be avoided. The first is assuming that behaviour is solely determined by worldviews. The second suggests that worldviews play a role in shaping actions and, therefore, precede any action. The third mistake is maintaining an essentialist and unchanging view of worldviews that disregards both the individuals holding these views and their interactions with the social world. When actors possess well-defined beliefs about identity, justice, and truth, along with a powerful plan to achieve their goals, they possess a compelling narrative. For instance, narratives portraying the world as a cosmic battlefield with absolute enemies and the actors as heroic warriors tend to mobilize people for violent or confrontational actions (Sheikh and Juergensmeyer, 2020).

The term "worldview" originates from the word "Weltanschauung," which was initially employed by Immanuel Kant in his book titled *Critique of Judgment* (Sheikh, 2018a). Sheikh finds worldview and ideology as often used interchangeably but points out important differences. Ideology typically refers to established political ideas and is heavily influenced by Marx's conception of ideology as an expression of material interests and power. In this view, ideology distorts reality and conceals true conditions. The idea of ideology is commonly used in literature when trying to uncover the real intentions behind what people say, which are often related to maintaining or gaining power and privilege. Studies of ideology often privilege textual analysis over practice and definitional claims over empirical evidence.

On the other hand, when we check out worldviews, it is important to look at the big picture. This means taking a wider view that includes an insider's attempt to understand what a particular worldview is all about. It involves exploring its social, ethical, political, and spiritual aspects and seeing how they fit together to make a complete and meaningful picture. Unlike the typical approach to studying ideology, worldview analysis doesn't aim to prove or disprove the ideas people have. Instead, its focus is on bringing those ideas to the forefront for examination. The aim is to grasp what people personally believe about the reality. What's important are the ideas they express, the terms they bring up, the pictures they create, and the ways they tell their overall stories. To grasp an epistemic worldview or how an actor sees and understands the world, one must figure out how their beliefs about reality work and fit them into their social environment. Secondly, it needs to see how these people and their beliefs connect with the social and power structures of their world (Juergensmeyer and Sheikh, 2013; Sheikh, 2018).

The Case of the Taliban

The majority of research on the Taliban primarily involves focusing on the dimension of warfare, examining their actions and the results rather than exploring the beliefs that drive them. Additionally, there are various challenges when studying the Taliban. It is important to consider the interests of different parties, including the United States, and to recognize their view of Afghanistan, which is often based on knowledge developed during colonial times. It is also essential to think about the strong influence of Eurocentric perspectives before attempting to learn about the Taliban. Nonetheless, researchers have made efforts to understand the Taliban in different ways and have made significant contributions to the existing literature.

According to Ruttig (2012), the Taliban have their origins in tribal society but also follow a broader Islamist ideology that goes beyond individual tribes. This supratribal ideology enables the Taliban to garner support from various tribal and ethnic groups. Furthermore, the use of Islamic references helps the Taliban unify different groups within their ranks (pp. 131–132). He says that the Taliban draws from three distinct networks: religious, political, and tribal, and chooses from these networks as the situation demands, whether it is for mobilization, support, or solidarity (Ruttig, 2012, pp. 118–119).

Linschoten and Kuehn (2012) thoroughly examine the Taliban in comparison to Al Qaeda, highlighting their significant differences. They closely analyze these distinctions across various aspects, including educational backgrounds, the economic environment, ideological foundations, and cultural backgrounds. Their findings emphasize that Al Qaeda's ambitions stretch globally, while the Taliban's vision remains closely tied to Afghanistan. Through an in-depth analysis, the book challenges the common belief of an unbreakable link between these groups, labelling it a strategic mistake in the Afghanistan conflict (Linschoten and Kuehn, 2012, p. 328). While this specific study is profoundly significant, its primary focus is limited to a comparative analysis of the two groups and their differences.

In his thesis, Linschoten (2016) explores the historical development of the Taliban's identity by primarily drawing insights from original sources. This investigation examines how the Taliban perceive themselves and how this self-perception shaped their governance in Afghanistan. It also underscores the dynamic nature of the Taliban's identity, emphasizing that it isn't a fixed concept. The central theme revolves around how the collective identity of the group influences the personal identities of its members. The impact of religion, culture, and institutions on the Taliban's identity is also examined

(p. 12–16). Notably, the author points out the presence of preconceived notions that influence researchers when attempting to understand the roots and agenda of the Taliban (Linschoten, 2016, p. 11). One main aspect of the Taliban, which he highlights, is the institution of Ameerul Mu'mineen that aided them in centralization. Another vital element is their strong cultural identity, stemming from a blend of religious and Pashtun traditions, which bound the group together. Additionally, he emphasizes the importance of duty among the Taliban, seen as a source of motivation. The author also stresses the role of the theology of Jihad and the prevalence of Deobandi education among the members. Furthermore, he notes the movement's dynamic nature, experiencing multiple changes over time. He points out that the Taliban elevated the status of Ulema or religious scholars. He further encourages future researchers to look deeper into the Taliban's religious education and ideology (Linschoten, 2016, pp. 286–298).

Farrell and Giustozzi (2013) look at the issue from the standpoint of fighters. By conducting interviews with fighters, commanders, and elders in the Helmand province, the study provides insights into the Taliban's gradual comeback and the evolving nature of their tactics for both warfare and governance. The study highlights the importance of understanding the relationship between the Taliban and the local population, as well as the role of religious scholars in obtaining social support for the movement.

Giustozzi (2019) digs into the complex dynamics of the Taliban insurgency in Afghanistan. His in-depth work examines the Taliban's strategies, tactics, motivations, and the forces shaping the conflict. It mentions the Taliban's relationships with the Afghan population. The book also points out the dynamics of the Taliban's internal leadership structure and the role that ideology, religion, and local politics play in their decision-making processes.

The efforts of the Taliban to achieve legitimacy in governance are comprehensively examined by Terpstra (2020). He asserts that the existence of a foreign enemy is the primary factor that confers legitimacy to rebel groups, and he demonstrates how this legitimacy was established and maintained, employing a careful examination of three phases of Taliban rule.

In his seminal work, Malkasian (2021) provides a comprehensive examination of past studies on the Taliban and argues that previous literature has failed to fully acknowledge the central role that the narrative of 'Islam' and 'resistance to foreign occupation' has played in the Taliban's success.

The Taliban did not have an official viewpoint on state and governance substantiated by a doctrine before. Only after their takeover of Kabul have more ideas emerged from official statements and other sources due to the increased authenticity of the information. Even the information from the collective translated texts of the Taliban reader is hard to verify, because many previous Taliban websites were taken down. Now, with numerous websites and official representatives on social media, it is possible to analyze the relationship between previously assumed worldviews and the currently affirmed ones and their influence on their policies and actions. The book by the Chief Justice of the Taliban, Abdul Hakim Haqqani, also serves as a supplement to earlier works and adds more coherence to the Taliban's worldview.

As we have seen, the existing literature has focused on various aspects of the Taliban, including their origins, beliefs, motivations, governance, and relationships with different groups. Researchers have also explored their tactics, strategies, and efforts to gain legitimacy. They have looked at how the Taliban use culture and religion to serve their goals. As we discussed earlier, the core conceptual framework of the chapter is epistemic worldview analysis, which examines the Taliban through their own perspective and how they perceive the world. This will give us a clearer understanding of why they currently act as they do. Also, most studies treat ideology instrumentally as a tool for pursuing strategic interests rather than an essential driver in itself. The agency and rationality behind belief-based actions are often discounted. Meanwhile, those focused on theology tend to simply assert that religion causes certain behaviours without examining mediating processes. Additionally, there is very little study on the political ideas of the Emirate.

Given the Taliban's significant emphasis on the Ulema, or religious scholars, it is essential to examine the works of figures like Abdul Hakeem Haqqani. His recent book, titled *Imarah al Islamiya wa nidaamuha* (*Islamic Emirate and Its System*), represents a significant doctrinal development, especially since it is endorsed by the current Supreme Leader, Hibatullah Akhundzada. Examining other statements, including those issued by Hibatullah and earlier supreme leaders, official letters, and statements, provides a comprehensive understanding of the Taliban's worldview. The study also considers other sources, such as speeches and statements by other senior Taliban officials. An analysis of recurrent narratives and themes in these texts helps identify key components of the Taliban's worldview and how they rationalize their system of rule and policies.

How to Understand the Taliban

By looking through the lens of the nation-state, the Taliban, or the Islamic Emirate of Afghanistan[1] (IEA), is seen as completely devoid of any perspective that is worth understanding. However, adopting this approach could lead to missing many insights regarding distinct or alternative perspectives that the Taliban holds of the world. Examining the speeches and writings of Taliban leaders reveals that they interpret events in accordance with their religious interpretations, contrasting with secular countries, and they utilize a particular religious perspective of social reality to justify their activities. Furthermore, the Taliban interprets their knowledge of religion in accordance with the unique social and political contexts in which they operate. This aligns with Sheikh's (2018a) opinion that worldview analysis is applicable to a wide range of phenomena, apart from violent behaviour, and can be used as entry points to understanding diverse views of the world (p. 157).

The Taliban's violent actions are always framed by them in the religious term of Jihad, and, most importantly, they obtained wide support from the population who share many aspects of their religious worldview, without which their August 2021 takeover wouldn't have been possible. According to Lugo et al. (2013), almost everyone in Afghanistan (99%) among the Muslim population expresses a desire for Sharia to be the official law of the land (p. 9). However, this doesn't mean that most of the population supports all the activities of the Taliban. Nonetheless, this reinforces the chances of the Taliban obtaining support from the population with such a mindset. Furthermore, the Taliban are bonded with people through their tribal, religious, and national identities and are interwoven into society (Ruttig, 2012).

Along with this social setting, as Juergensmeyer and Sheikh (2013) pointed out while defining sociotheology, the Taliban depict themselves as servants of God who are carrying out divine orders, as evidenced in their documents. Drawing again from their ideas, the motives and goals of the Taliban are represented in religious language. In accordance with the ideas of sociotheology, the acknowledgment of the religious dimension of politics can be observed in the Emirate of the Taliban, where they recognize religion beyond personal beliefs intertwined with public life.

There are some particular reasons why the Taliban was selected for this case analysis. One reason is that it is a religiously driven violent actor that can also be categorized as a Jihadist entity and fits well with the sociotheological approach. Even though it has transitioned into a government now, religion is still the supreme influential element for the Taliban's Emirate. The second reason is the uniqueness of the Taliban with respect to all other Jihadi movements or armed non-state Islamist actors. It is a nationalist movement with an adherence different from Salafi Jihadism and draws from both Deobandi and Salafi thoughts. Another reason for choosing the Taliban for this case study is that this is the sole such Jihadi movement in recent decades that became militarily successful and transformed into a government by the end of the war. At the same time, groups like ISIS met their demise in terms of territorial control by the end of the war and the overall weakening of the group as a whole.

What has helped the Taliban in its resurgence and, ultimately, victory is its unique worldview. It involves many representations, images depicting their ideas and goals, practices that have been carried throughout the war, and patterns of operationalizing their actions, which can also be considered to be socially embedded worldviews. Even though epistemic worldview analysis talks a lot about conducting direct interviews to grasp the worldview of actors, Juergensmeyer (2018) has also included the idea of collecting knowledge from existing sources of people who are experts on that specific actor or from textual analysis (p. 31). This chapter does exactly the same and mainly analyzes sources like *The Taliban Reader* (a collection of translated articles and statements of the Taliban), the book by Chief Justice of the Taliban Abdul Hakim Haqqani (*Islamic Emirate and Its System*), decrees, orders, and instructions of Taliban's Supreme Leader (Ameerul Mu'mineen[2]) from 2016 to 2023. Other documents from Taliban websites and social media posts of Taliban officials were also examined. The following are the five major principles that reflect the Taliban's perspective on the state, identified through the analysis of relevant materials.

1. State of Guidance and Divine Sovereignty

Abdul Hakim Haqqani (2022) considers the Islamic Emirate a "State of Guidance." He differentiates between states focused on taxation and material gain versus states focused on religious or moral guidance and argues that the Islamic Emirate is the latter – aimed at guiding people towards Allah and Islamic principles (p. 20–21). The three key features of this "State of Guidance" are an independent judiciary based on Islamic law, an Islamic army to enforce order, and governance by divine law (Shariah). Specifically, the interpretation of Shariah is referred to early Muslims and religious scholars (Haqqani, 2022, pp. 20–24). By quoting Al Samood[3] and Zabihullah,[4] Stenersen (2010) says that the Taliban considers the Islamic regime to be the only correct system of government, which they believe is the solution to all of Afghanistan's problems (p. 51).

During a speech in Russia, Amir Khan Muttaqi (Ministry of Foreign Affairs, Islamic Emirate of Afghanistan, 2023) talked about the crisis Afghanistan is going through. He said that these issues came due to the adherence to foreign models and rules by previous Afghan governments without considering their geography, history, culture, religion, and social values.

The theme of divine sovereignty recurs across the Taliban's statements and edicts. Their documents reject secular nationalism, arguing that ultimate sovereignty lies only with God. This shapes their dismissal of external governance models like democracy as violating God's authority. Rejection of secular laws is another central theme in Haqqani's book. Haqqani argues man-made laws are baseless compared to Shariah. However, he also says that the customs of the people should be observed and allowed if they don't contradict the principles of Shariah. Adherence to Hanafi[5] jurisprudence is also a necessary element, according to Haqqani, which he mentions is the school of thought common to most Afghans (Haqqani, 2022, pp. 37–39).

The Taliban do not accept systems that are not based on Shariah law, but they have not opposed living alongside these systems within the international state framework. This can be seen in many of their past statements and declarations. The letter to the Shanghai Cooperation Organization demonstrates this interest in cooperation and interaction with other countries (Gopal and Linschoten, 2017, p. 41). Furthermore, the ongoing discussions about seeking recognition from the UN and engagement with other countries also reflect this perspective. The Taliban's mindset was previously evident on their websites. For example, they stated, "Islamic Emirate of Afghanistan respects and adheres to all rules and principles ratified by the UN provided that they do not contradict the teachings of Islamic Shariah" (Linschoten and Kuehn, 2018, chap. 48). In all their mentions of coexistence with non-Shariah systems, they consistently add the condition, "as long as they do not contradict Shariah." However, they do not explain the specifics of this Shariah framework.

2. Rooted in Religious Nationalism With the Idea of "Ummah"

When we look at the literature about the Taliban, we can see that they are deeply rooted in their religious beliefs and only operate within the boundaries of Afghanistan. However, they also connect themselves to the broader Muslim community worldwide through the concept of Ummah (Muslim community). It is important to mention that the Taliban has never launched an attack beyond Afghanistan's borders. Moreover, when stating the prerequisites for the Ameerul Mu'mineen in a previous version of the Taliban's constitution, they explicitly state that the leader must be an Afghan citizen born to Afghan parents[b] (Linschoten and Kuehn, 2018).

At times, they emphasize Islam as a common shared identity, linking them with other armed actors. When Osama bin Laden was killed, the Taliban issued a statement honouring him as a martyr for his sacrifices in Afghanistan and for the Palestinian cause. They mentioned his fight against what they saw as Christian and Jewish aggression in the Islamic world and also emphasized their shared faith and common cause. In this particular statement, they chose not to discuss bin Laden's affiliation with Al Qaeda, possibly to avoid potential political ramifications. However, they did not hesitate to offer commentary on him as an individual Muslim. In another statement, they described his death as part of a "crusade against the Islamic Ummah for the past decade," reaffirming their connection to the concept of Ummah (Linschoten and Kuehn, 2012, pp. 341–342).

However, there has been a change in this pattern. When Al Qaeda's leader, Zawahiri, was killed recently by a drone attack in Kabul, the Taliban did not show the same kind of honour and didn't even acknowledge his death. Instead, they simply stated that an investigation is ongoing. (Knopp et al., 2023, p. 48). Their change in approach can be explained by being practical rather than having a fundamental shift in their stance toward these transnational groups. They are currently in a governing position and want to avoid strong criticism that might come from admitting their connection with Al Qaeda, which would go against the terms of the Doha Agreement.

The Islamic Emirate of Afghanistan (IEA) in its recent statement[7] stresses the importance of the Islamic Brotherhood in their request to neighbouring countries, urging them to show kindness to Afghan refugees (Mujahid, 2023). In many statements and speeches, we can observe this link to the concept of the Ummah, along with the firm commitment to Afghan nationalism.

Multiple documents prohibit regional, ethnic, and linguistic biases and cronyism, instructing to focus on piety and religious brotherhood instead. This subordinates other identities to a common religious identity (Clark, 2011). The Taliban considers Afghanistan to be both a religious land and a homeland – *balad dini wa watani* (Stenersen, 2010, p. 56).

From numerous reports, it is evident that militants from Tajikistan, Xinjiang, Uzbekistan, and Arab regions have taken refuge in Afghanistan under the Taliban government. This presence is rooted in the religious connections of the Ummah. However, Taliban officials have consistently denied the existence of these groups, refraining from disclosing their names (Knopp et al., 2023, p. 42). As such, there exists a complex interplay between the nationalism and transnational connections of the Taliban. Currently, the territorial and Afghan identity aspects seem confined within nationalistic terms. Nevertheless, when it comes to beliefs and a sense of Ummah or community, these boundaries often extend globally.

3. Religious Justification and Divine Ordainment of Their Actions

The Taliban's worldview is predominantly framed in religious ideas and justifications. Here, when we look further, we can see that the Taliban justifies their acts through a specific understanding of religious reality, as Sheikh (2020) pointed out (pp. 111–121). The Taliban documents repeatedly refer to pursuing "Allah's satisfaction," obeying "God's orders," and establishing "Allah's religion" as the purpose behind their "Jihad" and governance. Examples include decrees of the Supreme Leader about prisoners of war, cooperating with the virtue/vice department, prohibition of punishment and filming without a court order, and so on (Afghanistan Analyst Network, 2023, pp. 6, 11, 27). Justifications for many rules and policies are substantiated using religious references and principles of Shariah law. For example, the importance of obedience in the code of conduct is supported by framing it as a "religious duty" (Clark, 2011, p. 8).

All the codes of conduct start by elaborating on the virtues and religious obligations of Jihad. It is described as the "greatest worship" that will lead to "dignity" (Clark, 2011, pp. 2, 15, 25). This suggests Jihad forms a core part of the Taliban's worldview as the means to establish their political vision, which is divinely mandated. Also, that does not mean that all of their actions are driven by religious ideals. The Taliban follows many of the regular practices of other states as well. The upholding of diplomatic protocols with the Chinese ambassador is one example (Al Jazeera, 2023).

4. Pragmatism in Governance

Some problematic orders, like prohibiting working for the Afghan government, which were present in the 2006 layha were removed from later codes of conduct, suggesting pragmatism. Similarly, NGOs and such organizations which were banned in 2006 layha were later allowed to operate with some control over them (Clark, 2011, pp. 11, 21, 26). But decrees about university education order appointing Islamic scholars for oversight underscores that pragmatism has limits grounded in religious principles (Afghanistan Analyst Network, 2023, p. 65).

5. Ameer ul Mu'mineen as the Final Decision-Maker

The Amir ul Mu'mineen, or supreme leader within the Taliban, holds the highest power in the Emirate, also serving as the ultimate judicial authority. The Amir also plays a pivotal role in maintaining unity within the ranks, because every fighter regards him as the ultimate leader. The process of choosing the Amir as the state leader begins with a group of influential individuals known as "*Ahl al hall wal aqd*" who play a pivotal role in endorsing the candidate. Subsequently, the general populace adheres to this decision, guided by the principle of "listening and obeying" (Haqqani, 2022, p. 61).

Osman and Gopal (2016) mention an interview with Mullah Wakil Ahmad Mutawakkil from 1996 in which he explained that decisions within their group are made following the guidance of Amir ul Mu'mineen, and they don't think it is important to consult with others. They believe that this method is in line with their religious beliefs, and they follow the leader's opinion, even if it is his decision alone. Wakil Ahmad also mentioned that if he disagrees with a decision, the government can't implement it (p. 17–18).

Taliban places great importance on following their leadership. This is evident in numerous speeches, interviews, and statements. In a document titled "Obedience to the Amir" by Mufti Ludhianvi,[8] which offers advice to Taliban members, he emphasises that obeying the Amir is as crucial as breathing for survival. He also stresses that every Taliban member should understand that any shortcoming in obeying the Amir is equal to a shortcoming in Islam. Furthermore, he notes that any decline in the commitment to obeying the Amir weakens the implementation of God's system. In an earlier draft of the Taliban's constitution, they designated the Ameerul Mu'mineen as holding the highest position of authority[9] (Linschoten and Kuehn, 2018).

Recently, the Supreme Leader, Hibathullah Akhunzada, approved the prohibition of women's education in Afghanistan. Despite the presence of moderate factions within the Taliban who supported education, they were unable to oppose this measure because of their unwavering loyalty and obedience to the position of the supreme leader.

Conclusion

In conclusion, as religious armed actors become more prominent globally, understanding their worldview is crucial for policymakers, analysts, and scholars. This chapter attempts to unveil an alternative worldview diverging from the established Westphalian nation-state paradigm. This includes a range of entirely different ideas regarding state, governance, leadership, sovereignty, and so on. Understanding this is essential not only to comprehend the rationale behind the actions of the Emirate of the Taliban but also to make sense of a new world that is emerging, wherein the state and government framework may not be the same as in past centuries. Religious armed groups, such as Al Shabaab in Somalia and JNIM in the Sahel region, are gaining strength, a testament to the evolving geopolitical milieu. Therefore, understanding the worldview of these actors is significant because they would play increasingly consequential roles in future interactions with nation-states.

Notes

1 The Islamic Emirate of Afghanistan is the name that the Taliban use for their government. They adopted this name during their rule from 1996 to 2001. After their retreat from provincial capitals in 2001, the Taliban maintained a parallel government with the same name, overseeing various departments of operation and governance. This name has persisted since then, even after the Taliban's takeover of Kabul in 2021.
2 Ameerul Mu'mineen is an Arabic term that translates to "Leader of the Believers." This title was initially used for the first four Caliphs who governed Arabia following the death of Prophet Mohammed. It continued to be utilized in the Umayyad and Abbasid Caliphates. In 1996, when the Taliban took control of Kabul, they bestowed the same title, Ameerul Mu'mineen, upon their leader, Mullah Mohammad Umar. After him, Mullah Akhtar Mansoor and the current leader, Hibatullah Akhunzada, also assumed the same title.
3 *Al Samood* is the magazine of the Taliban.
4 Zabihullah Mujahid is the official Spokesperson of the Islamic Emirate of Afghanistan (IEA).
5 Hanafi jurisprudence, founded by Imam Abu Hanifa, is one of the four major schools of Sunni Islamic law.
6 *Taliban Reader*, Chapter 57 – Constitution (Article 53).
7 Document No. 395, Dated 31/10/2023, Official Spokesperson, Commission for Cultural Affairs, Islamic Emirate of Afghanistan.
8 *Taliban Reader* – Chapter 57 – Constitution -Article 52.
9 *Taliban Reader* – Chapter 27 – Obedience to the Amir – Extracts from Mufti Ludhianvi's Obedience to the Amir (Advice to Taliban members).

References

Afghanistan Analyst Network. (2023). *Decrees, Orders and Instructions of his Excellency, Amir Al-Mu'minin.* (Translated from the official Gazette published by the Ministry of Justice, Islamic Emirate of Afghanistan). Available at: www. afghanistan-analysts.org/en/wp-content/uploads/sites/2/2023/07/Decrees-order-of-Taleban-amir-English.pdf (Accessed: 18th August 2023).

Al Jazeera. (2023, September 13). Taliban gives a warm welcome to China's new ambassador to Afghanistan. Available at: www.aljazeera.com/news/2023/9/13/taliban-gives-a-warm-welcome-to-chinas-new-ambassador-to-afghanistan

Clark, K. (Trans.). (2011). *The Layha: Calling the Taleban to Account* (Translated from *The Layha* published in Pashto by the Islamic Emirate of Afghanistan in 2006, 2009 & 2010). Afghanistan Analysts Network. Available at: www. afghanistan-analysts.org/wp-content/uploads/downloads/2012/10/Appendix_1_Code_in_English.pdf

Farrell, T., and Giustozzi, A. (2013). The Taliban at war: Inside the Helmand insurgency, 2004–2012. *International Affairs*, 89(4), 845–871. https://doi.org/10.1111/1468-2346.12048

Fox, J. (2001). Religion as an overlooked element of international relations. *International Studies Review*, 3(3), 53–72. https://doi.org/10.1111/1521-9488.00244

Giustozzi, A. (2019). *The Taliban at War: 2001–2021.* New York: Oxford University Press.

Gopal, A., and van Linschoten, S. (2017). Ideology in the Afghan Taliban. *Afghanistan Analysts Network*. Available at: www.afghanistan-analysts.org/wp-content/uploads/2017/06/201705-AGopal-ASvLinschoten-TB-Ideology.pdf (Accessed: 15th October 2023).

Haqqani, A. H. (2022). الإمارة الإسلامية ونظامها (*Islamic Emirate and Its System*). Darul Uloom Shara'iyyah. Available at: https://archive.org/details/20220824_20220824_1134 (Accessed: 2nd August 2023).

Haynes, J. (2021). Religion in international relations: Theory and practice. In J. Haynes (Ed.), *Handbook on Religion and International Relations* (pp. 5–23). Northampton, MA: Elgar.

Juergensmeyer, M. (2013). The sociotheological turn. *Journal of the American Academy of Religion*, 81(4), 939–948. https://doi.org/10.1093/jaarel/lft049

Juergensmeyer, M. (2018). Thinking sociologically about religion and violence: The case of ISIS. *Sociology of Religion*, 79(1), 20–34. https://doi.org/10.1093/socrel/srx055

Juergensmeyer, M., and Sheikh, M. K. (2013). A Sociotheological approach to understanding religious violence. In M. Juergensmeyer, M. Kitts and M. Jerryson (Eds.), *The Oxford Handbook of Religion and Violence* (pp. 620–644). New York: Oxford University Press.

Knopp, B. M., Niewijk, J., Tariq, Z. H., and Wright, E. C., Jr. (2023). *Comparing Taliban Social Media Usage by Language: Who's Speaking and What's Being Said.* Santa Monica, CA: RAND Corporation. Available at: www.rand.org/pubs/research_reports/RRA1830-1.html (Accessed: 11th October 2023).

Lugo, L., Cooperman, A., Bell, J., O'Connell, E., and Stencel, S. (2013). *The World's Muslims: Religion, Politics and Society.* Pew Research Center. Available at: www.pewresearch.org/religion/wp-content/uploads/sites/7/2013/04/worlds-muslims-religion-politics-society-full-report.pdf (Accessed: 5th November 2023).

Lynch, C. (2014). A Neo-Weberian approach to studying religion and violence. *Millennium*, 43(1), 273–290. https://doi.org/10.1177/0305829814545150

Malkasian, C. (2021). *The American war in Afghanistan: A History.* New York: Oxford University Press.

Ministry of Foreign Affairs, Islamic Emirate of Afghanistan. (2023, October 1). Statement by IEA Foreign Minister Mawlawi Amirkhan Muttaqi at the Moscow Format Consultations, September 29, 2023, Kazan, Tatarstan. Available at: https://mfa.gov.af/en/statement-by-iea-foreign-minister-mawlawi-amirkhan-muttaqi-at-the-mosow-format-consultationsseptember-29-2023kazan-tatarstan/(Accessed: 10th November 2023).

Mujahid, Z. [@Zabehulah_M33]. (2023, November 1). Declaration of the Islamic Emirate on Afghan Refugees in Pakistan and Other Countries. Twitter. Available at: https://twitter.com/Zabehulah_M33/status/1719630782824583525

Osman, B., and Gopal, A. (2016). Taliban views on a future state. *Center on International Cooperation*. Available at: www.academia.edu/28493005/Taliban_Views_on_a_Future_State

Philpott, D. (2009). Has the study of global politics found religion? *Annual Review of Political Science*, 12(1), 183–202. https://doi.org/10.1146/annurev.polisci.12.053006.125448

Ruttig, T. (2012). How Tribal are the Taliban? In S. Bashir and R. D. Crews (Eds.), *Under the Drones: Modern Lives in the Afghanistan-Pakistan Borderlands* (pp. 102–135). Harvard University Press.

Sandal, N. A., and James, P. (2011). Religion and international Relations theory: Towards a mutual understanding. *European Journal of International Relations*, 17(1), 3–25, https://doi.org/10.1177/1354066110364304

Sheikh, M. K. (2012). How does religion matter? Pathways to religion in international relations. *Review of International Studies*, 38(2), 365–392. https://doi.org/10.1017/S026021051100057X

Sheikh, M. K. (2018a). Worldview analysis. In M. J. Juergensmeyer, S. Sassen, M. B. Steger and V. Faessel (Eds.), *The Oxford Handbook of Global Studies* (pp. 157–172). New York: Oxford University Press.

Sheikh, M. K. (2018b). The significance of worldview analysis for social sciences. In M. J. Juergensmeyer and M. K. Sheikh (Eds.), *Entering Religious Minds: The Social Study of Worldviews*. London: Routledge.

Sheikh, M. K. (2019). The significance of worldview analysis for social sciences. In M. K. Sheikh and M. Juergensmeyer (Eds.), *Entering Religious Minds* (pp. 111–121). New York: Routledge.

Sheikh, M. K., and Juergensmeyer, M. (Eds.). (2020). *Entering Religious Minds: The Social Study of Worldviews*. New York: Routledge.

Stenersen, A. (2010). The Taliban insurgency in Afghanistan-organization, leadership and worldview. *Norwegian Defence Research Establishment (FFI)*. Available at: https://ffi-publikasjoner.archive.knowledgearc.net/bitstream/handle/20.500.12242/2408/10-00359.pdf (Accessed: 13th October 2023).

Terpstra, N. (2020). Rebel governance, rebel legitimacy, and external intervention: Assessing three phases of Taliban rule in Afghanistan. *Small Wars & Insurgencies*, 31(6), 1143–1173. https://doi.org/10.1080/09592318.2020.1757916

Thomas, S., Tutu, D., and Tutu, D. M. (2005). *The Global Resurgence of Religion and the Transformation of International Relations: The Struggle for the Soul of the Twenty-First Century*. New York: Palgrave Macmillan.

Van Linschoten, A. S. *Mullah Wars: The Afghan Taliban between Village and State, 1979–2001*. [PhD Thesis, Kings College London]. Available at: https://kclpure.kcl.ac.uk/ws/portalfiles/portal/60838634/2016_Van_Linschoten_Alex_Strick_0202417_ethesis.pdf (Accessed: 23rd September, 2023).

Van Linschoten, A. S., and Kuehn, F. (2012). *An Enemy We Created: The Myth of the Taliban-al Qaeda Merger in Afghanistan*. New York: Oxford University Press.

Van Linschoten, A. S., and Kuehn, F. (Eds.). (2018). *The Taliban Reader: War, Islam and Politics in Their Own Words*. New York: Oxford University Press.

5

PIECED PEACE IN AFGHANISTAN

Evaluating the Peace Processes for Ending the Conflict in Afghanistan Post-2014

Chayanika Saxena

It is said that politics is the continuation of war by other means. In that case, the politics of peace in Afghanistan appears to have become that front on which different stakeholders still play out their rivalries. The deal between the United States of America and the Taliban, which was signed in Doha on February 29, 2020, and the intra-Afghan dialogue that followed in its wake in early September 2020, are amongst the many peace processes that have been initiated to settle the multi-scalar disputes in which Afghanistan remains embroiled. While holding a credible promise for reconciliation, there are impediments to this peace process, like the friction between the Taliban and the Afghan government or the accusations of deliberate harm to the American forces by Russians (Prothero 2020) and Iranians (Cohen 2020), which continue to hold the process to ransom to different geopolitical exigencies.

Similarly, the past experiments with peacebuilding in Afghanistan –from the late 1980s right up to now – are far from inspiring because they met with little success. In light of this, the current round of negotiations looks tenuous at best. However, as Abdullah Abdullah, Chairman of the High Council for National Reconciliation (HCNR), had recently said, "four decades of war does not mean that Afghanistan (sic) cannot solve the conflict" (Gallagher 2020). In this chapter, I look at three major peace processes that were initiated since the drawdown of the American and international forces from Afghanistan in 2014. These are the *Murree Process* (2015); the *Quadrilateral Coordination Group on Afghanistan* (QCG 2017); and the *Moscow-Format* (2016–18).

Interestingly, all these negotiations had two things in common. Firstly, the presence of the Taliban or at least an outreach to this insurgent-cum-political group by the state-stakeholders involved in these respective dialogues/

DOI: 10.4324/9780429281631-7

processes. Secondly, the indifferent treatment meted out to India at all these platforms. India was neither invited to the Murree Process nor QCG. Similarly, India's delayed inclusion in the Moscow-Format and its subsequent 'non-official' participation in it signalled its displeasure both with talking to the Taliban and with the slight it had received at the Russian hands.

In what follows, I will discuss the dynamics of each of these three peace processes individually, prefacing it with a discussion on the American involvement in Afghanistan and the course it had followed up to 2014. I will also evaluate India's reaction to these negotiations, in brief, as part of this discussion. It must be mentioned here that while these aborted missions may not have buildable takeaways to offer, they can offer insights into the issues that prevented them from taking off, and which must be avoided to give the in-progress intra-Afghan dialogue a sustainable start. This chapter will conclude with an evaluation of the critical developments that have taken place since the signing of the Doha Agreement[1] earlier this year.

For now, it is hard to predict the course of the looming peace process, especially at a time when new and old bottlenecks continue to make the path to peace meandering and tortuous. It is not unlikely that the current negotiations, which happen to be in a state of slow movement if not no movement at all, might run into a dead end just as the previous processes did. That said, the evolving situation in Afghanistan, as I have discussed elsewhere (Saxena 2020), is one in which the Taliban will continue to the strengthen its position as a legitimate political player on the back of international support. As this insurgent movement gains a firmer place on the political landscape of this war-torn country, it will also throw up interesting challenges for countries like India that are still reluctant to talk to the Taliban. On India's part, its hesitance is rooted both in its perilous encounters with this group in the past (ex. IC-814 hijack), and its present concerns regarding the Taliban's evidenced support to the South Asian chapter of Al-Qaeda (UNSC 2020). However, as the Taliban assumes an inevitable political presence in Afghanistan, it will only be in India's strategic interest to acknowledge that its existing approach towards this group might have actually "had its day" (Aneja 2020).

America's Afghantsy and Aftermath

In October 2001, the US began an international military operation in Afghanistan in response to the attacks carried out by Al-Qaeda on American soil on September 11. These attacks, which are more commonly known as '9/11', were the deadliest for the United States since the attack on Pearl Harbor during the Second World War in 1945 (The Commission 2004). Denting the prolonged unipolar moment that was enjoyed by the US since the end of the Cold War (S. Smith 2011), these attacks revealed the growing might and reach of the various transnational, non-state terrorist outfits that ultimately catapulted the problem of terrorism onto the global stage. What until September 11, 2001, was taken to be a quasi-global phenomenon, terrorism in general and Islamist terrorism in particular became a global concern. This realisation, in turn, necessitated the creation of a collective front against terrorism, wherein as many as 136 countries offered their diplomatic and military support to the US (US Department of State 2001). Interestingly enough, this 'global war on terror' (GWOT) gave a non-state entity like Al-Qaeda a territorial dimension and identified it with a nation-state, Afghanistan.

This *statisation* of global terrorism became an attempt to territorially demarcate and manage what was essentially an *aterritorial* and *non-state* phenomenon and which may have contributed to the eventual failure of the United States-led 'crusade' against it (Carroll 2018). Without going into the details of the problems that affected this trans-statal initiative (see Malkasian 2020), it will be sufficient to say that the GWOT had no clear objective (Leonhard 2005) or "spatial and temporal limits" (Humanitarian Policy Group 2003, 4) and accomplished very little in terms of minimising terrorism. Far from it, the countries that were placed at the centre of this global war still lie wasted socially, politically and economically. Moreover, they have been transformed into 'incubators' (Gerges 2005) of other, 'newer' terrorist outfits such as the Islamic State (IS; in Iraq and Syria) and the Al-Qaeda in the Indian Subcontinent (AQIS; along the Af-Pak borderlands).

If the Afghanistan of the 1980s proved to be the 'Soviet Union's Vietnam' (Cohen 1988), history repeated itself for the Americans twice over. The conflict in Afghanistan in the twenty-first century has proven to be intractable, not the least because of American misjudgements. On the one hand, its expeditionary counterinsurgency practices could not stem the insurgency, partly also because of Pakistan's proven duplicitousness. On the other hand, the American efforts at nation-building in Afghanistan were mostly a hotchpotch of misguided efforts that did not match requirements on the ground and unduly militarised its foreign aid (Spear 2016). Furthermore, the American investment in Afghanistan, which according to some estimates exceeds the Marshall Plan in adjusted value (Groll 2014), has been affected by local and trans-local corruption, mismanagement and persisting insurgency, amongst other things (SIGAR 2020). Standing at a gigantic figure of USD 2 trillion (Watson Institute 2019), the American contributions have been no more than a "money pit" (Brinkley 2013), particularly in the absence of domestic wherewithal in Afghanistan to deal with the incoming financial flows (Zürcher 2012). In addition to breeding institutional and individual corruption (Marquette 2011), the American decision to mobilise regional 'warlords' as part of both counterinsurgency and redevelopment initiatives may have contributed to the consolidation of what I have described as "centripetally-centrifugal forces"[2] (Saxena 2018), undermining the legitimacy of the national government(s) further.

While there was nothing inherently erroneous in the American intention of rebuilding Afghanistan, their approach was "devoid of a fundamental understanding of Afghanistan" (Whitlock 2019). As a result, it will not be misplaced to suggest that most of the aid and assistance provided by the US has "gone in vain" (ibid.). In light of these aid-related failures, deliberate misleading of the American public by different political leaders (ibid.), war fatigue (Myers 2020) and the like, it was only desirable for the US to want to "get the hell out of Afghanistan" (Stein 2018). A change in the mandate came after years of military surge, resulting in the drawdown of the American and the North Atlantic Treaty Organisation (NATO)-led International Security Assistance Forces (ISAF) from Afghanistan in 2014. However, the drawdown did not mean the end of the involvement and presence of foreign forces in Afghanistan. Instead, the mandate of the international military support transformed from one that was primarily offensive, called *Operation Enduring Freedom*, to one that combines a mix of training to the Afghan and limited, but very controversial (see UNAMA 2019), air support. The new mission that began primarily under the American auspices – also known as *Operation Resolute Support* – has been the bone of contention between the US and the Taliban and was central to the Doha Agreement.

Preceding the Doha deal, there were three separate occasions on which international, regional and domestic actors came together to discuss the terms and prospects of peace in Afghanistan. Although these processes/dialogues were not able to accomplish much, they, interestingly, witnessed direct outreach to the Taliban. These initiatives included the *Murree Process* (2015); the *Quadrilateral Coordination Group on Afghanistan* (2017); and the *Moscow-Format* (2016–18). I turn to each of them individually in the following sections.

Murree Process

"A mishandled peace process might only be able to produce a few rounds of talks, but would most likely break down before achieving anything", wrote Borhan Osman (2015) in the aftermath of the Murree Process that went kaput. Set up to bring the leadership of the Taliban, including both the members of the *Rehbari Shura* (Leadership Council) in Quetta and the Political Office in Doha, to the table of talks, this process was hampered by an alleged breach of trust, violation of secrecy and immense Pakistani pressure (ibid.).

Following on the heels of the American/ISAF drawdown in 2014, the Murree Process began with a much-publicised meeting between the representatives of the Afghan government's High Peace Council (HPC) and the Taliban during the month of Ramadan in July 2015, ostensibly in the hope of building on the holiness of this Islamic month to start putting an end to the war.

Far from it, the process could not even last beyond the first round of meetings and was grounded on account of the death of the *Rehbar* (Supreme Leader) and the founder of the Taliban movement, Mullah Omar. Interestingly enough, his demise, which had been speculated for a long time, was given an official endorsement in the middle of the ongoing peace process. While it is likely that the official acknowledgement of Omar's death was intended to be leveraged to further arm-twist the Taliban into talking with the Ashraf Ghani-led National Unity Government (NUG), it did not create the desired effect. On the contrary, the hoped-for weakening of the Taliban movement brought with it its own set of troubles, including an increase in overall violence (in Afghanistan) and factionalism (within the Taliban) that only inhibited the peace process (Smith 2015).

The rift between the Quetta and Doha offices also became more pronounced during and after the Murree Process and continues to date. It is important to note here that the Qatar office, which exists as an 'unofficially-official' (*Associated Press* 2013) political outpost of the Taliban, was established to create some distance between this Afghan Taliban and its facilitators in Pakistan. As a result, while the differences between the Pakistan-based *Shura* and the Qatar-based political office were likely to have always existed "the Taliban's (sic) projection of coherence in their communications and internal policies was put in question" (Osman 2015) in the run-up to the Murree Process. According to reports, the political office of the Taliban was unwilling to participate in a process that was being extorted out of them on the Pakistani command (AFP 2015). That the Taliban's leadership in Quetta was warned with 'consequences' if they did not participate in the Murree dialogue made the Pakistani 'sleight of hand' (Osman 2015) quite evident. Moreover, other factors such as the lack of secrecy around the talks and the presence of Pakistan's intelligence agency, *Inter-Services Intelligence* (ISI), personnel at the same table as the Afghan and Taliban delegation may have contributed to the early demise of this process (ibid).

The role of regional and international state actors also needs a mention here. The US, which had just withdrawn a massive portion of its troops from Afghanistan, was putting pressure on Pakistan to get the Taliban to talk. The Chinese involvement, on the other hand, was being sought for two different but interconnected reasons. Firstly, before the Murree Process, the Taliban delegation, along with ISI representatives, had met with Chinese officials in Urumqi in May 2015 on the back of China's apparent interest to mediate between the Afghan government and the insurgent group (PTI 2015). Given its hands-off approach in Afghanistan, China has managed to remain equidistant from both the Afghan government and the Taliban while maintaining sustainable relations with both of them. Hence, it is not surprising that the Pakistani-orchestrated Murree Process made space for China as an 'observer' along with the US.

Secondly, the Afghan government under President Ghani had its geopolitical reasons for vetting the Chinese involvement in the Murree Process. As part of his "five-circle foreign policy" (Katju 2015), President Ghani sought to recalibrate his government's approach to the Afghan conflict, which necessitated an outreach to China – a country in the first circle – for assistance. Within the NUG's geopolitical matrix, the conflict in Afghanistan was viewed as a consequence of state rivalry. Early on in his first term itself, the then (and current) president of Afghanistan was clear about the need for "two kinds of peace" (Qureshi 2015) – one with the Taliban and the other with Pakistan, which according to him, is in an "undeclared state of war" with Afghanistan (ibid). The externalisation of the Taliban-led insurgency to another state (actor), thus, continued the trend of the *statisation* of the global war on terror at the same time as it convinced Afghanistan to appeal to China to rein in on its 'all-weather ally', Pakistan. The Murree Process, in a way, marked the beginning of the Chinese involvement in the peace processes that have happened in Afghanistan ever since, including the now-defunct Quadrilateral Coordination Group, at which I look next.

Quadrilateral Coordination Group

Even for a failed process, the Murree Process had failed beyond redemption. It did not have much to offer apart from reinforcing the need to proceed with negotiations for peace in good faith; a lesson that was so obvious that it did not need reiteration. It was, perhaps, for this reason that the nation-states that were a part of the Murree Process decided to come together once again and form a Quadrilateral Coordination Group (QCG).

Composed of four state actors – Afghanistan, China, Pakistan and the US – the QCG's objective was to "consider mutual efforts to facilitate an Afghan-led and Afghan-owned peace and reconciliation process to achieve lasting peace and stability in Afghanistan and the region" (Embassy of Pakistan 2016). Meeting for the first time in January 2016, this group had sprung up on the sidelines of the fifth Heart of Asia Conference-Istanbul Process (HoA) that was organised in Islamabad in December 2015. Given that HoA had been in operation since 2011, and had provided a wider, international platform to "address the shared challenges and interests of Afghanistan and its neighbours (sic) and regional partners" (HoA 2011), the formalisation of the parleys on the sidelines into an official, peace-negotiating group may have sent out the following signals. One, the emergence of QCG shortly after the collapse of the Murree Process could have been read as an attempt on the part of the US, China and Pakistan to keep the reigns of the larger Afghan peace process in their hands. Two, the formalisation of this four-state group may have even dented the sanctity of the HoA-Istanbul Process by keeping the other participating countries out of the loop. Considering that the achievement of peace in Afghanistan has been as much of a geopolitical battle (Saxena 2017), it is not hard to see why the inception of QCG became a source of strategic concern for the excluded countries such as India.

Meeting in rapid succession in early 2016, the QCG intended to make use of the emergent split within the Taliban's ranks and draw out those who were in favour of reconciliation to the table of talks. The distinction between the 'conciliatory' and 'irreconcilable' Taliban was reminiscent of the difference that was once drawn between the 'good' and 'bad' Taliban by Pakistan and endorsed by the US (Doucet 2016). According to Thomas Ruttig (2016), the Afghan government's insistence on distinguishing between the different factions of the Taliban was a strategy that sought to

> Widen the split among the Taliban (sic) . . . based on two hopes. Firstly, that either Pakistan, with China's prompting, will succeed in bringing the Taleban mainstream faction of Mullah Akhtar Muhammad Mansur to the Islamabad talks or, alternatively, persuade other groups (for example Rassul's faction or Hezb-e Islami) to join the talks.

Needless to say, India vehemently opposed such distinctions, but its opposition fell on deaf ears on both occasions.

While the QCG may have failed to bring the Taliban to talk directly to the Government of Afghanistan, Ghani's emphasis on differentiating the proverbial good apples from the bad ones was able to draw out the erstwhile mujahideen commander, *Gulbuddin Hekmatyar*, into the public fold. That said, the Taliban continued to remain out of reach even up to 2017 when the QCG met for the sixth time in Muscat. The killing of Mullah Akhtar Mansour, the new *Rehbar* of the Taliban, in an American drone strike in the Pakistani province of Balochistan, may have spelt out the demise of the quadrilateral group even as Mansour was being painted as an "obstacle to the peace and reconciliation" by the US (Al Jazeera 2016).

The gradual frittering away of the QCG in the light of geopolitical exigencies, including the debilitating relations between the US and Pakistan, once again showed that the achievement of peace in Afghanistan is affected by factors that are patently not-Afghan. As such, it has not been surprising to see regional and trans-regional states taking the lead to set up different peace processes *for* Afghanistan instead of lending active and concrete support to the processes initiated by Kabul itself (ex. The Kabul Peace Process). These international involvements, however, may have been made necessary by the very nature of the conflict(s) in Afghanistan as being multi-scalar. Thus, as the conflict(s) in Afghanistan jumped scales, so did the dialogues, processes and negotiations to put an end to the decades-long war in the country, including the Moscow-Format which I discuss next.

Moscow-Format

The Moscow-Format, which started taking shape in 2017 parallel to other initiatives, including the negotiations between the US and Taliban, is another example of an exogenous initiative that was taken to bring peace *to* Afghanistan. As such, there was little new about the Moscow-Format. Like the other negotiations that preceded it, the Moscow-Format was a multi-nation, trans-regional attempt to restore peace to Afghanistan. However, what may have set it apart from the other initiatives was the lack of official involvement of the Government of Afghanistan, on the one hand, and the full-fledged participation by the Taliban, on the other.

Unlike its predecessors, the Moscow-Format was a remarkable development insofar as it was able to get the members of Afghanistan's political opposition and representatives of both the Qatar and Quetta offices of the Taliban at a single table. In fact, as Ekaterina Stepanova (2019) notes, the Russian-brokered rounds of talks in February 2019 were the "first significant direct contact between leaders of the former Northern Alliance and the Taliban since the former helped oust the latter from power in Kabul in late 2001". Furthermore, the Russian leadership in these peace negotiations marked both the revival of its involvement in the domestic happenings of Afghanistan after a hiatus of almost thirty years as well as an evolution in its foreign policy vis-à-vis Central Asia (Blank and Kim 2018) and its role in other trans-regional conflicts like the one in Syria amongst other things (Bhadrakumar 2017).

Held concurrently to the waning QCG-led negotiations, the Moscow-Format was essentially an outgrowth of the trilateral discussions that began taking place between Russia, China and Pakistan in 2016. The coming together of China, Russia and Pakistan was, perhaps, a result of their "common strategic interest in the region, which is that a peaceful and stable Afghanistan is conducive to the security of all three countries" (Tiantian 2016). At the same time, "Russia's involvement in the mechanism also serves as a 'reminder' to India over New Delhi's tilt toward Washington" (Fu Xiaoqiang quoted in ibid.) Pakistan, on its part, had much to gain from this trilateral camaraderie too. Symbolically, the emergence of this association with Russia, which has been as much of an "all-weather friend" to India (Sajjanhar 2020), was enough to ruffle the feathers of its neighbour and regional adversary. More tangibly, Pakistan was once again able to insert the 'good' Taliban into the Afghan peace process, particularly at a time when the US President Donald Trump was blowing hot and cold towards Pakistan. Unlike the failed Murree Process or the dormant QCG, the Russia-China-Pakistan trilateral discussions, and the Moscow-Format subsequently, promised some movement. The emergent trans-regional consensus on Afghanistan provided an appropriate opportunity to Pakistan to internationalise its domestic strategies that relied on getting the 'good' Taliban into power in Afghanistan.

Neither the trilateral grouping nor the Moscow-Format was the doing of the Pakistani machinations alone. Internationally, as I have noted elsewhere, "the dwindling American interest in battles in 'near abroad' under the Trump administration and an increasing possibility of application of sanctions/restrictions on Pakistan managed to get Russia and Pakistan closer (DRUZHBA-VI)" (Saxena 2017). Moreover, China and Russia too had their vested interests involved in getting a new peace process started under their leadership. On the one hand, China was no longer shy about playing the role of a mediator in bringing the war in Afghanistan to an end. On the other, the Russians too made no bones about recognising Taliban as an "Afghan-centric social movement" (ibid.) that could be enlisted to ward off the increasing threat posed by the IS in Central and South Asia. Hence, the purported entry of the IS into the picture and the increasing Russian involvement on its pretext; China's wariness towards rising radicalisation on its western flank and threat to its multi-billion-dollar China-Pakistan Economic Corridor (CPEC) project; and the continued absence of a discernible and determined US policy towards Afghanistan provided Russia and China reasons to team up with Pakistan to bring the Afghan conflict to an end in ways they desired.

The trilateral group began its discussions in 2016, leading eventually to a meeting in December of the same year. It was during this meeting that Russia, China and Pakistan concurred on the need to adopt a "flexible approach to remove certain figures from sanctions lists as part of efforts to foster a peaceful dialogue between Kabul and the Taliban movement" (Hobson 2016) but without keeping the Afghan government in tow. Evidently upset over this slight, particularly because NUG had sought the inclusion of the new Taliban leader, Mohammad Habaitullah Akhundzada in the UN sanctions list a month earlier, the Government of Afghanistan rejected the Russian-Chinese-Pakistani calls for going soft on the Taliban. Subsequently, the Afghan government also made it clear that the talks for peace with the Taliban "can only be held on its soil" (Mitra 2017).

From being a trilateral meeting to becoming a six-state international exercise, the Moscow-Format held its second meeting in February 2017 and then with five other Central Asian countries in April 2017, taking the total count of the member-states at this forum to eleven. It was at the second meeting that India and Afghanistan were made a part of the Moscow-steered peace process, assuaging Indian concerns about the increasing closeness between Pakistan and Russia. That said, Russia's evident outreach to the Taliban was not received well either by India or Afghanistan. Consequently, the subsequent round of talks under the Moscow-Format in November 2018, in which the Taliban was present, was resented by both countries. They registered their displeasure by sending 'non-official' representations to the meeting. It must be mentioned here that while India's decision to be non-officially present "was taken in close coordination with the Afghan side" (Meher 2018). However, it was not taken either "to impress Afghan NUG or disappoint Russian but as a matter of principled stand towards peace in Afghanistan" (ibid.) which was relayed by India in a Joint India-Russia Statement in October 2018.

"The spectacle of a former invading power hosting old foes was, indeed, remarkable", noted Zahid Hussain (2018). However, other more remarkable things that happened at the forum too, even as the Moscow-Format did not gather official support from both Afghanistan and the US. As mentioned previously, the Moscow-Format brought many of the former antagonists to the table of talks, including Russia, the former Afghan Mujahideen, and the Taliban. Brokered by the Moscow-based Centre for the Afghan Diaspora, the two-day dialogue in November 2018 may not have transformed the different stakeholders into brothers and sisters in arms. But it did provide an opportunity to the Afghan delegates and the Taliban's representatives to reiterate their commitments and spell out their red lines under one roof. The presence of women Afghan delegates, such as Fawzia Koofi, in the same room as the Taliban, was undoubtedly a symbolic breakthrough. However, we must be cautious about reading too much into it. Similarly, in an iconic scene that has since been in the headlines, a Taliban delegate leading the Islamic prayer with the members of the Afghan opposition and the other Taliban representatives in the same frame, showed an increase in the confidence of this insurgent group.

There were plenty of reasons for the Taliban to feel confident about its position in the evolving political scenario in Afghanistan. The Moscow-Format, which was patently an international forum unlike the Murree Process and QCG, was the first such occasion on which the Taliban came face to face with official/non-official delegates from eleven countries. At the same time, the absence of the Afghan government from this two-day dialogue and the participation of other Afghan delegates simply as the "citizens of Afghanistan" (Hamid Karzai quoted in Reevell 2019) appeared to have vetted the Taliban's refusal to talk to anyone in power in the country. The Taliban has not been shy in describing the existing governmental setup in Afghanistan as illegitimate, impotent and a sham. As such, its persistent naysaying on talking to the Afghan government(s) stood endorsed as different national and international stakeholders gathered together in Moscow to discuss the prospects of peace in Afghanistan with only token, non-official presence of the Ghani-led NUG at the forum. Also, while the Moscow discussions were underway, the Taliban was negotiating a deal with the US to work on putting an end to the decades-long conflict. Once again, the exclusion of the Afghan government from these negotiations gave a further boost to the Taliban's position within Afghanistan's political matrix, allowing it to appear in Moscow and re-appear on Afghanistan's political landscape on its terms.

Faustian Bargain?

On September 8, 2019, the President of the USA, Donald Trump, was hoping to earn his own 'Camp David' moment by bringing the war in Afghanistan to a halt. Apparently, in a 'secret meeting' that he had planned with the 'major leaders' of the Taliban, and separately with the President of Afghanistan, Trump was willing to provide concessions against a promise for reduction in violence by the Taliban and the initiation of an intra-Afghan dialogue (Baker, Mashal, and Crowley 2020). However, in a style that has become typical of his presidency, President Trump tweeted a hasty decision and refused to engage with the Taliban for the latter's failure to adhere to a ceasefire and "build false leverage" (Donald Trump quoted in Crowley, Jakes, and Mashal 2019). Commenting on an attack carried out by the Taliban in Kabul a day earlier, Trump lamented, and perhaps rightly so, that if the Taliban "cannot agree to a ceasefire during these very important peace talks . . . then they probably don't have the power to negotiate a meaningful agreement anyway" (ibid.). The death of an American soldier in this attack and the open opposition to negotiating with the Taliban, including murmurs that came from within the Trump administration (Donati, Bender, and Nelson 2019), may have weighed upon the US President to declare the talks with this insurgent group as "dead, as far as I (Trump) am concerned" (Donald Trump quoted in PTI 2019b).

However, the talks did not die a silent death. Far from it, they were revived in November 2019 when Trump made his first visit to Afghanistan since entering office in 2016. Speaking from the Bagram Airbase, where he met with the American soldiers on Thanksgiving Day, Trump made it clear that while the talks were back on track, they were contingent upon the Taliban's commitment to maintaining a ceasefire while the negotiations were on. He further added that "we (America) are going to stay until such time as we have a deal or we have total victory, and they (Taliban) want to make a deal very badly" (Donald Trump quoted in PTI 2019a). In hindsight, these negotiations could have taken place decades ago had the US not embraced a miscalculated and a too rigid stance on not talking to the Taliban. Instead, the US continued to engage in a military confrontation with this insurgent group, making the American war in Afghanistan the longest war that it has fought outside its shore.

The signing of the Doha Agreement on February 29, 2020, brought the confrontation between the US and Taliban to an effective halt while making space for the intra-Afghan dialogue to take place. The agreement was brokered by an Afghan-American, Zalmay Khalilzad, who was appointed as the US Special Representative for Afghanistan Reconciliation by the Trump administration with a singular focus "to get the Afghans and the Taliban to come to a reconciliation" (Mike Pompeo quoted in Kelemen, Hadid, and Romo 2018). A year and a half into his appointment, Khalilzad was able to make good on his promise and deliver an agreement that since then has become historical for different reasons. As part of the agreement, three interconnected verticals were put in place. On the one hand, the US committed to withdrawing its troops from Afghanistan within fourteen months from the signing of the agreement. In return, the US has sought assurances from the Taliban that no part of Afghanistan will be used by "any group or individual, including al-Qa'ida . . . to threaten the security of the United States and its allies" (Department of State 2020). On the other, it also paved the way for the different Afghan stakeholders to initiate intra-Afghan negotiations, which may bring the enduring war(s) in Afghanistan to an end.

It is important to note here that while the Doha Agreement may have refused to acknowledge the claim of the Taliban both to and as an Islamic Emirate, it granted it a semblance of international political legitimacy that it had sought for long. At the same time, the Doha Agreement bypassed the official Afghan government entirely and instead envisaged a peace process between the different "Afghan sides" (ibid.). The American decision to keep the Ghani-led NUG out of the agreement may have been taken to appease the Taliban whose stern opposition to and dislike for the existing constitutional setup in Afghanistan is well known.

Ideally, the intra-Afghan negotiations should have started on March 10, 2020, per the Doha Agreement. However, long past the deadline, these negotiations began only on September 12, 2020, when the delegation of the Afghan government led by Abdullah Abdullah came face to face with the Abdul Haqim Ishakzai-chaired contingent of the Taliban in Doha. As was expected, the talks opened to a lot of fanfare and witnessed participation from many countries, including India. But since then, the momentum appears to have been lost. Beset with multiple problems, including those concerning the protocols of the negotiations, principles and other formalities in the present, and those that had disrupted the schedule in the past such as disputes over the mandated prisoner exchange and initial differences over the results of the 2019 presidential elections and the composition of the new Afghan government; the path to intra-Afghan dialogue remains treacherous. On top of that, the Taliban's persistent use of violence against the Afghan military and government, despite no official declaration of its annual spring offensive, has generated reasonable doubts over the group's commitment to the peace process. As the goalposts keep shifting, the fate of the intra-Afghan negotiations continues to hang in the balance, particularly while neither side is willing to let go of its leverage. Whereas the current Ghani-led Afghan government has once again refused to release the remaining high-profile Taliban prisoners despite an endorsement from the *Loya Jirga*, the Taliban, on its part, has kept up its attacks in the major city centres (ex. Balkh on August 25), in a clear violation of the spirit, if not the letter, of the Doha Agreement.

No actor, at least overtly, would like to posture itself in favour of continued conflict in Afghanistan. With a military solution to the conflict being both undesirable and impractical, intra-Afghan negotiations appear to be the only way out of the violence that has endured in this country for over forty years. As such, the talks between Kabul and the Taliban appear to hold some promise, although it is still unclear as to how they will pan out. And while it is true that the American carrot-and-stick policy might be able to get the different Afghan sides to the table of talks, it will not be enough to broker peace. Recalling what Bruce Riedel (2015) had written while the Murree Process was still in its initial stages, the war in Afghanistan, which is more than four decades old now, "will not (sic) end because the White House says it is over". It will be over only when the different stakeholders, and particularly Afghans, want it to end and allow peace to run a sustainable course. While all this may sound too proper and poetic, it is a fact that lasting peace has never been achieved unless the situation is ripe enough for the antagonistic parties to realise the need to stop fighting (Sadr 2019).

As the previous rounds of exogenous peace negotiations have shown, the piecing of the peace processes in Afghanistan has happened at the altar of varied vested interests. The cross-scalar nature of the conflict(s) has ensured that the achievement of peace in Afghanistan also divides national, regional and international stakeholders into various camps, with each side demanding a piece of the peace they desire. The US-Taliban agreement and the ongoing intra-Afghan negotiations may offer some hope. However, the actors involved in the process are still unwilling to see eye to eye on many counts. Affected by varying and often antagonistic calculations, peace for peace's sake in Afghanistan may continue to remain elusive unless a deal is struck as part of the current intra-Afghan negotiations in all earnestness. That said, a deal in and of itself will mean little if it is not matched by genuine and honest efforts to turn a new page in the history of Afghanistan.

Notes

1 The Doha Agreement is officially known as the "Agreement for Bringing Peace to Afghanistan between the Islamic Emirate of Afghanistan which is not recognized by the United States as a state and is known as the Taliban and the United States of America". It was signed on February 29, 2020.
2 The phrase centripetally centrifugal forces and its implications for Afghanistan have been explained by the author as the following: "where an attempt is (sic) made to grab power and resources from the centre by the regional warlords not with the intent of ruling the centre but to rule their regions better". For more information, see the corresponding reference.

References

AFP. 2015. "Doubts and Divisions among Commanders as Taliban Talk Peace." NDTV. www.ndtv.com/world-news/doubts-and-divisions-among-commanders-as-taliban-talk-peace-780856.

Aneja, Atul. 2020. "The Taliban Movement Has Changed, Says Russian Presidential Envoy for Afghanistan." The Hindu. www.thehindu.com/news/international/

the-taliban-movement-has-changed-says-russian-presidential-envoy-for-afghani-stan/article31761493.ece.

Associated Press. 2013. "Taliban Close Qatar Office in Protest at Flag Removal." The Telegraph. www.telegraph.co.uk/news/worldnews/asia/afghanistan/10169161/ Taliban-close-Qatar-office-in-protest-at-flag-removal.html.

Baker, P., Mashal, M., and Crowley, M. 2020. "How Trump's Plan to Secretly Meet with the Taliban Came Together, and Fell Apart." The New York Times.

Bhadrakumar, M.K. 2017. "Will India Sit down with Pakistan and Taliban to Discuss Peace in Afghanistan?" The Scroll2. https://scroll.in/article/832332/will-india-sit-down-with-pakistan-and-taliban-to-discuss-peace-in-afghanistan.

Blank, Stephen, and Younkyoo Kim. 2018. "Making Sense of Russia's Policy in Afghanistan." Paris. www.ifri.org/en/publications/etudes-de-lifri/russieneireports/making-sense-russias-policy-afghanistan.

Brinkley, Joel. 2013. "Money Pit: The Monstrous Failure of US Aid to Afghanistan." World Affairs 175 (5): 13–23.

Carroll, James. 2018. "The War on Terror as the Launching of American Crusade." Lobe Log. https://doi.org/10.2139/ssrn.2506321.

Cohen, Richard. 1988. "The Soviet's Vietnam." The Washington Post. www.washingtonpost.com/archive/opinions/1988/04/22/the-soviets-vietnam/5e7fde43-6a0c-46fb-b678-dbb89bcb720b/.

Cohen, Zachary. 2020. "US Intelligence Indicates Iran Paid Bounties to Taliban for Targeting American Troops in Afghanistan." CNN Politics. https://edition.cnn.com/2020/08/17/politics/iran-taliban-bounties-us-intelligence/index.html.

Crowley, M., Lara Jakes, and Mujib Mashal. 2019. "Trump Says He's Called Off Negotiations with Taliban after Afghanistan Bombing." The New York Times. www.nytimes.com/2019/09/07/us/politics/trump-taliban-afghanistan.html.

Department of State. 2020. "Agreement for Bringing Peace to Afghanistan between the Islamic Emirate of Afghanistan Which Is Not Recognized by the United States as a State and Is Known as the Taliban and the United States of America." US Department of State. www.state.gov/wp-content/uploads/2020/02/Agreement-For-Bringing-Peace-to-Afghanistan-02.29.20.pdf.

Donati, Jessica, Michael C. Bender, and Craig Nelson. 2019. "Divided White House Prompted Trump to Call Off Taliban Talks." The Wall Street Journal. www.wsj.com/articles/afghan-government-praises-trump-suspension-of-u-s-taliban-negotiations-11567956075.

Doucet, Lyse. 2016. "Afghanistan Confronts a New Threat from IS." BBC. www.bbc.com/news/world-asia-pacific-35406434.

Embassy of Pakistan. 2016. "Joint Press Statement First Meeting of the Quadrilateral Coordination Group on Afghan Peace and Reconciliation Process Independence Day Flag Hoisting Ceremony Held at Embassy of Pakistan Washington D. C." Joint Press Statement. https://embassyofpakistanusa.org/press-releases-01-11-2016/.

Gallagher, Adam. 2020. "Negotiations Are the Only Way to End Afghan Conflict, Says Abdullah." USIP. www.usip.org/publications/2020/06/negotiations-are-only-way-end-afghan-conflict-says-abdullah.

Gerges, Fawaz A. 2005. The Far Enemy: Why Jihad Went Global. Cambridge: Cambridge University Press.

Groll, Elias. 2014. "The United States Has Outspent the Marshall Plan to Rebuild Afghanistan." Foreign Policy. https://foreignpolicy.com/2014/07/30/the-united-states-has-outspent-the-marshall-plan-to-rebuild-afghanistan/.

HoA. 2011. "Heart of Asia – Istanbul Process." HoA. https://doi.org/10.1002/ecy.1259.

Hobson, Peter. 2016. "Russia, Pakistan, China Warn of Increased Islamic State Threat in Afghanistan." Reuters. www.reuters.com/article/us-afghanistan-taliban-russia-pakistan-c/russia-pakistan-china-warn-of-increased-islamic-state-threat-in-afghanist....

Humanitarian Policy Group. 2003. "Humanitarian Action and Global War on Terrorism: A Review of Trends and Issues." London. www.odi.org/sites/odi.org.uk/files/odi-assets/events-documents/4089.pdf.

Hussain, Zahid. 2018. "The Moscow Format." Dawn. www.dawn.com/news/1445504.

Jazeera, Al. 2016. "Afghan Taliban's Mullan Mansoor 'Killed in US Strike.'" Al Jazeera. www.aljazeera.com/news/2016/05/taliban-leader-killed-drone-strike-160521204020111.html.

Katju, Vivek. 2015. "Ghani and India: Circles of Separation." Gateway House. www.gatewayhouse.in/ghani-and-india-circles-of-separation/.

Kelemen, Michele, Diaa Hadid, and Vanessa Romo. 2018. "Zalmay Khalilzad Appointed as U.S. Special Adviser to Afghanistan." National Public Radio. www.npr.org/2018/09/05/641094135/zalmay-khalilzad-appointed-as-u-s-special-adviser-to-afghanistan.

Leonhard, Robert R. 2005. "The Evolution of Strategy in the Global War on Terror." Baltimore. www.jhuapl.edu/Content/documents/Strategy.pdf.

Malkasian, Carter. 2020. "How the Good War Went Bad." Foreign Policy. www.foreignaffairs.com/articles/afghanistan/2020-02-10/how-good-war-went-bad.

Marquette, Heather. 2011. "Donors, State Building and Corruption: Lessons from Afghanistan and the Implications for Aid Policy." Third World Quarterly 32 (10): 1871–1890. https://doi.org/10.1080/01436597.2011.610587.

Meher, Manabhanjan. 2018. "India's Approach towards Moscow Format Consultations." Foreign Policy News. https://foreignpolicynews.org/2018/12/09/indias-approach-towards-moscow-format-consultations/.

Mitra, Devirupa. 2017. "At Russia-Led Regional Talks, Afghanistan Says Talks with Taliban Can Only Be Held on Its Soil." The Wire. https://thewire.in/external-affairs/afghanistan-taliban-talks-russia.

Myers, Chandler. 2020. "Mirroring Vietnam's Failures in Afghanistan: DOD's Descent into War Fatigue." War Room. https://warroom.armywarcollege.edu/articles/war-fatigue/.

Osman, Borhan. 2015. "The Murree Process: Divisive Peace Talks Further Complicated by Mullah Omar's Death." Afghan Analysts Network, no. August 5: 1–13. www.afghanistan-analysts.org/the-murree-process-divisive-peace-talks-further-complicated-by-mullah-omars-death/.

Prothero, Mitch. 2020. "Russia Did Pay Extremists to Attack US Soldiers in Afghanistan, According to 3 Separate Taliban Sources." Business Insider. www.businessinsider.in/politics/world/news/russia-did-pay-extremists-to-attack-us-soldiers-in-afghanistan-according-to-3-separate-taliban-sources/articleshow/76735595.cms.

PTI. 2015. "Afghan Taliban Leaders Meet Secretly in China: Report." The Economic Times. https://economictimes.indiatimes.com/news/defence/afghan-taliban-leaders-meet-secretly-in-china-report/articleshow/47413160.cms?from=mdr.

———. 2019a. "Trump Announces Resumption of Peace Talks with Afghan Taliban." The Economic Times. https://economictimes.indiatimes.com/news/defence/trump-announces-resumption-of-peace-talks-with-afghan-taliban/articleshow/72289800.cms.

———. 2019b. "Trump Says US-Taliban Talks Are 'Dead.'" The Week. www.theweek.in/wire-updates/international/2019/09/10/fgn60-trump-taliban-talks.html.

Qureshi, Ahmad. 2015. "Pakistan in State of Undeclared War with Afghanistan: Ghani." Pajhwok Election. www.elections.pajhwok.com/en/2015/05/24/pakistan-state-undeclared-war-afghanistan-ghani.

Reevell, Patrick. 2019. "Taliban and Senior Afghan Politicians Hold Talks in Moscow, Upsetting Government." ABC News. https://abcnews.go.com/International/taliban-senior-afghan-politicians-hold-talks-moscow-upsetting/story?id=60852053.

Riedel, Bruce. 2015. "The Longshot Taliban Talks." Brookings Institution. www.brookings.edu/opinions/the-longshot-taliban-talks/.

Sadr, Omar. 2019. "Political Settlement of the Afghanistan Conflict: Divergent Models." Kabul.

Sajjanhar, Ashok. 2020. "How Should India Respond to Russia-China-Pakista Triad?" ORF. www.orfonline.org/expert-speak/how-should-india-respond-to-russia-china-pakistan-triad/.

Saxena, Chayanika. 2017. "Concerting for Peace in Afghanistan: Will the 'Meeting of Six' Have a Tune to Play?" CLAWS. https://archive.claws.in/1714/concerting-for-peace-in-afghanistan-will-the-meeting-of-six-have-a-tune-to-play-chayanika-saxena.html.

———. 2018. "Afghanistan's Irresolvable Conflict: Destructive Obsession with Everything Strategic." Indian Strategic Studies. https://nationalinterest.org/blog/the-buzz/watch-out-china-indias-navy-wants-200-warships-13340.

———. 2020. "Why India Must Engage Pro-Actively in Afghanistan." 9DashLine. www.9dashline.com/article/why-india-must-engage-pro-actively-in-afghanistan-FHqTb.

SIGAR. 2020. "Quarterly Report to the United States Congress." Kabul. www.sigar.mil/pdf/quarterlyreports/2020-07-30qr.pdf.

Smith, Graeme. 2015. "Taliban Factionalism Rises after Mullah Omar's Death." International Crisis Group. www.crisisgroup.org/asia/south-asia/afghanistan/taliban-factionalism-rises-after-mullah-omar-s-death.

Smith, Steve. 2011. "The End of the Unipolar Moment: September 11 and the Future of World Order." SSRC. https://essays.ssrc.org/10yearsafter911/the-end-of-the-unipolar-moment-september-11-and-the-future-of-world-order/.

Spear, Joanna. 2016. "The Militarization of United States Foreign Aid." In The Securitization of Foreign Aid, edited by Stephen Brown and Jörn Grävingholt, 18–41. London: Palgrave Macmillan. https://doi.org/10.1007/978-1-137-56882-3_2.

Stein, Jeff. 2018. "Donald Trump's Desire to 'Get the Hell Out' of Afghanistan Amid Taliban Gains Could Lead to Catastrophe." Newsweek. www.newsweek.com/2018/10/26/donald-trump-get-hell-out-afghanistan-amid-taliban-gains-catastrophe-1132203.html.

Stepanova, Ekaterina. 2019. "Russia and the Afghan Peace Process." PONARS Eurasia Policy Memo. www.ponarseurasia.org/memo/russia-and-afghan-peace-process.

The Commission. 2004. "The 9/11 Commission Report: Final Report of the National Commission on Terrorist Attacks upon the United States." National Commission on Terrorist Attacks Upon the United States. Washington, DC. https://doi.org/10.2307/20034163.

Thomas, Ruttig. 2016. "In Search of a Peace Process: A 'New' HPC and an Ultimatum for the Taleban." Afghanistan Analysts Network. www.afghanistan-analysts.org/in-search-of-a-peace-process-a-new-hpc-and-an-ultimatum-for-the-taleban/.

Tiantian, Bai. 2016. "China, Russia, Pakistan Hold Trilateral Talks on Afghanistan Issue." Global Times. www.globaltimes.cn/content/1026031.shtml.

UNAMA. 2019. "UN Urges Parties to Heed Call from Afghans: Zero Civilian Casualties." UNAMA. https://unama.unmissions.org/un-urges-parties-heed-call-afghans-zero-civilian-casualties#:~:text=UNAMA attributed 83 percent, the armed conflict in Afghanistan.

UNSC. 2020. "Letter Dated 19 May 2020 from the Chair of the Security Council Committee Established Pursuant to Resolution 1988 (2011) Addressed to the President of the Security Council." United Nation Security Council. Washington, DC. https://doi.org/10.1017/S0020818300014144.

US Department of State. 2001. "The Global War on Terrorism: The First 100 Days." Washington, DC. https://2001-2009.state.gov/s/ct/rls/wh/6947.htm.

Watson Institute. 2019. "US War Spending in Afghanistan." Costs of War.

Whitlock, Craig. 2019. "At War with the Truth: The Afghanistan Papers." The Washington Post. www.washingtonpost.com/graphics/2019/investigations/afghanistan-papers/afghanistan-war-confidential-documents/.

Zürcher, Christoph. 2012. "Conflict, State Fragility and Aid Effectiveness: Insights from Afghanistan." Conflict, Security and Development 12 (5): 461–480. https://doi.org/10.1080/14678802.2012.744180.

6

STATE BUILDING IN TALIBANIZED AFGHANISTAN

Lessons From History

Arezou Nooristani

Introduction

The state building process in third world and backward countries has a difficult and winding path ahead. Many internal and external factors often make this process a long-term challenge. The history of Afghanistan and the ongoing events in the country indicate that the process of state building in Afghanistan from the last hundred years to now is problematic due to various factors, including poverty, economic dependence on external aid, ethnic diversity, ruling traditions and external interventions. After the rule of Amanullah Khan for more than a decade in Afghanistan, when fundamental steps were taken towards state building, it can be said that the actions and strengthening of institutions and the growth of agents in the direction of state building have been more prominent during the two decades of the republic. The incident of September 11, 2001 (9/11) and as a result the attention of the world to Afghanistan is one of the most important incidents in the history of Afghanistan. In modern Afghanistan, after September 11, international and domestic efforts were made to strengthen institutions, which are considered important elements of state building: reestablishment of the Afghan National Security Forces of more than 300,000, efforts for institutionalization of democracy, separation or division of powers, including revitalizing of judicial and legislative systems, constitution, social equality and civil rights, strengthening of economic institution, distribution of new and valuable money, directing functional foreign policy and women's meaningful presence in political and social affairs are the characteristics of the two decades of republic effort toward state building.

But the question is, why did the achievements of twenty years and the joint efforts of the international community and the Afghan government fall apart and the Taliban remerge?

DOI: 10.4324/9780429281631-8

To answer this question, in this article, with a historical look at the state building process in Afghanistan in the past hundred years, the most important factors and obstacles in the state building process, which include ethnic diversity, the dogma of Islam and external interventions, are discussed.

Conceptual Framework

State building as a social and political concept is a creation of Western scientific societies, which was entered into scientific and academic circles after 1990. In political literature, state has a multi-dimensional meaning: as a country that has territory, population, government and sovereignty. State means the governing body or the executive branch, which includes the cabinet. Alternatively, the government means the creator of the executive, legislative and judicial branches. Broadly, state building means the creation of legislative institutions, executive institutions and institutions in charge of judicial affairs (Khalili and Fardoqi, 2017). Some consider state building to be the ability to accumulate power for the integration of institutions, while others consider state building to increase the capacity of political, economic and social institutions for the progress and development of a country. And some consider state building to be the process of government authority and government control to create civil order (Hatami, 2011). Among all these statements, according to the author, state building is the strengthening of political and social institutions and all sub-institutions that help in creating order and progress of the society. On the other hand, state building means the rule of order that comes from the heart of the law and prevents chaos, collapses the islands of power inside the country and brings prestige and increases the dignity of its citizens abroad.

Modern state building is mostly a product and offspring of seventeenth-century Europe. Western European states of the seventeenth century had several important indicators, which at that time and even now are considered to be the primary components of the formation of a state. Firstly, the seventeenth century modern states of Europe had definite territorial boundaries. Secondly, by creating a financial and administrative organizational system, they dominated all the economic activities that took place under their rule. Thirdly, they provided diplomatic services beyond its borders by establishing the first embassies. Fourthly, they accomplished accumulation, concentration and monopoly of power by the government, which is considered the most important element of absolute government (Hatami, 2011; Khalili and Fardoqi, 2017). Therefore, the process of modern state building is the formation of the first absolute states that started in the seventeenth century and continued until the nineteenth century. This process was formed first in Europe and gradually spilled over to non-European countries.

In 1970, various literatures entered the scientific circles about this phenomenon. There are many theories about state building. Some scholars consider state building to be an internal process that has matured due to the internal forces of a country in its natural context, and no external forces were involved in this process. Such a process will undoubtedly reach its peak after going through ups and downs and experiencing war and peace and with the management of the domestic agents it comes to its stable point. Seventeenth-century European states and onwards is a good example of this natural process of state building. On the other hand, a number of experts believe that state building is the result of the efforts of external or international factors, in which not the internal forces of a country, but foreign factors played a role in state building (Khalili and Fardoqi, 2017). In some cases, efforts to build a state by foreign forces have been successful; Germany can be mentioned as a successful model. However, in various cases, this process has come to a dead end (Dobbin et al., 2003). Accordingly, in such a process, it is possible that a lot of money is injected into the countries for state building by foreign forces, but the desired result is not obtained. Afghanistan is one of the good examples of this model, which is discussed in detail in the rest of the article.

Likewise, some scholars consider war to be a driving indicator in state building. Otto Hintze (1975) is one of the early theorizers of this approach that considers the role of war in state building. He considers war to be the driving force of history, and accordingly, he considers state building to be the result of this phenomenon. He also states that the geopolitical location and the military threats caused by this phenomenon are another factor in the formation of the modern state and the diversity of the new system. In addition, he considers that the more sensitive the geographical location of a political unit is, the more likely war and military threats are, and it is likely to result in absolute bureaucratic state formations (Hintze, 1975). Tilly (1990) is another scholar in this approach who played an important role in the popularity of this approach. According to him, war has created states and states have created war. He states that in Europe, where the war for power is one of its prominent features, and every faction tried to take a bigger share in this conflict, the nation state performed better than other competitors in mobilizing resources in the war. The nation state carried out the mechanism through the bureaucratic system, the tax collection system and another institution-based functionality of which other competitors were not capable. He also considered the type of closed and open system and the ability of units to use geographical location to be another factor in this case (Tilly, 1990). In other words, he expressed that the level of economic ability in extracting resources and following trade and mastering agriculture along with geopolitical position in early modern state building was essential (Tilly, 1990; Hatami, 2011).

Additionally, another approach explains state building as an offspring of economic and social changes in Europe. The scholars of this approach consider state building to be the result of changes in the feudal system or in connection with it. This approach illustrates that the weakening of the landed class or aristocracy in the face of peasant revolt and the rise of bourgeois trade on the other hand led the landowners to find themselves in a trade-off with the kings, who were concentrating power. Such situation led to the development of the of state-building. This approach, unlike the first approach, which stated war as the cause of the formation of absolute governments, consider state building to be the result of changes in the feudal system or in connection with it, as a result of which the king gained control over the state after the control of the landowner over the peasant. On the other hand, the culmination of the crisis among the landlords over the expansion of spheres of influence and the growth of the urban bourgeoisie facilitated the formation of the state. Founding offices for the regulation of tax affairs, urban police, courts and trade regulation are the pattern of the state growth in that time. At this time, the state was not only bargaining with the feudal lords and the bourgeoisie to regulate affairs, but behind these negotiations, it tried to destroy them and dominate them as well (Hatami, 2011). Immanuel Wallerstein's (1975) views can also be considered in the socio-economic approach of state building. While some scholars considered the formation of the absolute state to be the result of the crisis in feudalism, Immanuel Wallerstein considered the early formation of the modern state to be the result of the transformation of the feudal production method and growth, the capitalist mode of production and trade with the help of the bourgeois class. Therefore, he considered the strength of the early modern state in England and France to be the result of their proper functioning in the economic and capitalist fields, which was obtained from the collapse of feudalism and its fractures (Wallerstein, 1975; Hatami, 2011).

Contrary to the foregoing two approaches, which considers early modern state-building in the context of war, crisis in feudalism and the growth of capitalism, or has an objective-experimental and pragmatic view of state-building, another approach, which is based on cultural and social elements, explores the construction of absolute states before entering the experimental stage in the context of cultural and intellectual developments. Among the theorists of this approach, the views of Groski are worthy of consideration. He points out the role of the church and clergy in establishing the foundations of the absolute government. According to him, at the beginning of the modern era, we are witnessing the growth of countless laws and regulations that absolute governments were unable to implement everywhere. At that time, clergymen, religious preachers and elders of the church became moral mediators who supervised the implementation of laws even in the most remote places and controlled people's lives. Protestant reforms in the field of helping the poor and educational reforms in Protestant areas prepared the ground for providing educational and literacy services for the poor, and in this way, it became possible for the subalterns to read the Bible. The next part of the church's help with the government was in the legitimacy of the government's laws in the field of sex and marriages. The church helped make these laws public and registered marriages. All of these measures provided the basis for the government's increasing control over people's lives, and in this context, the church and clergy came to the aid of this institution. Accordingly, this approach regards the emergence of the state as dependent on cultural and social developments, which over time will form the foundations of a strong state (Groski, 2003).

As stated, state building in Europe has reached the stage of evolution in the context of political, social and cultural developments. Experts and theoreticians consider this evolution with historical reasons and experiences, in the context of war, crisis of feudalism or following intellectual and social developments in Europe. In other words, state building in Europe is a process formed from the bottom up: people, religious groups, women, executives and all sections of the society have played a role in the interactions of the transformation stage and have brought this process to the fruitful stage. However, this issue is not true for third world countries, especially non-Western countries. Third world and non-Western countries were mainly formed after the Second World War, and this is one of the main indicators of separation between the early states formed in Europe and the countries created after the Second World War. Accordingly, in the Europe of the seventeenth century, the authoritarian absolute government should have the ability to consolidate power in the implementation of affairs, and sufficient power was considered one of the primary and important components of the government; otherwise, weak governments would simply collapse. While after World War II, international laws such as respect for sovereignty and non-interference guaranteed the immunity of newly created countries.

Another important thing in this regard is creating boundaries. European states were able to define their own borders, while in third world countries, especially non-Western countries and governments that were formed based on colonial forces, their national borders have been separated by colonial powers (Rahimi, 2021). In other words, many third world states were built with the support of foreign powers. Therefore, state building in these countries is defined more in the structure of the project than the process (Qanbardoost, 2016). The foreign forces involved in the process have acted according to the values, norms and beliefs that they themselves believe in, or that their respective governments are based on; in non-Western countries, they have acted with the same approach that ultimately resulted in. It has been far from expected or fragile. A good example of this process is Afghanistan after 2001. I will discuss this in detail in the next sections of the article.

History of State Building in Afghanistan

1. Early Twentieth Century

The history of the formation of the state in Afghanistan can be divided into seven historical milestones: 1) the formation of Afghanistan by Ahmad Shah Durrani in 1747, 2) the establishment of the modern state and the determination of the geographical boundaries of Afghanistan during the royal governments until the time of Amir Abdul Rahman Khan (1880–1901), 3) the independence of Afghanistan by Amanullah Khan (1919) and the growing stage, 4) the attack of the Soviet Union and the formation of the communist government, the beginning of jihad and civil wars in Afghanistan, 5) the formation of the Mujahidin government and then the emergence of the Taliban group, 6) the establishment of the new government after the Bonn agreement (2001), 7) August 15, 2021, which coincided with the fall of the Islamic Republic of Afghanistan and the reinstatement of the Taliban.

Afghanistan is a country with an ancient history, which has experienced countless difficulties during its political and social life. The foundations of Afghanistan were determined for the first time by Ahmad Shah Abdali. After the death of Nader Afshar, Ahmad Khan Abdali founded the current Afghanistan, which was named the Khorasan region at that time. He spent most of his life in campaigns to the east and west of Afghanistan, and the scope of his rule sometimes extended northward to the Jayhoon River, southward to the Sea of Oman, westward to Khorasan in present-day Iran, and eastward to India and the Tibetan mountain range (Rahimi, 2012). The territorial integrity of Afghanistan was endangered due to the conflict between Timor Shah's sons, especially Mahmood Shah, over the acquisition of the kingdom. At that time, due to the importance of the geographical location of Afghanistan, the British extended its influence to the current borders of Afghanistan in order to prevent the influence of Tsarist Russia and other European colonial countries in India, which resulted in three bloody wars between Afghans and British between the years 1839 and 1919, which became known as the first, second and third Afghan-British wars.

The era of Amanullah Khan is considered a golden page in the history of Afghanistan. After Afghanistan's independence from the British, Amanullah Khan took effective steps in the field of state building. In 1923, the first constitution of Afghanistan was approved, in which the rights of individuals were reserved. In addition to that, fifty other supplementary laws were compiled, which were called *Nizamnameh*, according to which the limits and competencies of government and judicial organizations were determined. The judicial system was considered one of the most important systems to strengthen the governance system. Before this law, mullahs and clerics were in charge of the country's judicial affairs. With the approval of this law, the mullahs were expelled from the traditional judicial system, which later angered the mullahs and clerics and caused them to rebel against the government. Slavery and taking people into captivity was abolished. One of the most important measures of the Amani period in the field of state building was providing educational opportunities for women, who make up half of the population of the society (Mohsen, 2014).

In 1922, the first school where French teachers taught was established, followed by other schools. Queen Soraya, the wife of Amanullah Khan, supervised all matters related to women's education. It was in this direction that in 1920, Mastoorat School, the first girls' school, and in 1921, Ismat High School, which was later renamed Malali High School, was established. Dozens of young girls were sent to Turkey for nursing and medical training. Amanullah Khan attempted "unveiling hijab" to women for the first time and women were allowed to dress in a modern way and appear outside (Tanin, 2005). The reforms of the Amani period continued strongly and this situation was dangerous for England and the enemies of Amanullah. Based on this, by using the traditional and religious spirit of the clerics, conspiracies were formed against him and the reform process of Amanullah Khan was called anti-religion (Tanin, 2005). The clerics rioted and formed a new government led by Habibullah Kalakani. As a result, the growing process of state building stopped, and as a result, Amanullah Khan was exiled to India and then to Italy. Habibullah Kalakani, who was an uneducated person, took the power.

From the first days, the government of Habibullah Kalakani faced resistance from the different corners of the country as a result. After the nine-month rule of Habibullah Kalakani, the government fell to General Nadir Khan in 1929. Zahir Tanin in his book considers the role of Britain in Nadir Khan's victory and says, "Nadir Khan's victory was not the result of internal factors alone, but he was aware of the interest of the British towards him and took advantage of this issue. In order to consolidate peace in the border tribes and prevent the ideological influence of Russia, the British were interested in seeing Nadir Khan instead of Shah Amanullah" (Tanin, 2005: 68). In this period, the second constitution of Afghanistan was approved in 1931, in which religious people were given government positions for the first time. Although the type of kingdom was defined as constitutional, however, the power was in king's hand. This period in the process of governance is considered a period of suffocation and coercion of the people (Safiq, 2015).

Nadir Khan was shot by a student named Abdul Khaliq Hazara. After his death his nineteen-year-old son Zahir Shah took over the government from 1933 to 1973. Although he was apparently the king, his uncle Hashim Khan and then his other uncle Shah Mahmood were in charge of the state matters. New educational plans and global peace are the characteristics of this era. But on the other hand, poverty and weak economy continued to affect the people of Afghanistan. In 1947, Shah Mahmood was appointed prime minister, and during his tenure, partial democracy was introduced. Elections were held to select mayors and two years later, similar elections were held for the National Assembly. In 1950, the Free Press Act was passed and there was a period of political unrest as a number of private weeklies tried to portray the dreams of liberal intellectuals (Mohsen, 2014). In this period the issue of Pashtunistan became important, and when Dawood Khan became prime minster, this turned the direction of Afghanistan's foreign policy to the another direction: Afghanistan became directly controversially in touch with Pakistan.

In 1963, feeling the danger caused by the strengthening of relations between Afghanistan and the Soviet Union during Dawood's leadership in the field of Pashtunistan, Zahir Shah decided to normalize relations with Pakistan and democratize the government structure. He persuaded Dawood to step down and asked Mohammad Yusuf, an outsider of royal blood, to form a new government (Tanin, 2005). In 1963, Dr. Yusuf became prime minister and numerous changes occurred in the state building process. The following year, a new constitution was approved by the Loya Jirga. In this constitution, Afghanistan was declared a "constitutional kingdom". The National Assembly (Wolesi Jirga), provincial assemblies and municipal councils were directly elected through general elections in secret. One third of the members of the Senate (Mishrano-Jirga) were elected in a similar way, one third were indirectly elected by provincial councils and one third were appointed by the Shah. The Shah nominated the members of the cabinet, but they were only approved by the vote of the parliament, to which they were also accountable. Members of the Shah's family, including his paternal uncles and cousins, were banned from politics. Judges were appointed by the king, but they were independent in practice. At that time, the media and parties were given freedom and people could express their views freely (Tanin, 2005).

The state building process in Afghanistan entered a new phase with the white coup of Dawood Khan in 1973. Dawood Khan, who was also Zahir Shah's cousin, ended the royal system during a white coup while the Shah was on a leisure trip in Europe (Haqjoo, 2001). The republican government was formed under the influence of the National Revolutionary Party. The president was elected for a six-year term with two thirds of the votes of the Loya Jirga. The National Assembly was established for only four months in a year. Although Dawood Khan had comprehensive and long-term plans for the development and prosperity of Afghanistan, the foreign influence and interference in Afghanistan's affairs by the powers of the time made him unable to implement his plans to the end. Dawood Khan had a good relationship with the Soviet Union from being prime minister until the presidency. But he maintained closeness with the Americans. It is interesting to note that the economic projects are supported by Americans, like the *Kajaki* electricity transmission project. He also had ties with Iran, like taking loans from Iran, which was America's ally in the region at that time.

The removal of the elites of the People's Democratic Party from the cabinet and key government positions caused the Soviet Union to distrust Dawood Khan and provide a platform for the overthrow of his government (Mesbahzadeh, 2009). In 1978, the People's Democratic Party of Afghanistan killed Dawood Khan and his family members during a bloody coup, and the new communist leaders formed a one-party government: "A new form of government of the Democratic Republic of Afghanistan" in which the legislative and judicial powers were completely under the influence of the executive branch under the name "Revolutionary Council". In 1980, the Interim Constitution, which was the basic principles of the Democratic Republic of Afghanistan, was approved. The stated goal was to guide Afghans to create a humane society free from the exploitation of others. This constitution was based on the existing political structure. The rights of free speech, sanctity of the home and peaceful assembly were once again guaranteed. People were accused, arrested and punished only according to the law. People were considered innocent until they were found guilty in court. The People's Democratic Party considered itself the representative of the working-class party, which was identified as "the leader and guide of the social force and the government". The government pledged to take care of the youth in order to bring the family, especially mothers and children, under special protection. Not only the religious freedom of the followers of Islam, but also of other beliefs were guaranteed.

This constitution represented an ideal, but had the least impact on the Afghan society as a whole. The promotion of Marxist ideology and the use of unfamiliar words such as socialism, democratic and feudalism were completely unfamiliar to the traditional society of Afghanistan Mesbahzadeh, 2009). On the other hand, widespread killings by the intelligence services, made people suspicious about the government because it was mainly consist of atheists. All this made the foundations of the government weak inside and provided the ground for religious movements under the leadership of the Mujahidin. In 1992, with the defeat and withdrawal of the Soviet forces from Afghanistan, the People's Democratic Republic, which had become the Republic of Afghanistan during the time of Dr. Najibullah, was abolished by the Mujahidin, and instead the Islamic State was governed by a leadership council and the Mujahidin Council. The leadership council immediately banned the activities of the Watan Party. However, in the absence of unity between the previous Mujahidin organizations, conditions of political chaos and civil war dominated Afghanistan. Provinces were governed by the non-accountable councils to the Kabul government, and neighboring countries advanced their interests by relying on united national groups. By late 1992, there was no clear vision of a unified administration, an end to the war or a new constitution.

2. The Mujahidin Government (1991–2001)

After the defeat of the Soviet forces in Afghanistan and their departure from the country, the fourteen-year war was ended. However, this time was the beginning of another full-scale misery and destruction for the people of Afghanistan. Following the power struggle between the jihadist groups, as a result, with the mediation of Pakistan, the Mujahidin leaders signed the "Peshawar Resolution" in 1992 in the presence of Nawaz Sharif, the Prime Minister of Pakistan. The purpose of that resolution was to specify a framework for the temporary and transitional status. According to that decision, Sibghatullah Mojaddedi should have been the head of the Islamic State for two months. After that, Burhanuddin Rabbani had to become the head of the Islamic State for four months. Burhanuddin Rabbani, the head of the Islamic State, should have established the "Reconciliation Council" (Ahle-Hal-o Aqd) within four months of his term of responsibility to introduce an eighteen-month interim government, and after that make preparations for general elections and the establishment of a comprehensive national government. But in 1992, this council extended Burhanuddin Rabbani's rule for another eighteen months (Hamidzada, 2020). The formation of the Islamic State did not solve this problem, and the war between Gulbuddin Hekmatyar and the Nazzar Council led by Ahmad Shah Massoud continued, which resulted in the emergence of the Tehreek-e-Taliban in 1994 in Kandahar and their rise to power in 1996 in Kabul.

3. The Taliban Movement (1994–2001)

As mentioned earlier, the withdrawal of the Soviet forces and the end of the occupation promised peace and tranquility for the people of Afghanistan. But it didn't take long for the conflict between Jihadi leaders over the division of power and Afghanistan's descent into the civil war which paved the way for foreign intervention and taking Afghanistan to a new misery. The formation of Tehreek-e-Taliban can be analyzed from two dimensions: firstly, factors such as internal disturbances, people's frustration, Jihadi leaders' struggle for power, poverty and the destruction of Afghanistan's economic infrastructure, and exhaustion from the existing atmosphere created the ground for accepting the force (Tanin, 2005). The Taliban, who considered themselves a spontaneous force, with the slogan of ending corruption, killing and looting, establishing universal justice and consolidating Islamic justice in the form of a group of students who were mainly trained in Pakistani religious schools, under the leadership of Mullah Muhammad Omar, first appeared in Kandahar and southern provinces and quickly reached other provinces (Tamanna, 2009). From another perspective, many consider the Taliban to be a planned project created by the United States of America, Saudi Arabia and Pakistan. This group includes factors such as preventing the influence of Iran and strengthening the anti-American revolutionary spirit, the change in US strategy towards the region and the Greater Middle East Initiative for the United States, Saudi Arabia's concern about convergence, alignment and the increasing activity of political parties mainly consisting of Shiites, Iran's order and through this channel Iran's extensive influence in Afghanistan, and Pakistan's political and economic goals to connect to the world markets and Central Asia through Afghanistan and also to prevent India's influence in Afghanistan, which are seen as a reason for aligning with the goal of forming the Tehreek-e-Taliban.

With the capture of Kabul in 1996, the Taliban declared the type of government as an Islamic Emirate based on Hanafi jurisprudence (Karimi and Khadimi, 2016). The Taliban controlled about 90% of the territory of Afghanistan, but the provinces of Panjsher, Badakhshan and Takhar were under the command of Ahmad Shah Massoud. Afghanistan's internal institutions and economic infrastructures had completely collapsed during the civil wars and the governance system was practically inflamed and paralyzed. Such a broken government was inherited by the Taliban, and during their five-year rule, the Taliban, who were unaware of governance, added to this fragility. All institutions were managed by mullahs, schools and offices were closed to women, the freedom of the press and media was completely denied and the atmosphere of suffocation, force, violence against people, unemployment, poverty and hunger increased. Due to the problems of access to basic health services, the infant mortality rate reached the highest rate in the world at 25%, and one in four children died before the age of five (Clayton, 2021). The people of Afghanistan needed humanitarian aid from the United Nations and foreign non-governmental organizations. The Taliban regime, while applying a strict policy based on "Islamic rules", was skeptical of foreign aid organizations. In the summer of 1998, the Taliban closed the offices of all foreign aid organizations and the offices of the United Nations in this country and ended their activities. The United Nations accused the "Islamic Emirate of Afghanistan" of preventing the delivery of food aid to 160,000 civilians who were facing a hunger crisis. In the foreign dimension, except for countries such as Pakistan, the United Arab Emirates and Saudi Arabia, which recognized the Taliban, the rest of the countries had severed their diplomatic relations with Afghanistan, and Afghanistan was in international isolation (Mohsen, 2014).

4. September 11 and the Shaping of a New State in Afghanistan

During the rule of the Taliban, Afghanistan had become a safe haven for terrorists. The presence of Osama bin Laden, the leader of the Al-Qaeda terrorist network in Afghanistan, and the September 11, 2001 attacks on the World Trade Center in New York, led to the formation of the international coalition to fight against terrorism led by the United States of America. These forces captured Kabul in 2001 within twelve days of siege. The creation of a temporary administration came out from the decision of the Bonn Conference to the creation of a transition period, which occurred during the Loya Jirga, was at the top of international decisions. The interim administration was formed for six months and this was the first manifestation of state building in this period. After six months of the interim administration, based on the decision of the Loya Jirga, a transitional administration was formed. This was the second step in the direction of state building in new Afghanistan, and in fact, the transitional administration was a transition from the chaotic and abnormal situation of shaky institutions to stability. In addition to the main task of the transitional government, which was to prepare for the Loya Jirga of the Constitution and then launch the elections, ensuring border security, preventing terrorists from Afghanistan, restoring Afghanistan's traditional role as a regional transit route, supporting women and minorities and controlling drug trafficking are its other important tasks (Tamanna, 2009).

After the approval of the constitution in 2004, the presidential elections, which were considered an important step in strengthening democracy, were launched, as a result of which Hamid Karzai won 51% of the votes and assumed the position of president. The second important step in the field of state building was the parliamentary election that was held in 2005, and a large number of women and men competed for 249 parliamentary seats. On the other hand, to strengthen the economic prosperity of Afghanistan, holding international conferences with the support of the United States was prioritized. The Tokyo conference (2002), London conference (2006), Berlin conference (2004), etc. to attract international aid, were among the measures to strengthen the foundations of the government (Khalili and Fardoqi, 2017). In order to defend the territorial integrity and not to turn Afghanistan into a safe nest of terrorists, the international community, in cooperation with the Afghan government, founded the National Army and the National Police, with the number of army forces reaching 195,000 (MOD, 2021) and the number of police forces reaching 157,000 (Mohamadi, 2013). Four rounds of presidential elections and three rounds of parliamentary and provincial council elections were also held. Although these processes were not without defects, these steps were important for democratization and the practice of democracy. In addition to the extensive role of women in governmental and non-governmental institutions, sending students abroad, establishing the Independent Human Rights Commission, Independent Election Commission and Independent Administrative Reform Commission and creating institutions for better management of affairs are all important measures in line with institutionalization. It is considered the government of Afghanistan.

5. Doha Negotiations and Taliban Regaining Power

In 2006, the Taliban gradually rose again and carried out sporadic attacks such as roadside mine explosions, suicide attacks, burning schools and guerrilla attacks in Kabul and the southeastern provinces. With this operation, they tried to challenge the collective order and security and the central government. These attacks intensified with the withdrawal of foreign forces, especially after 2014, and every day at least a hundred people lost their lives due to suicide and explosive attacks by the Taliban (Khalili and Fardoqi, 2017). At the same time, the former president Hamid Karzai and the next president Mohammad Ashraf Ghani repeatedly invited the Taliban to negotiate, but until 2019, the Taliban did not show a green light or seriousness. In 2019, the Doha negotiations between the Taliban and Zalmay Khalilzad, the US representative for Afghanistan peace affairs, were seriously discussed and ended in the same year with the consensus of the parties to establish a ceasefire under the title of "reducing violence". These negotiations were resumed in 2020. Zalmay Khalilzad and Mullah Abdul Ghani Baradar, the political deputy of the Taliban group, signed "The Agreement for Bringing Peace to Afghanistan" during a ceremony in Doha, the capital of Qatar (Clayton, 2021). Based on this agreement, it was decided that 5,000 Taliban prisoners from Afghan government prisons and 1,000 hostages and captives who were in the hands of the Taliban would be released and intra-Afghan talks would also begin (Clayton, 2021).

During the negotiations and finally the agreement with Washington, the Taliban group was able to remove some of its senior members from the UN blacklist and release more than five thousand prisoners, including "400 dangerous criminals", from Afghan prisons. Also, the Taliban were able to free Anas Haqqani, the son of founder of the Haqqani Network and deputy leader of this group Mulla Hibatullah Akhundzadeh, from the prison of the National Security Directorate of Afghanistan and take them to Qatar. After the agreement and signing of the Doha Treaty with the United States, the Taliban stopped their attacks on foreign forces, but intensified the war against the Afghan security forces and civilians. The years 2020 and early 2021 were the bloodiest years for the people, especially the defense and security forces of Afghanistan. During the massive attacks of the Taliban, civilians were losing their lives every day, and on the other hand, the Taliban group did not agree to continue negotiations with the negotiating team of the Afghan government and kept the war fronts warm (Irani, 2021). The increasing attacks of the Taliban on the one hand, the weakness in the morale of the security and defense forces, corruption and mismanagement in the government on the other hand, in addition to the abandonment of the Afghan people by international friends, finally caused that after the fall of the major cities like Herat, Mazar-e-Sharif and Kandahar, when President Ashraf Ghani fled Afghanistan, Kabul fell to the Taliban and Afghanistan's nascent democracy was razed to the ground.

Rulers and the Cause of the State Collapse in Afghanistan

Ruler	Year of rule	Cause of the fall
Amanullah Khan	1919–1929	• Conflict between traditionalism/Islamists and modernism • British intervention (Amanullah khan wanted to change Afghanistan to independent and developed country) • Ethnic tension
Habibullah Kalakani	1929 (nine months)	• Ethnic tension • Civil war
Nadir Khan	1929–1933	• Assassinated for his ethnic discrimination
Zahir Shah	1933–1973	• Coup by Sardar Dawood Khan
Sardar Dawood Khan	1973–1978	• *Sawr* Revolution by the People's Democratic Party • Russian intervention
Noor Mohammad Taraki	1978–1979	• Coup by Hafizullah Amin • Russian intervention
Hafizullah Amin	1979 (four months)	• Was killed by the Russians
Babrak Karmal	1979–1986	• Resignation with the pressure of Russia
Dr. Najibullah	1987–1992	• Civil war by Mujahidin supported by US/Pakistan
Sibghatullah Mojaddedi	1992–1992 (three months)	• Period completed
Burhanuddin Rabbani	1992–2001 (1996–2001 the government was in exile)	• Peaceful transition
Mullah Mohammad Omar	1996–Sept. 2001	• Attack by the international coalition led by US
Hamed Karzai	2001–2014	• Completion of the presidency
Mohammad Ashraf Ghani	2014–Aug. 2021	• Escape from the country after entry of the Taliban to Kabul
Mulla Hibatullah Akhundzadeh	Aug. 2021 to date	• NA (But came to power with support of US)

Major Challenges for State Building in Afghanistan

1. Ethnic Diversity

Afghanistan is a multi-ethnic and pluralistic country. At different times, the issue of ethnicity has been the cause of the overthrow of the government or a challenging element in the direction of state building. Although the common people of Afghanistan have lived together and accepted each other in the corners of the country for many years, in the last forty years, especially during the civil wars, the leaders of the political parties have used the issue of ethnicity as a tool to build position and power. Through this channel, they increased the ethnic divisions among the people and also created a link between politics and ethnicity and made several groups of people from a single nation at certain times. In the state-building process, the issue of power sharing among different ethnic groups, such as Pashtuns, Tajiks and Hazaras, has been a problem. The conflict over the division of power can be seen in the history of the last hundred years, but the peak of ethnic tensions in Afghanistan, which resulted in civil wars and the bloodshed of thousands of Afghans, goes back to the withdrawal of Soviet forces and the beginning of regulatory wars over the power. Different parties, based on their ethnicities, demanded the greater share of power, and as a result created civil war.

After the collapse of Dr. Najibullah's presidency, according to the decision of the Mujahidin (Ahl-e Hal-o Aqd) Council, the term of the government's rotating presidency was set for three months, and every three months, the leader of one of the Jihadi organizations took over the government. Sibghatullah Mojaddedi, the leader of National Salvation Front, was appointed the first head of the Afghan government. After spending three months as president, he handed over the responsibility to Burhanuddin Rabbani, the leader of Jamiat-e-Islami, which is the strongest party of Tajik descent in Afghanistan. The extension of these three months by the Ahl-e Hal-o Aqd Council, and as a result of not handing over the government to the next leader after three months, as well as the presence of the Northern Alliance in power on the one hand and the lack of satisfaction of Gulbuddin Hekmatyar, the leader of the Islamic Party of Afghanistan, in the position of prime minister on the other hand, resulted in civil war. The conflict that caused the displacement of about five million Afghans and hundreds of thousands of deaths. These losses and people's dissatisfaction paved the way for the emergence of the Taliban, whose style of governance was unpopular in Afghanistan (Sardarnia, 2014).

One of the major criticisms of the Taliban in two periods of their government is the issue of their mono-ethnicity. The Taliban group is mainly composed of the Pashtun people, and the people in charge of the first-level management structures are mostly from the same ethnicity. This issue has become a problem among other ethnic groups and is one of the major criticisms of this group. In the current Taliban cabinet, there is an Uzbek, "Qari Abdul Salam Hanafi", the deputy head of the prime ministry, and two Tajiks, "Qari Fasihuddin", the chief of the army staff, and "Qari Din Mohammad Hanif", the acting minister of economy, of Tajik origin. An important point to consider in this regard is that the Taliban is mainly an ideological group, and the criterion for selecting and dividing power among them is to be a Talib rather than a Pashtun (Hussaini, 2022). Accordingly, in the selection of cabinet ministers to the lowest levels of civil servants, the most important criterion is to be ambitious or loyal to the belief in their intellectual and functional ways.

2. Foreign Interventions, Lessons From History

According to the hundred-year history of the modern government in Afghanistan, it can be seen that foreign interventions have had the greatest impact in overthrowing the government and systems. Historical experience has shown that external intervention is the main challenge in the process of state building: from 1919 to 2021, sixteen regimes have been experienced in Afghanistan. Among these sixteen regime changes, ten have been by foreign intervention directly; in other words, 62.5% of the changes were based on foreign intervention.

The era of Amanullah Khan is considered an important point in the modernization of Afghanistan. The rapid process of reforming Afghanistan and establishing extensive relations with the world was a concern for the British. Regaining independence from England on the one hand, and modernizing Afghanistan inspired by Kemal Atatürk's reforms in Turkey on the other hand, led England to believe that the continuation of this process would lead Afghanistan to prosperity and the needlessness of foreign aid. As a result, Afghanistan would be self-reliant and necessarily cut off the British hand from Afghanistan forever. Accordingly, the British, using the traditional religious spirit of the Afghan people, in collusion with high-ranking government officials, and through the influence and encouragement of mullahs and clerics, tried to overthrow the system. Habibullah Rafi, an Afghan historian as quoted in Tanin's book, says the British circulated fake photos showing the queen with bare legs on her trip to Europe, and that "it was a shocking image for the people inside Afghanistan" (Tanin, 2005: 67).

He added, "Britain could not tolerate a free and successful Afghanistan, lest India, which was under British occupation, be inspired by this freedom and progress and revolt against them" (Tanin, 2005: 67). That is why Britain did everything it could to destroy the Afghan government and especially the queen. By spreading Queen Sorya's half-naked edited photos among the people, they tried arouse the religious sentiments of the people and in this way prove the king and his wife to be infidels and atheists. Amanullah Khan's close relationship with the Soviet Union, especially after the signing of the Afghanistan Peace Treaty with the Soviet Union in May 1921, which was caused by the alarm of the British presence, was the reason that Britain was really worried for India (Tanin, 2005).

After Amanullah Khan, Habibullah Kalakani took charge of the government. After the nine-month period of his rule in 1929, Nadir Khan, who was allied with the British, took over the government until 1933. After his death, his son Zahir Shah came to power in 1933 and until the presidency of Sardar Dawood Khan (1973), the Afghan government had political stability for more than four decades. The first instability of Sardar Dawood Khan's government dates back to the establishment of the People's Democratic Party of Afghanistan, which was previously established during the reign of Zahir Shah and the presidency of Sardar Dawood. Although this party had a significant effect in bringing Sardar Dawood Khan to power, later this same party caused the overthrow of his government. By returning to power as the president (1973–1978), Dawood Khan sought to gain full control of power and brought about a major change in Afghanistan's foreign policy. In addition to suppressing religious conservatives and pro-monarchy liberals, he also gradually removed the leftists who collaborated in the coup over the course of a year or two and closed down all nineteen non-governmental newspapers (Husain, 1983).

This change was quite tangible until 1975. By traveling to Iran and Arab countries, including Saudi Arabia, which had become rich from oil extraction, Dawood Khan tried to attract new economic aid. In an ambitious move, the Shah of Iran promised a loan of two billion dollars to Kabul, and by mediating between Afghanistan and Pakistan, the US silenced the grounds for solving the Pashtunistan problem. During this period, Dawood not only didn't open the old wound with Pakistan, but the relations between the two countries became a warm friendship in the summer of 1976 (Husain, 1983). In this way, Afghanistan distanced itself from the Soviet Union after twenty years of friendship. In 1978, Dawood also traveled to non-aligned countries, including Pakistan, Saudi Arabia and Yugoslavia.

At the same time as the tension between Afghanistan and the Soviet Union was increasing, Dawood Khan was trying to align himself with the Parcham party, and the Soviets were trying to reunify the Khalq (People Party) and the Parcham by applying pressure. Finally, the reunification of the two sides of the Democratic Party was realized in 1977. This was at the same time as Dawood Khan's last trip to the Soviet Union, when his verbal argument with the Soviet leader, Leonid Brezhnev, brought the relations between the two countries to a critical stage. The tendency towards America and the policy of getting out of the Soviet influence caused the People's Democratic Party, which was under the influence of the Soviet Union and supported by the

Soviet Union, to overthrow the government of Sardar Dawood in a bloody coup and assassinate him and all his family members. After this coup, the People's Democratic Party of Afghanistan took power.

Noor Muhammad Taraki was the first president of the People's Democratic Party of Afghanistan. He reached this position with the support of party members and also the Soviet government. But over time, relations between Taraki and the Soviets gradually soured, and the Soviet leadership found it increasingly difficult to work with him. The KGB held Taraki largely responsible for the widening split between the Khalq faction, under his own leadership, and the Parcham faction, led by Babrak Karmal. On the other hand, the Soviet leadership found it somewhat easier to work with Karmal than to work with Taraki. On the other hand, the inner party turmoil, which extended to the supporters of both the Khalq and the Parcham factions, resulted in "ideological sabotage" to the Communist Party and leaders (Mohsen, 2014). This was also one of the main concerns of Moscow. The Soviet and KGB leaders, who were worried about the vicious power struggle between the two factions of the Khalq and the Parcham within the party, asked Taraki to change his behavior towards the Parcham faction, but Taraki did not take the request seriously. Ignoring Moscow's request, Taraki imprisoned a large number of Parcham sympathizers and sent their leader Karmal, who was more trusted in the KGB than Taraki, as ambassador to Czechoslovakia to prevent rebellion. Another important thing that worried Taraki was the strengthening of the prominent member of the party, Hafizullah Amin. With the influence he had on the party, he was appointed to the position of deputy prime minister and later prime minister. He was appointed as the Minister of Defense and had a high influence within the military. During Taraki's recent trip to the Soviet Union, the Soviets saw him as a threat to the party due to the suspicion of Amin's closeness to America, and planned to overthrow him. When Amin came to know about this issue, he took the lead from Taraki and killed him by several military forces and took the government himself (Mohsen, 2014).

Although Hafizullah Amin was a powerful man of the People's Democratic Party and on the other hand, he influenced the military forces, he was not trusted and accepted by the Soviet Union due to the suspicion of being close to Pakistan and the US. Accordingly, the plan of poisoning him by the Soviet agents in Afghanistan was carried out several times, but it failed. Finally, there was a coup against him in Taj Beyk Hill, where Amin lived, and he was killed by the Soviet forces along with his two sons, and Babrak Karmal came to power (BBC, 2009). Although Babrak Karmel was in power at the same time as the Soviet occupation and his government lasted for six years, but with the inauguration of Mikhail Gorbachev as the President of the Soviet Republic, the country's policies regarding Afghanistan changed and preparations were made to oust Babrak Karmal from power. Karmal was removed from the general secretary of the People's Democratic Party in 1986, and he was dismissed from the presidency by Dr. Najibullah in October of the same year (Shafai, 2019). It is said that Viktor Petrovich Plichka, a powerful Russian adviser to Karmal, along with two members of the People's Democratic Party's political bureau, visited him and asked him to sign his resignation.

Two Examples of State Building Failure in Contemporary Afghanistan

1. Najib's Presidency, War and the Beginning of the Collapse of State Institutions

Dr. Najibullah, whose presidency coincided with the withdrawal of Soviet troops from Afghanistan, took serious measures and reforms in the structure of the government. His actions include removing the word "Democratic" from the name of the system, changing the name of the People's Democratic Party to the Watan Party, a party whose members were called secular by religious people, and most importantly, announcing the plan of national reconciliation, which is based on peace and integration. He pointed out that all Afghans should forget the past and come together in a new structure. Of course, it should be noted that his latest plan came to a dead end. The Mujahidin, who received logistical and training support from the US and Pakistan during the Jihad and wanted to seize power in any way, rose up to fight against the regime and did not accept this plan. As a result of the chaos and riots in the provinces and its expansion to Kabul, Dr. Najibullah took refuge in the United Nations office and the Mujahidin formed the Islamic State (Daimirian, 2021). The lack of accordance between the Mujahidin groups to reach a centralized government led to the mediation of regional countries and the United Nations, which led to the signing of the Peshawar Agreement between the Mujahidin groups for power sharing. However, the complexity of the situation and especially Hekmatyar's opposition led to the start of a fierce battle in Kabul, the capital of Afghanistan. In that four-year battle that lasted until 1996, an important part of Kabul's infrastructure was destroyed and nearly 50,000 people were killed (Daimirian, 2021).

The chaos that came out of the Jihad period and the Mujahidin government led to the formation of the Taliban in 1994. The Taliban, with the direct support of Pakistan and Saudi Arabia, entered a new phase in the history of Afghanistan that has never before been seen in history. Although the Taliban government had inherited a ruined government, their government was not structured and organized in any way. They did not have the legitimacy and structure of a government, neither domestically nor in the international environment, and their governance was more similar to the management of a religious school. This semi-government was finally overthrown in 2001 with the attack of the United States and the coalition of the international community, within a week, and a new order took its place. With the fall of the Taliban, a new era of state building led by the US and NATO began in Afghanistan. This presence lasted nearly twenty years, which cost the United States 2.26 trillion dollars (Clayton, 2021). Four hundred thousand Afghans and 2,500 American soldiers lost their lives in this two-decade war. The peak of the US military presence in Afghanistan was in 2011, when the number of US soldiers in this country reached 110,000 (Clayton, 2021), but this massive presence could never destroy the Taliban. Since an important part of the international aid was spent on the payment of salaries as well as military aid, Afghanistan's infrastructure was never developed to the extent that the Taliban could be seriously pushed back.

On the other hand, during these two decades, the heads of government could not establish a serious balance between different parties and ethnic groups. Therefore, in 2017 withdrawal from Afghanistan was placed on the agenda of the "Donald Trump" government. At this time, the process of negotiations with the Taliban was started by Zalmay Khalilzad, the US special envoy for Afghanistan peace in Doha, Qatar, which finally led to the signing of a peace agreement between the two sides. In this conference, the Afghan government was absent. In fact, the Doha Agreement laid the foundation for the failure of the Islamic Republic, which was established at the financial cost and lives of thousands of Afghan and international soldiers. With Joe Biden entering office, the withdrawal process of the US forces was accelerated and with this process, the Taliban forces began to advance rapidly. The advance, which coincided with the rapid withdrawal of foreign forces, quickly disintegrated the structure of the Afghan military forces. Despite the high cost spent on equipping these forces, it seemed that they could resist for up to six months, but in the end, after Ashraf Ghani's escape from the country, Kabul and the twenty-year-old order fell in less than a week.

2. The Taliban Regime

The Taliban unexpectedly took power on August 15, 2021. On August 17, amid growing chaos and panic, Taliban spokesman Zabihullah Mujahid held a press conference and promised to form an inclusive government. He also assured the charities, the security of the embassies and the right of women to work and study according to Sharia laws.

Since the capture of Kabul by the Taliban, the situation at Kabul Airport had been tense. Meanwhile, on August 26, a suicide attack took place at Kabul International Airport, killing dozens of civilians trying to leave the country. ISIS terrorist group Khorasan branch took responsibility for this attack. After the terrorist attack on Kabul International Airport on August 29, the United States carried out a second drone strike targeting suspected ISIS terrorists, but an Afghan family of ten people, including children, were killed

(Aikins, 2022). On August 31, America withdrew from Afghanistan, and this marked the end of more than two decades of American war in Afghanistan. After one year of Taliban rule, regardless of the relative improvement of security in the provinces, the economic situation of Afghanistan has completely collapsed and the people are in a bad livelihood situation. The gates of schools are closed to girls and women are completely removed from the scene of political and social activities. In government offices, instead of experts and officials of the previous government, mullahs are appointed, and the governance system is in the hands of mullahs who graduated from religious schools. The Taliban has not only the lack of international legitimacy, but also they are not accepted within the Afghan society.

The Taliban and the Dogmatic Recitation of Islam

Since its inception, Afghan society has been strongly religious and traditional. Since the establishment of Afghanistan until now, the institution of religion has played a fundamental and important role in the government. Throughout history, many kings called themselves the Amir of Muslims in order to gain people's satisfaction and to make religion appear at the top of governance. In the past, the prefix of Amir was considered to be the name of the kings, on the one hand, to attract the support of the people in line with the ruler's support, and on the other hand, it was considered a trick for the continuity and strength of the foundations of the government. Before Amanullah Khan came to the kingdom, the previous kings addressed themselves as Amir, and according to that, the Amir was considered the shadow of God on earth (Mohsen, 2014). Everything that the Amir did was considered to be in the direction of the welfare of the country, and so on. Religion and religious reading were considered the main pillar of the government. In the last hundred years, the institution of religion has played an important role in empowering groups or, on the contrary, in overthrowing the government. The important base and historical indicator of the role of religion and clerics in overthrowing the government can be examined during the reign of Amanullah Khan and later during the government of the People's Democratic Party. Amanullah Khan was the first king in Afghanistan who strongly sought to modernize Afghanistan. In the first step, he removed the prefix Amir from his name and addressed himself as the king of Afghanistan, unveiling the hijab for women, allowing the presence of the king's wife in public, opening the social space for women, promoting modern culture in big cities like Kabul and hundreds of other reform programs. The clerics considered the Shah as infidels and rebelled against the system, and as a result, with the Shah's exile to Italy, the government fell into the hands of Habibullah Kalkani, who considered himself the Kadem-e Din Rasoulolla (Servant of Islam Religion) (Tanin, 2005).

Another important example of the role of religion in overthrowing the government was during the government of the People's Democratic Party, which led to the occupation of Afghanistan by the Soviet Union. After taking power, the People's Democratic Party took a series of actions that were unacceptable to the traditional Afghan society. The leaders of this party were considered by the people in the villages and countryside to be puppets of the Soviet Union and atheists. With the 7 Sawr (April) coup and then the invasion of Afghanistan by the Red Army, the residents of Afghanistan, most of whom were religious, felt that their identity and culture were under serious threat, and therefore resorted to radical literature to defend their beliefs and values. They were forced to resort to war and violence in order to defend their homeland and identity.

In order to strengthen the motivations and religious beliefs against the "wave of atheism and irreligion", the "religious scholars" enjoyed a special status in the society and religious sciences were placed at the top of the priorities. Because the conditions for learning religion were not available in Afghanistan, thousands of students of religious studies were engaged in Islamic education in schools in Pakistan and Iran, and later most of them (Sonnni in religion) joined the Taliban. While the elites of the political Islam movement succeeded in mobilizing the people against occupation and aggression, they were strangely unable to theorize. They had to use the works of Islamist thinkers from other countries to present a different and up-to-date understanding of Islam; but until the end, they remained intellectually dependent and needy and did not show any creativity. Major Islamists in Afghanistan during this period (Islamic Jamiat and Hizb-e-Islami) saw themselves as adhering to the ideological foundations of Maududi and Seyyed Qutb. They greatly benefited from the terminology of these two thinkers and considered Islam to be a comprehensive religion with a complete system in the fields of politics and economics. They considered today's capitalist and socialist societies to be ignorant societies (Abaas and Shakouri, 2018).

With the march of the Red Army to Afghanistan, the leaders of the Islamic movements felt empowered more than before. Because now they could easily convince the Muslims that their struggle is right and they need their help. It was that human aid and weapons poured in from all over the Islamic world that strengthened the Islamists. This approach led to the emergence of political Islam in Afghanistan in response to the "Marxist-Leninist wave of atheism and anti-religion", which was also supported by some regional and world powers. The growth and spread of political Islam affected the traditional culture of this country and made it vulnerable, but the alternative offered by political Islam was not very pleasant. Political Islam in Afghanistan tried to present a different understanding of Islam by using new concepts, but it could not come up with a theory: it always fed on the works of thinkers from other countries and remained intellectually dependent. This theoretical poverty caused them to become disillusioned when the Mujahidin or the Taliban took over the government and were unable to manage the country's problems, because they did not have a written strategy and plan for the period after the overthrow. The failure of the Islamists in Afghanistan has instilled the idea in the minds of the people that political Islam is more useful for subversion than for reconstruction (Mohammad Ali and Shafai, 2017).

With the Taliban gaining power, a sharp and closed version entered Afghanistan's governance. The Taliban are perhaps one of the few ideological groups in the world whose way of governing and dealing with the people is completely primitive and based on dogmatic and closed views of Islam. During the last four decades, religious schools have provided free combat power for the war in Afghanistan. Even taking advantage of the power of mobilizing schools in Afghanistan and Pakistan was considered the winning card of the Taliban in the twenty-year war with the Islamic Republic of Afghanistan, and now these schools have become the focus of the Taliban's attention. On several occasions, the senior officials of the Taliban clearly stated that education in religious schools is of special importance in accordance with schools and universities. Mullah Mohammad Yaqub, the Taliban's defense minister and the son of Mullah Omar, the founder of the Tehreek-e-Taliban, had stated that not having a certificate or an academic degree for his forces, but Jihad, was the principle of being recruited into government offices (Afghanistan Int, 2022). A large number of Taliban leaders and their forces have graduated from religious schools in Pakistan. Darul Uloom Haqqaniyyah and Jamia Uloom Islamic School are two important schools that played a major role in training and developing the mental foundations of the Taliban. Based on the teachings that the Taliban have acquired in these schools, the basis of all interactions of the Taliban in the field of governance is based on Islam. Quran and Sharia have the basic legal status in their governance; in other words, implementing political Islam in the entire governance process is a fundamental principle for them. The Ministry for the Propagation of Virtue and the Prevention of Vice of the Taliban (Amr Be Maroof Va Nai Az Munkar), not only in relation to governance issues, but also the personal affairs of people's lives, men's beards, women's clothes and other matters are under supervision and investigation.

Therefore, it was based on such a harsh view of Islam that during the first period of this group's rule, people were extremely disgusted and dissatisfied with their performance. But the atmosphere of suffocation, force and coercion did not allow raising the voice. On the other hand, Afghanistan is the only country in which there is a unit under the title of martyrdom or "suicide" department in the Ministry of Interior. The Taliban consider the insurgent groups to be one of the main pillars of their system; therefore one of the first actions of Sirajuddin Haqqani, the Minister of Interior of the Islamic Emirate, was to establish this unit to protect the borders. These forces were previously responsible for suicide attacks against the Afghan government (8pm, 2022).

In addition, in the state building process, women participation plays major role. Under Taliban rule, women as a vast bulk of the society have been marginalized from social, political and economic processes.

Conclusion

State building in underdeveloped countries has always faced difficulties. Afghanistan, as one of the underdeveloped countries and always exposed to political transformation, has experienced many ups and downs in the state building process. From the kingdom of Amanullah Khan (1919) to the twenty years of democracy (until 2021) with the support of the international community, state building has sometimes intensified and sometimes experienced stagnation. Experience has proven that external factors and foreign interference have had the greatest impact on overthrowing or coming to power of Afghan governments in the last century. Although the multiplicity of ethnic groups in Afghanistan and the problems caused by ethnic pluralism or the abnormal economic situation have caused disruptions in the process of state building. The history of Afghanistan has proven that whenever the society is growing and progressing, external factors and foreign interventions have caused that half-life process to not reach maturity.

The re-emergence of the Taliban after twenty years in 2021 is an example of this bitter reality. Although the Taliban inherited a government in which the system and institutions were ready and active in advance, the management of the system by mullahs who have studied only in the field of religion in schools and have no use of modern science, and are still specialized in the institution for which they do not have relevant specialization, will cause problems for the functioning of this institution in the long run. Also, even though the international community has provided them with the opportunity to negotiate and lobby indirectly, the Taliban government has not been recognized at the international level, and domestically, it is not recognized as illegitimate based on the law or any other mechanism. Apart from this, the increasing poverty in the country, the brain drain, the closure of girls' schools, the economic failure of the country and the increasing social and political gap between the people, make the prospect of state building in Afghanistan under the Taliban rule full of darkness.

References

8pm. (2022). Deputy Interior Minister of the Taliban: "Suicide Unite Is Our Honor". 8pm News Paper. https://8am.af/deputy-interior-minister-of-the-taliban-kandak-suicide-is-our-honor/.

Abaas, A.T., Shakouri, A. (2018). The Role of Darul Uloom Deoband in the Formation of Religious Extremism: The Case Study the of the Tought Foundations of Taliban. Journal of Cultural Relations, 4 (8). pp 109–130.

Afghanistan International. (2022). Taliban Members without Education Should Be Employed in Government Offices. www.afintl.com/202201289698.

Aikins, M. (2022). Times Investigation: In U.S Drone Strike, Evidence Suggests No ISIS Bomb. The New York Times. www.nytimes.com/2021/09/10/world/asia/us-air-strike-drone-kabul-afghanistan-isis.html.

BBC, P. (2009). Biography of Hafizullah Amin, from Birth to Death. BBC Persian. www.bbc.com/persian/afghanistan/2009/12/091222_a-jadi-6th-profile-amin.

Chi, T. (1990). Coercion, Capital and European State. Oxford: Basil Blackwell.

Clayton, T. (2021). U.S. Military Withdrawal and Taliban Takeover in Afghanistan: Frequently Asked Questions, Congressional Research Service. https://crsreports.congress.gov/product/pdf/R/R46879.

Daimirian, M.A. (2021). Lessons Learned from the Intra-Afghan Peace Negotiations of the 1980s and 1990s. Kabul: Heart of Asia Society.

Dobbin, J. et al. (2003). America's Role in Nation Building from Germany to Iraq. Pittsburgh: RAND. www.rand.org/content/dam/rand/pubs/monograph_reports/MR1753/RAND_MR1753.pdf.

Groski, P. (2003). The Disciplinary Revolution, Calvinism, Confessionalism and the Growth of State Power in Early Modern. Chicago: Chicago University Press.

Hamidzada, H. (2020). Afghanistan in the Fourteenth Solar Century; Civil War. Published in 8pm Newspaper. https://8am.af/afghanistan-in-the-fourteenth-solar-century-civil-war/.

Haqjoo, M. (2001). Afghanistan and Foreign Interferences. Ghom: Majlesi Publications.

Hatami, A. (2011). Different Theories of State Building: Towards a Theoretical Framework. Journal of Political Science, 6 (3).

Hintze, O. (1975). Military Organization and the Organization of the State. The Historical Essay of Otto Hintze, Ed. F. Gilbert. New York: Oxford University Press. p. 183.

Husain, S.I. (1983). [Review of Afghanistan under Soviet domination 1964–81; The Afghan Syndrome, by A. Hyman and B. S. Gupta]. *Pakistan Horizon*, 36 (4), pp. 141–146. www.jstor.org/stable/41394206.

Hussaini, J. (2022). Analysis of the Structure of the Taliban Cabinet and the Future Perspective. East Institute of Strategic Studies. www.iess.ir/fa/analysis/2778/.

Irani, J. (2021). How and Why Did America and the Taliban Reach an Agreement? Persian Independent. www.independentpersian.com/node.

Karimi, M., Khadimi, H. (2016). Genealogy of Takfiri Currents A Case Study of the Taliban Movement in Afghanistan. Islamic Awakening Studies Quarterly, 5 (9).

Khalili, M., Fardoqi, M.B. (2017). Dual Construction of State Building in Afghanistan. *Politics Quarterly*, 47 (3), pp. 647–657.

Mesbahzadeh, M.B. (2009). Brief History of Afghanistan. Kabul: Aftab Publication.

Ministry of Defense. (2021). The Current State of the National Army. https://mod.gov.af/dr/%D9%88%D8%B6%D8%B9%DB%8C%D8%AA-%D9%81%D8%B9%D9%84%DB%8C-%D8%A7%D8%B1%D8%AF%D9%88%DB%8C-%D9%85%D9%84%DB%8C.

Mohamadi, Z. (2013). Afghan Security Forces; Number and Equipment. BBC Persian. www.bbc.com/persian/afghanistan/2013/06/130618_k04_afghan_security_force_info.

Mohammad Ali, M.A, Shafai, A. (2017), Discourse Analysis of Caliphate-Oriented Islam in Afghanistan. *Islamic World Political Research Quarterly*, 2 (8), pp. 1–214.

Mohsen. (2014). Brief History of Afghanistan Five Decades. Kabul: Mohsen Publication. https://ia801906.us.archive.org/27/items/history-of-afghanistan-past-5-decades-revised-may-2016/History%20of%20Afghanistan_Past_5_decades_Revised_May 2016.pdf.

Qanbardoost, M. (2016). Study of State Building Theories in Western and Islamic Civilizations. Third National Conference on Modern Islamic Civilization, Tehran.

Rahimi, M.R. (2021). Deconstructing the Official Discourse State Formation in Afghanistan. In Persian. Kabul: Amiri Publication.

Rahimi, S.M. (2012). The Process of Formation of Afghanistan's Political Borders. Geopolitics of Afghanistan, Blog of Afghanistan Geopolitics Association. https://geo-af.blogsky.com/.

Safiq, S. (2015). History of Constitutionalism in Afghanistan. Jama-e-Baz Afghanistan Newspaper. www.tribunezamaneh.com/archives/85173.

Sardarnia, K., (2014). Social Challenges of Modern State Building in Afghanistan. *World Political Research Quarterly*, 3 (3), pp. 37–63. www.sid.ir/fa/journal/ViewPaper.aspx?id=248928.

Shafai, A. (2019). Soviet withdrawal from Afghanistan; What Did Gorbachev Say to Najib? BBC Persian. www.bbc.com/persian/afghanistan-47227857.

Tanin, Z. (2005). Afghanistan in the 20th Century 1900–1996. Tehran: Mohammad Ibrahim Shariati Afghanistani.

Wallerstein, I. (1975). The Modern World System. New York: Academic Press.

PART III

Afghanistan and Major Powers

7

THE US ROLE IN AFGHANISTAN

A Critical Overview

Dhananjay Tripathi

I: Introduction

Inspired by the 'end of history' thesis of Francis Fukuyama (1989) and encouraged by the information technology boom in the early 1990s, the US had taken a pivotal role in structuring the post-Cold War new world order. Earlier, the fall of the Berlin Wall (1989) and the subsequent collapse of the Soviet Union (1991) had overpowered the ideological resistance of socialism to capitalism and established the US as a sole military and economic superpower. Proving its strategic superiority, in the post-Cold War world, no single power or coalition of powers was in the position to pose a potential threat to the security of the US (Gaddis 1991). In brief, after the end of the Cold War, the US emerged as an uncontested leader of the world. Even though the international community largely acknowledged the US leadership, one can see a contradiction in the USA's approach to world politics on close examination. Despite having the centre stage, it failed to reorient the world order and made a few strategic blunders. The case in discussion, i.e. Afghanistan, is a good example. Examining the US involvement in Afghanistan from 2001 to 2021, it is difficult to accept that the USA has succeeded in its efforts in Afghanistan. The US promised a stable, peaceful, and modern Afghanistan when it entered Afghanistan in 2001; at the time of its abrupt exit in 2021, no one can believe that any of these objectives have been achieved.

This paper makes an effort to evaluate the role of the US in Afghanistan. The motive is to understand how the situation unfolded in a direction that led to the lethal terrorist attacks on the sole superpower of the world. It was beyond comprehension that a non-state actor would inflict such an injury on one of the most militarily advanced countries in the world. The same

DOI: 10.4324/9780429281631-10

non-state actors in Afghanistan prior to 9/11 were largely ignored by the US. Further, this chapter also discusses the US retaliation to the terrorist strike through its war against terror to analyse its almost two decades of active engagement in Afghanistan.

It is interesting to note the change in the US's power position in the last two decades when it remained entangled in Afghanistan. When the US entered Afghanistan to eliminate terrorism, it was referred to as the unchallenged power of the world. After the exit in 2021, scholars and policymakers term the world more multipolar, with the US as one of the strong poles. In short, it is now accepted that the world is no longer unipolar, with the US as the unquestioned leader. The assertive rise of China and the Russia-Ukraine war are some of the more concrete examples that should be seen in relation to the USA's position in world politics.

In the next part, we will discuss the US's role in the post-Cold War world for better clarity and academic rigour. As argued earlier, there is a link between the US power ascendency and Afghanistan. The following section will give us some better insight into this intriguing connection.

II: Post-Cold War World Order: The Role of the US

After the collapse of the Soviet Union, it was believed that the new world order would be economically more integrated than ever, with no or withering confrontation to the free-market economy. The victorious power of the Cold War ultimately tried to propagate the ideas of Adam Smith, who advocated in his celebrated work *An Inquiry into the Nature and Causes of the Wealth of Nations* (1776) that a functional and free-market economy is the ultimate cure for all socio-economic problems (Harvey 2005). It will not be an exaggeration if one concludes that in the post-1991 era 'the superiority of free market capitalism seemed to carry the irrefutable weight of historical proof' (Centeno and Cohen 2010).

The unprecedented support for establishing the World Trade Organization (WTO) (1995) is a testimony to the fact that most nation-states endorsed the new post-Soviet world order. The disintegration of the Soviet Union opened a prospect for the US to pursue its international economic agenda of liberalisation and globalisation. There was almost negligible opposition to the US and neo-liberalism.

The Eastern European countries, allies of the erstwhile Soviet Union, also readily accepted the liberal economic system and democracy. Even countries like China and India have chosen the course of liberalisation to integrate their economies with the world economy (Nayak 2008; Naughton 1995). Thus, the post-Cold War international economic order was driven primarily by the US, and it was relentlessly accepted by the other states as well as the related non-state actors. The US has succeeded in promoting the liberal economic system in the post-Cold War world order. Notably, the US defended the capitalist system, both at the practical and theoretical levels, throughout the era of the great divide between the socialists and the capitalists (Panitch and Gindin 2012). Washington excelled in the process and was conversant with the minute details of these ideological contests. Furthermore, there were fewer takers for the command economic model practised and propagated by the Soviet Union (Bisley 2004).

In regard to international economics, the US was fine because it had the necessary expertise to deal with the situation; only the level of engagement had changed. The scope and scale of work have considerably increased because, from a leader of a bloc, the US, after the demise of the Soviet Union, became the sole superpower of the world. While the US power had increased, so had its role in world politics. The new international reality makes it evident that the US needs to reorient its foreign policy to meet new tests. Trained in the Cold War system of strategic competition, the US foreign policy establishment failed to deal with the work on alternative security issues. Ideally, the US would have moved from conventional to non-conventional security matters. However, the fundamental shift had never happened according to the general expectation, and non-conventional security failed to draw the attention of the policymakers despite its popularity in the academic circles. 'On a practical plane, the termination of the Cold War threatened to unleash what would be a wrenching transformation in the conceptual and bureaucratic foundations of foreign policy' (Brands 2008: 1).

At this historic juncture, the US had not relinquished its ambitious foreign policy to establish its complete hegemony in the world, militarily and culturally. This is often described as the US effort to build an 'empire' rather than adopting a policy for long-term peace and stability of the world system (Agnew 2005). Due to the early temptation for domination and in order to promote the interest of specific lobbies, the US struggled to alter the power politics in the post-Cold War phase and involved itself in many complex disputes (Schwenninger 1999). To mention a few examples, one was the North Atlantic Treaty Organization (NATO) decision to expand eastwards in Europe by giving membership to countries that are geographically close to Russia. Moscow vehemently opposed the eastward enlargement of NATO, because it was perceived to be a hidden ploy to militarily encircle Russia. Initially, Russia was inclined to get close to the West, but things changed after the expansion of NATO towards the East. The Russian political elites united against this move of the US. 'For Russia's fragmented political life, this phenomenon is rare indeed, although it should be mentioned that the consensuses was built by those who had different (sometimes mutually exclusive) explanations of and motives for their opposition to NATO enlargement' (Baranovsky 2001).

Russia registered its concern about NATO getting closer to its borders. This can be inferred from Russia's New Military Doctrine (NMD), released in 2010. According to point 8 of the NMD,

> The main external military dangers are . . . the desire to endow the force potential of the North Atlantic Treaty Organization (NATO) with global functions carried out in violation of the norms of international law and to move the military infrastructure of NATO member countries closer to the borders of the Russian Federation, including by expanding the bloc.[1]

We know that ultimately, it is the NATO expansion question that triggered Russia's belligerent response, and it invaded Ukraine.

Likewise, critics are also of the view that the US had decided in haste when it jumped into Iraq in 1991. The decision to attack Iraq, in this regard, was primarily assumed to be taken by geo-economic considerations rather than motivated by purely normative considerations (Frank 1990). As a matter of fact, the US applied different yardsticks, one for friendly and another for antagonistic states (Przybylowicz and Jan Mohamed 1991). There are undemocratic regimes in West Asia, and Washington generously backs some of them.

After the end of the Cold War, West Asia was perceived as a region of the American sphere of influence (Brzezinski 1991). Therefore, the US immediately swung into action after the invasion of Kuwait by Iraq. On 2 August 1990, Iraq attacked and occupied Kuwait to push its agenda directly in the region. 'The economic problems that Iraq faced after the war with Iran, the territorial disputes with Kuwait and even Iraqi claims on the whole or part of Kuwait, and the conflict over oil quotas with OPEC and Iraq's accusation and Kuwait's counter-accusation over exploiting the Rumaillah oil fields, all are critical factors in the crisis' (Hassan 1999: 5).

The Iraqi attack on Kuwait shook the world because it was at a time when everyone was talking of the rule-based peaceful world order. The international community deplored the Iraqi invasion of Kuwait, but evidence suggests that the US was not keen on resolving the crisis diplomatically and preferred a military solution.

After the invasion of Kuwait, on 6 August 1990, the United Nations Security Council (UNSC) passed resolution 661, imposing severe economic sanctions against Iraq; on 8 August, US President Bush, in a televised speech, announced to send US troops to Saudi Arabia. This is just one part of the strategy, but the arrival of the US troops to Saudi Arabia left little room for parley. Further, UNSC resolution 665 permitted the use of naval power to implement the embargo on Iraq, and it opened the way for the US to deploy naval ships. Later, UNSC resolution 678 authorised military action (Khan 1994). The US took the lead in attacking Iraq and was supported by its international partners. In this way, first the Kuwait War and later the Iraq invasion by the international coalition forces led by the US destabilised West Asia. While Saddam Hussein was defeated, the war in West Asia was used by the Islamic fundamentalists to project the West as an enemy.

These are two examples of the significant foreign policy decisions of the USA and both reveal how it intended to promote its interest and not the rule-based international order. With the NATO enlargement, the US lost an opportunity to bring Russia into the Euro-Atlantic security structure. This unnecessarily alienated Russia, when after the collapse of the Soviet Union it desired to be a part of the West. Notwithstanding its earlier move to establish a cordial relationship with the West, Russia slowly drifted in a different direction. The gap at present is historic, since Russia and the West are fighting with each other in Ukraine. Likewise, the US-led coalition's invasion of Iraq made Saddam Hussein a hero amongst those Arab citizens who viewed the West as the enemy. The main argument was that the US adopted an uncompromising policy towards the occupation of Kuwait by Iraq but maintained silence on Palestinian suffering.

Although Arab states did not support Saddam Hussein, he became popular among the Muslim communities, particularly among the radical sections. At the same time, the Saudi national and veteran of the Afghan war Osama bin Laden raised the issue of the American presence in Saudi Arabia. 'In fact, Bin Laden had become anti-American to the core – and anti the Saudi monarchy soon after they invited US troops to take part in the first gulf-war' (Shahzad 2011: 74). After solid opposition, bin Laden was forced to leave Saudi Arabia. He struggled to establish a base in a couple of countries, such as Sudan, from where he finally arrived in Afghanistan around 1996. It was a volatile Afghanistan, controlled mainly by the militant Taliban, from where bin Laden planned and executed the deadliest terrorist attacks on the USA.

III: Attacking the Invincible: A New Reality

According to the 9/11 Commission Report, the terrorist attacks on the US revealed four kinds of failures, namely imagination, policy, capabilities, and management. The 9/11 Commission Report is the official report of the National Commission on Terrorist Attacks Upon the United States. The report underlined that after the end of the cold war, there was a general sense of satisfaction and it was hard to perceive an attack from an organisation based in one of the poorest, most remote and least industrialised countries of the world. 'To us, Afghanistan seemed very far away. To members of Al-Qaeda, America seemed very close. In a sense, they were more globalised than we were' (The 9/11 Commission Report 2004: 379). The 9/11 Commission Report also acknowledged that there was no national debate on what was going on in Afghanistan, and it was a failure of imagination.

Afghanistan remained absent from international discourse until it became the most important battlefield during the Cold War. The country was almost destroyed due to the apparent show of strength by the two superpowers. In Afghanistan, Americans had discovered a 'Vietnam' for the Soviets. It was a tactical decision to keep the Soviet Union trapped in Afghanistan for a longer period (Khan 1987: 75). The USA's involvement in Afghanistan was an attempt to regain some space in Asia during the height of the Cold War. For the USA, Iran had slipped out of its influence after the Islamic revolution in 1979, and Afghanistan, during the same period, came under the direct control of the Soviet Union. This was a worrisome situation for a superpower with significant political and economic stakes in West Asia and the Islamic countries (Hartman 2002). 'The American President Carter who had down-played the Afghanistan issue during a foreign policy conference for Editors and Broadcasters in February 1979 started showing utmost concern after the Soviet invasion' (Haqqani 2013: 244). Then National Security Adviser (NSA) Zbigniew Brzezinski suggested to President Carter to give importance to the changing situation in Afghanistan – "could be a Soviet Vietnam". Brzezinski advocated the involvement of the US in Afghanistan, ignoring the string of Islamic fundamentalists that was attached to it because, in his viewpoint, in world politics, nothing succeeds like success, whatever be the moral aspects (Haqqani 2013: 245).

The US intervened in Afghanistan, supported anti-Soviet armed groups, took support from Pakistan in its efforts, and brought radical elements from the Arab region to counter atheist communists in Afghanistan. The US accomplished its objective in Afghanistan by compelling the Soviet Union to retreat.

Burdened by the decade-long futile but costly war in Afghanistan, the Soviet Union changed its international policy and opted for a rapprochement towards the West. However, internally divided and externally weak, the Soviet Union disintegrated in 1991. After the departure of the Soviet Union, Afghanistan lost its geopolitical relevance for the US but not for Pakistan, which continued to harbour ex-Mujahadeen and diverted some of them towards India, particularly into Kashmir.[2] Still, it was difficult to manage everything for Pakistan, and soon the whole of Afghanistan plunged into chaos. It was not only the armed, trained and motivated Afghans but a large group of foreign fighters who entered Afghanistan and became aimless after the defeat of the Soviet Union. Thus, after the complete Soviet withdrawal from Afghanistan (1989), several warring factions who otherwise were united against the communists started fighting amongst themselves. Internal turmoil and a deeply divided ethnic society provided space for the formation of the Taliban who declared to bring peace and stability in Afghanistan by strictly adhering to the Islamic code of governance (Zaeef 2010). Radicalised, organised, trained fighters and resolutely backed by Pakistan, the Taliban soon started gaining territorial control in Afghanistan. The Taliban became the single largest group controlling Afghanistan and was also officially recognised by Pakistan, Saudi Arabia, and the United Arab Emirates.

Although the Taliban occupied the majority of land in Afghanistan, it faced stiff resistance from the Ahmad Shah Massoud-led Northern Alliance. In its effort to control the country, Al-Qaeda also helped the Taliban and directly played a role in assassinating Massoud. This further strengthened the collaboration between the two. The world, particularly the US, had disregarded the closeness between these two organisations, namely the Taliban and Al-Qaeda, who were willing to adopt any tactics to achieve their goals. Both of these organisations were capable of carrying out suicide bombings and major terror attacks. Afghanistan, during this period, became the safest destination for international terrorists. Al-Qaeda and the Taliban together supported militant organisations in India, Russia, Central Asia, and China. Laskar-e-Taiba (LeT), Harakat-ul-Mujahideen (HuM), and Jaiah-e-Muhammad (JeM) are anti-India terrorist organisations with foreign recruits and had links both with Al-Qaeda and the Taliban. These organisations have indulged in many terrorist activities in India, particularly in Kashmir. Likewise, Chechen rebels were also associated with the Taliban. Mullah Omar, the leader of the Taliban, was a supporter of independent Chechnya. The Islamic Movement of Uzbekistan was also an associate of the Taliban and was active in Uzbekistan and Tajikistan. Extremists from Xinjiang region also have close contact with the Taliban and Al-Qaeda leaderships (Tripathi 2013).

The Taliban, with the help of Al-Qaeda, soon networked with terrorist organisations throughout the world. Winning the civil war in Afghanistan, eliminating every voice of dissent, cooperating with other terrorist organisations, and promoting the idea of Jihad throughout the world remained the significant objectives of the Taliban and Al-Qaeda. The US, preferably with the involvement of the international community, could have checked these unwarranted non-state actors rooted in Afghanistan and branched out to other parts of the world. Unfortunately, the US remained engaged in other projects related to empire building, as we have discussed earlier in this chapter. The US ignored the Islamic terrorists in Afghanistan, which also has had a deep grudge against the US. The realist orientation of the US foreign policy remained focused on exalting its own national interest where a few regions such as West Asia were given more prominence over the others. The major internal conflict, if it was not in the regions of interest of the US, was generally overlooked. Thus, the opportunity that came after the end of the Cold War to make the world a safe place for everyone through the involvement of different regional and international organisations was not utilised by the US. The US remained determined to promote the interest of the few because this is the key objective of its foreign policy based on the realist international relations theory. According to Robert Gilpin (2001), 'interest and policies of the state are determined by the governing political elite, the pressure of powerful groups within a national society' (Gilpin 2001: 18). This means that those who directly benefit from the system through its varied interpretations narrowly define national interest.

While trying to understand the new changes in the international system a decade before the end of the Cold War, Gilpin (1981) had made it clear that national elites and pressure groups do play a significant role in the making of the foreign policy. This was to maximise the profits by the functioning of the international system. According to Gilpin,

> The international system is established for the same reason that any social or political system is created; actors enter social relations and create social structures in order to advance particular sets of political, economic, or other types of interests. . . . Thus the study of international political change must focus on the international system and especially on the efforts of political actors to change the international system in order to advance their own interests . . . as in the case in any social and political system, the process of international political change ultimately reflects the efforts of individuals or groups to transform institutions and systems in order to advance their interests.
>
> *(Gilpin 1981)*

Gilpin, who subscribes to the state-centric view of international relations, has thoughtfully elaborated objectives of a realist foreign policy. The US during the Gulf War and in the succeeding period after the end of Cold War only threw its weight to enhance the gains of its selected elites at the cost of ignoring many severe matters in the world. Afghanistan was one such country where a number of things were underway, but it did not receive any attention from the sole superpower. As analysed by Zain,

> Between 1991–1996, the non-Afghan Jihadis either returned to their countries or spread out to other conflict zones such as Tajikistan, Azerbaijan, Chechnya, Bosnia, Somalia, Kashmir, occupied Palestinian territory and Pakistan. . . . During the Taliban period, most of the non-Afghan guerrillas returned to Afghanistan with fresh recruits and established a permanent base under the command of Al Qaeda.
>
> *(Zain 2006: 83)*

In order to consolidate its position in some regions, the US played the role of an irresponsible leader in the unipolar international system. By crass justifications of national interest for all its acts in world politics, the US ignored Afghanistan, which eventually became a hub of international terrorism. The 'invincible' was finally attacked, and a non-state actor shattered the myth.

When problems in Afghanistan were simmering, the US failed to nip them in the bud and finally when it declared a war for 'enduring freedom' it was too late an option. To sum up, the 9/11 terrorist attacks were not only an intelligence failure but also an indication of a narrow foreign policy of the US, which was, to some extent, admitted in the 9/11 Commission Report.

IV: The War on Terror and Operation Enduring Freedom

The unprecedented attack on the sole superpower shook the faith of people in the international system the US tried to build after the end of the Cold War. With the 9/11 terrorist attacks, Al-Qaeda had openly challenged the leader of the unipolar world order. However, the international community expressed solidarity with the people of the USA and offered unconditional support to fight against the new threat of global terrorism. This was the second such opportunity in the post-Cold War era when Washington could have adopted an inclusive approach and acted in collaboration with the international community to start a conclusive battle for perpetually ending the menace of terrorism. Unfortunately, this time the neo-conservative administration of President George W. Bush missed this chance. The prominent neo-conservatives in President Bush's administration included Dick Cheney (Vice President of the US), Donald Rumsfeld (Secretary of Defense), and Paul Bremer (US diplomat).

For the neo-conservatives, the end of the Cold War made the world more fragile so that there was a need for decisive action even for minute threats, and pre-emptive strikes when necessary; and 9/11 only reinforced their theoretical suppositions. The neo-conservative administration in the US also tried to invoke religious sentiment after 9/11 because of their ideological belief (Rockmore 2011).

President Bush articulated his neo-conservative position in his address to Congress and the nation on 20 September 2001. The speech's content analysis can explain how President Bush tried to treat it as a holy war. This kind of justification in the academic world can be inferred from the work of Samuel P. Huntington and Bernard Lewis, who are the proponents of the 'clash of civilisation'. The following excerpts are from President Bush's speech (20 September 2001).

> The terrorists practice a fringe form of Islamic extremism. . . . the terrorists are traitors to their own faith. . . . these terrorist kill not merely to end lives but to disrupt and end a way of life. . . . they are the heirs of all the murderous ideologies of the 20th century. . . . either you are with us, or you are with the terrorists. . . . this is civilisation's fight. . . . the civilised world is rallying to America's side. . . . freedom and fear, justice and cruelty, have always been at war, and we know that God is not neutral between them.[3]

Thus, from a realist to a neo-conservative shift of the US foreign policy only complicated things. The religious overtone of the US President's speech after the terrorist attacks certainly had helped the cause of extremists in Afghanistan who wanted polarisation based on religion.

After the terrorist attacks, the US pressurised Pakistan to support its war in Afghanistan and started Operation Enduring Freedom, the command of which was given to NATO. Inside Afghanistan, the US got support from the Northern Alliance – the group that for a long time had been opposing the Taliban. Regional powers like India and Russia supported the US without joining the military coalition; even Iran did not raise any direct opposition. In this, at the regional level, only Pakistan was the least unwilling partner or coerced by the US to be part of the war against terrorism (Musharraf 2006: 201). Although reliance on Pakistan was the strategic compulsion of the US, it had repercussions. Pakistan clandestinely maintained ties with the Taliban, and this support substantially helped the Taliban and its affiliates in the moment of extreme crisis. The resurgence of the Taliban was made easy by Islamabad, which was accused of playing a 'double game' by the US (Laub 2013).

The Taliban and its associates, including Al-Qaeda and its top leadership, took refuge in the tribal belt of the Af-Pak border, from where they continued their terror operations inside Afghanistan. There is a different angle to this war, and it does not come within the purview of this paper, but one should critically look analyze the role of Pakistan to understand why the US, after an initial success in Afghanistan, faced strong resistance from the Taliban. While underlining the role of Pakistan in the resurgence of the Taliban, it is also important to note that President Bush lacked a concentrated effort to finish the war in Afghanistan. The US government, within a couple of years after starting Operation Enduring Freedom, started making a similar case for an attack on Iraq. The US with its formidable ally the United Kingdom (UK) had made pretext that Iraq was possessing weapons of mass destruction (WMD). Thereafter, in 2003, the US and its allies attacked Iraq. The WMD story was to evade the real intention from the general public that the war was for Iraqi oil (Moore 2004: 24).

The Iraq war was a great digression from the war against terror, and it also negated the initial gains made in Afghanistan. Politically as well, the US war on Iraq helped the dying Al-Qaeda because it vindicated the position of bin Laden that the US is against the Muslim world. 'Every additional day that the United States remains in Iraq is a boon for *Al Qa'ida* and the broader jihadist movement. On the other hand, *Al Qa'ida* and its allies would also exploit a US withdrawal that left Iraq in chaos' (Bayman 2007). The Iraq war also had its financial cost for the US. According to the Costs of War Project by the Western Institute for International Studies at Brown University, the war had cost US $1.7 trillion (Trotta 2013). This was happening at a time when the US had already started slipping into financial crisis. There are also reports that the Iraq war increased the terrorist attacks by seven times on a yearly basis; even if terrorist attacks in Iraq and Afghanistan were to be excluded, the attacks in other parts of the world increased by one third (Bergen and Cruickshank 2007).

Two simultaneous wars of equal intensities were difficult to manage for the US, particularly when, in the case of Iraq, the world was convinced that the purpose was something other than countering terrorism and eliminating WMD. After it was exposed that the UK and US tried to present an untenable case of Iraq possessing WMD, both governments lost their credibility. Since it got involved, therefore, it was not easy for the US to withdraw from Iraq. When it was necessary for the US to successfully finish its military campaign in Afghanistan by eliminating Al-Qaeda and the Taliban, it had taken on an additional burden of war in Iraq. While both wars were on in 2008, it came to the world's knowledge that $25 trillion of the US wealth had suddenly disappeared. 'The events that unfolded after the collapse of the financial giant Lehman Brothers, for the first time highlighted the weakness in the US economy' (Centeno and Cohen 2010). This was demonstrated by the then-weak regulatory mechanisms as far as finances and the entire banking system were concerned.

The US, which emerged as the sole superpower of the world after the demise of the Soviet Union, had not been able to maintain its position. This emerging world order for analysts like Zakaria (2011) is a 'post-American world'. It was accepted by Zakaria that in the new world order there are many rising powers. At this juncture, the popular American President Barack Obama made a number of relevant decisions on both the economic and foreign policy fronts. President Obama made it clear that the role of the US in the world politics should not be defined by the global war on terror (Brzezinski 2010). This was a new shift in the US policy and to give it a practical shape President Obama had rightly initiated the policy of withdrawing the US troops from Iraq so as to concentrate primarily on Afghanistan.

There were two major points in President Obama's Afghanistan policy: firstly, the recognition of the fact that the Pakistan-Afghanistan border was the central hideout of the Taliban and Al-Qaeda militants, and secondly, to increase the number of ground troops in Afghanistan to enhance the counter-terror activities (Ra'ees 2010). Although the policy of President Obama was based on ground estimations of the situation in Afghanistan, by this time, the Taliban and Al-Qaeda had jointly gained ground, regrouped, and learnt their lessons through their earlier defeat. Therefore, this policy of President Obama, despite being better than that of his predecessor, did not bring the desired results of defeating the Taliban. Ultimately, the US started exploring diplomatic ways to settle the war in Afghanistan. Negotiating a peace deal was ultimately considered a way forward for the US policy in Afghanistan.

V: The Sudden Exit

Amitav Acharya defines the new world order as 'multiplex' in which there will be 'multiple great and regional powers bound together in complex forms of interdependence'. This is because, for the first time after the end of the Cold War, the world's military power was not the world's economic power (Acharya 2014). The US is also facing contests on different fronts in world politics. In this context, the US's exit from Afghanistan becomes important for international relations students. When the US decided to suddenly exit from Afghanistan after making a deal with the Taliban, how should we read it? Here, the most critical point is how the people of Afghanistan look at it.

The Iraq war debacle, its economic recession, and the declining domestic public support for the war in Afghanistan are some hard realities for the US that cannot be discounted while making an analysis of its exit strategy. Under these circumstances, it would have been very difficult for any country to continue to support an unending war in a foreign land. Starting from President Obama, we have seen his two successors making a similar poll promise in regard to Afghanistan, and that was to end the war. The war in Afghanistan became the longest war for the USA in a foreign land that has both material and human costs. According to the calculation of Brown University, the US had spent nearly USD 2.31 trillion, excluding 'The United States government obligation to spend on lifetime care for American veterans and interest payments on money borrowed to fund the war' (Brown University 2022).

The American public, too, became wary of their military engagement in Afghanistan. According to a survey conducted in August 2021, almost '62 percent of the Americans thought the war in Afghanistan wasn't worth fighting' (Shortridge 2021). This figure was just the opposite of the public backing that the US government had when it declared war on terror. According to a survey conducted by the *Washington Post* a couple of days after the 9/11 terrorist attack, almost 93 percent of the US citizens were in the favour of military retaliation (Phillips 2021). Logically, the American government was left with little space to garner public endorsement for the war in Afghanistan.

The question is not on exit but on the sudden retreat leaving Afghanistan entirely in control of the Taliban. The return of the Taliban in Kabul after the gap of two decades was bitterly debated in terms of the Taliban 2.0. Today, when again, girls in Afghanistan are out of school and universities because of the Taliban, one needs to rethink whether this is really a Taliban 2.0. The Taliban after recapturing power, this time quite comfortably after making a deal with the US, showed no intention to change its ideological position on girls' education. The Taliban, after international criticism, assured critics that they would open the schools in March 2023, since it wanted to make certain changes in the curriculum. However, girls above the age of twelve are not even allowed in 2024 to enter the school premises to continue their studies.

Women in Afghanistan now cannot go to parks or gyms and are prohibited from entering swimming pools. Moreover, women were banned from working in domestic and international NGOs (Al Jazeera 2022). In the last twenty years, when the international forces were stationed in Afghanistan, there was an improvement in the overall literacy rate. In 2003, the number of girls' enrolment in secondary school was 6%, which increased to 40% in 2018 (Batha 2022). Likewise, women's presence in higher education increased from 5,000 students in 2001 to over 100,000 two decades later (UN News 2023).

There are many such concerns, like the domination of Pashtuns in the Taliban, whereas other ethnic communities were not included in the government. As mentioned in the introduction, Afghanistan is a multi-ethnic society, but the Taliban failed to accommodate others. The presence and growth of the Islamic State terror network in Afghanistan is also a cause of concern. With a lack of economic activities, there is a chance that it may again slip into a civil conflict. So, whatever had been developed in the last twenty years in terms of civil liberty and little economic activities, it may just erode until the international community steps in and puts some kind of pressure on the Taliban. The world cannot afford once again to disregard Afghanistan. It is more pertinent for the USA. While the sudden exit irked many in the world, the Biden administration, in a twelve-page report, blamed the earlier President Trump for leaving less scope for manoeuvring, and exit was the only option left. This could be part of the US's domestic political debate. However, it is a known fact that Americans wanted to get out of Afghanistan. It is not possible to permanently keep an army in a foreign country. Nonetheless, the point remains about the sudden exit that led to the collapse of the state institutions that were put in place by the US in Afghanistan.

VI: Conclusion

The international reality has altered from the time when the US entered into Afghanistan and when it exited from the country. Today, the US has to deal with Russia – a much more formidable enemy. The European countries are also putting their energy into handling the Russian invasion of Ukraine and will not have the appetite to give serious consideration to the developing humanitarian crisis in Afghanistan. The US exit from Afghanistan again left a void in the lives of many who had witnessed development in the last two decades. The Taliban, despite not having official legitimacy, now has communication with the international community, and this gives others an agency to pursue humanitarian causes in Afghanistan. To conclude, things might appear stable; nonetheless, it is still in volatile, and a few years from now will be important for the future of Afghanistan.

Notes

1 For more details, please see http://carnegieendowment.org/files/2010russia_military_doctrine.pdf
2 There are substantial evidences of Afghan militants being involved in the Kargil War.
3 For more details, please see www.911memorial.org/sites/all/files/President%20Bush%20Address%20to%20Congress%20and%20the%20nation%20on%20terrorism.pdf

Reference

Acharya, Amitav. 2014. 'The End of American World Order', *The Hindu*, May 29, www.thehindu.com/opinion/op-ed/the-end-of-american-world-order/article 6058148.ece (accessed on 29 May 2014).

Agnew, John. 2005. *Hegemony the Shape of Global Power*. Philadelphia: Temple University Press.

Al Jazeera. 2022. 'Afghan Women Barred from Gym, Taliban Official Says', *Al Jazeera*, https://www.aljazeera.com/news/2022/11/10/taliban-ban-afghan-women-from-gyms-and-parks-in-new-crackdown (accessed on 13 January 2023).

Baranovsky, Valadimir. 2001. 'NATO's Enlargement: Russia's Attitudes', www.eusec.org/baranovsky.htm (accessed on 28 May 2014).

Batha, Emma. 2022. 'Taliban U-Turn Leaves Afghan Girls Shut Out of School', *Reuters*, https://news.trust.org/item/20210831110425-cvykj (accessed 20 June 2023).

Bayman, Daniel. 2007. 'Iraq and the Global War on Terrorism', *The Brookings Institution*, www.brookings.edu/research/articles/2007/07/iraqterrorism (accessed on 2 June 2014).

Bergen, Peter and Paul Cruickshank. 2007. 'The Iraq Effect: War Has Increased Terrorism Sevenfold Worldwide', *Mother Jones*, www.motherjones.com/politics/2007/03/iraq-101-iraq-effect-war-iraq-and-its-impact-war-terrorism-pg-1 (accessed on 2 June 2014).

Bisley, Nick. 2004. *The End of the Cold-War and the Soviet Collapse*, New York: Palgrave Macmillan.

Brands, H. 2008. *From Berlin to Baghdad: America's Search for Purpose in the Post-Cold War World*, Kentucky: The University Press of Kentucky.

Brown University. 2022. Human and Budgetary Costs to Date of the US War in Afghanistan, https://watson.brown.edu/costsofwar/figures/2021/human-and-budgetary-costs-date-us-war-afghanistan-2001-2022 (accessed on 27 April 2023).

Brzezinski, Zbigniew. 1991. 'Selective Global Commitment', *Foreign Affairs*, www.foreignaffairs.com/articles/47136/zbigniew-brzezinski/selective-global-commitment (accessed on 29 May 2014).

Brzezinski, Zbigniew. 2010. 'From Hope to Audacity: Appriasing Obama's Foreign Policy', *Foreign Affairs*, 89 (1): 16–30.

Centeno, A. Miguel and Joseph N. Cohen. 2010. *Global Capitalism: A Sociological Perspective*, Cambridge: Polity Press.

Frank, G. Andre. 1990. 'Political Economy of North-South Conflict in Gulf', *Economic & Political Weekly*, 25 (37): 2043–2044.

Fukuyama, F. 1989. 'The End of History?', *The National Interest*, 16 (Summer): 3–18.

Gaddis, J. L. 1991. 'Toward a Post-Cold War World', *Foreign Affairs*, 70 (2): 102–122.

Gilpin, Robert. 1981. *War and Change in World Politics*, Cambridge: Cambridge University Press.

Gilpin, Robert. 2001. *Global Political Economy: Understanding the International Economic Order*, Princeton, NJ: Princeton University Press.

Haqqani, Hussain. 2013. *Magnificent Delusions: Pakistan, the United States, and an Epic History of Misunderstanding*, New York: Public Affairs.

Hartman, Andrew. 2002. 'The Red Template': US Policy in Soviet-Occupied Afghanistan', *Third World Quarterly* 23 (3): 467–489.

Harvey, David. 2005. *A Brief History of Neoliberalism*, Oxford: Oxford University Press.

Hassan, A. Hamdi. 1999. *The Iraqi Invasion of Kuwait, Religion Identity and Otherness in the Analysis of War and Conflict*, London: Pluto Press.

Khan, A. Rais. 1987. 'US Policy towards Afghanistan', *Pakistan Horizon*, 40 (1): 65–79.

Khan, Nasir. 1994. 'US Abuse of UN in Gulf War', *Economic and Political Weekly*, 29 (35): 2277–2282.

Laub, Zachary. 2013. 'Pakistan's New Generation of Terrorists', www.cfr.org/pakistan/pakistans-new-generation-terrorists/p15422 (accessed on 7 May 2014).

Moore, James. 2004. *Bush's War for Reflection: Iraq, the White House, and the People*, Hoboken, NJ: John Wiley & Sons.

Musharraf, Parvez. 2006. *In the Line of Fire a Memoir*, London: Simon & Schuster.

Naughton, Barry. 1995. *Growing Out of the Plan: Chinese Economic Reform, 1978–1993*, Cambridge: Cambridge University Press.

Nayak, S. Satyendra. 2008. *Globalization and the Indian Economy: Roadmap to Convertible Rupee*, Oxon: Routledge Press.

Panitch, Leo and Sam Gindin. 2012. *The Making of Global Capitalism: The Political Economy of American Empire*, London: Verson Publication.

Phillips, Amber. 2021. 'When and How Americans Started Souring on the War in Afghanistan', *The Washington Post*, https://www.washingtonpost.com/politics/2021/08/18/when-how-americans-started-souring-war-afghanistan/ (accesssed 24 October 2022).

Przybylowicz, Donna and Abdul Jan Mohamed. 1991. 'The Economy of Moral Capital in the Gulf War', *Cultural Critique*, 19: 5–13.

Ra'ees, Wahabuddin. 2010. 'Obama's Afghanistan Strategy: A Policy of Balancing the Reality with the Practice', *Journal of Politics and Law*, 3 (2): 80–93.

Rockmore, Tom. 2011. *Before and after 9/11: A Philosophical Examination of Globalization, Terror, and History*, New York: The Continuum International Publishing Group.

Schwenninger, R. Sherle. 1999. 'World Order Lost: American Foreign Policy in the Post-Cold War World', *World Policy Journal*, 16 (2): 42–71.

Shahzad, S. Syed. 2011. *Inside Al-Qaeda and the Taliban: Beyond Bin Laden and 9/11*, London: Pluto Press.

Shortridge, Anna. 2021. The US War in Afghanistan Twenty Years On: Public Opinion Then and Now, Council on Foreign Relations, https://www.cfr.org/blog/us-war-afghanistan-twenty-years-public-opinion-then-and-now (accessed on 12 October 2022).

The 9/11 Commission Report. 2004. *The 9/11 Commission Report Final Report of the National Commission on Terrorist Attacks Upon The United States*, Washington: US Government Printing Office Internet.

Tripathi, Dhananjay. 2013. 'Eurasian Nations Its Significant Role for Peaceful and Stable Afghanistan', *Special Report, Diplomatist*, September.

Trotta, Daniel. 2013. 'Iraq War Cost US More than 2 Trillion: Study', *Reuters*, www.reuters.com/article/2013/03/14/us-iraq-war-anniversary-idUSBRE92D0PG20130314 (accessed on 14 May 2014).

UN News. 2023. Afghan Girls and Women Made Focus of International Education Day: UNESCO, *UN News*, https://news.un.org/en/story/2023/01/1132637 (accessed on 8 August 2024).

Zaeef, S. Abdul. 2010. *My Life with Taliban*, Gurgaon: Hachette India.

Zain, F. Omar. 2006. 'Afghanistan: From Conflict to Conflict', *Pakistan Horizon*, 59 (1): 79–86.

Zakaria, Fareed. 2011. *The Post-American World and the Rise of the Rest*, London: Penguin Books Limited.

8

CHINA'S ENGAGEMENT WITH AFGHANISTAN

Quest for Security, Stability, and Strategy

Sankalp Gurjar

This paper discusses China's engagement with Afghanistan. It begins by situating China in the history of great power politics related to Afghanistan. China is the fourth great power after Imperial Britain, Tsarist Russia, and the United States (US) to take an active interest in the politics of Afghanistan. Unlike the other three powers, China is extremely wary about the deployment of Chinese troops in Afghanistan or to be seen to influence Afghan politics. It is rather content to expand its political diplomatic and economic engagement with the ruling regimes of Afghanistan.

This paper surveys China's relationship with Afghanistan since 1949 when the People's Republic of China (PRC) assumed power in China. It explains how China's security concerns about the Soviet Union prompted it to support Mujahidin forces in the 1980s. Despite supporting Mujahidin fighters in their Jihad, China remains deeply concerned about the spillover of the radical Islamic ideology into the Xinjiang region from Afghanistan. China's security anxieties about Xinjiang are a key driver of Chinese engagement with Afghanistan. For this purpose, China was not averse to reaching out to the Taliban in the 1990s and has continued to maintain contacts with the group. Since the US invasion of Afghanistan in 2001, China had supported the new regime. The paper argues that China is the only power which has maintained good relations with the Taliban as well as the Afghan governments (led by Hamid Karzai and Ashraf Ghani) in Kabul. In that way, China's domestic vulnerabilities are a major factor in influencing its Afghan policy.

China's interests in Afghanistan are not limited to the security and stability of Xinjiang. China is keen to extract resources such as copper and oil from Afghanistan. China would like to extend its ambitious foreign and strategic policy project, Belt and Road Initiative (BRI), to Afghanistan and in effect, reshape

DOI: 10.4324/9780429281631-11

the geo-economic map of the region. Concerns about the security and stability of Afghanistan have prevented the expansion of China's economic presence. China is also worried about the continued foreign presence in Afghanistan as well as Central Asia and would like to limit the influence of the US in the region.

The flow of drugs into the Xinjiang represents another important Chinese concern about Afghanistan. It is clear that China's engagement with Afghanistan is primarily driven by its security interests and concerns regarding the stability of Afghanistan. In the context of the BRI projects and massive investments in Central Asia, Pakistan, and Iran, it is imperative for China to ensure the security and stability in Xinjiang. Consequently, stability in Afghanistan and political reconciliation assume importance. China's efforts in Afghanistan are directed to serve these objectives. The paper discusses these issues in the subsequent sections.

I. Afghanistan and the Great Powers

For the last 200 years, Afghanistan has attracted the attention and interest of great powers. In the nineteenth century, Imperial Britain and Tsarist Russia were engaged in asserting their control over Afghanistan. Their competition was famously dubbed the 'Great Game' by well-known British writer Rudyard Kipling (Garrity, 2013). Tsarist Russia's advances in Central Asia, its interests in Afghanistan, and the consequent threats to the security of British Empire in India were the primary British concerns in Afghanistan. As a result, Britain fought as many as three wars with Afghanistan (1839–42, 1878–80, and 1919) and was constantly involved in efforts to install a regime friendly to the British interests (Tripodi, 2010). Britain, despite being such a powerful empire, could only achieve partial success. This pattern of military involvement, attempt to reshape Afghan politics, and competition between major powers to attain influence and subdue Afghans has repeated itself again and again without much success for other great powers as well.

In the twentieth century, until the 1970s, Afghanistan remained relatively neglected. Despite sharing borders with the mighty Soviet Union and its neighbours (Iran and Pakistan) becoming key American allies in the Cold War geopolitics, Afghanistan did not face the pull and push pressures of the superpower rivalry between the US and the Soviet Union. In 1979, the Soviet Union invaded Afghanistan and the country was pushed to the centre stage of the Cold War (Reuveny and Prakash, 1999). Consistent political instability within Afghanistan was a key factor that contributed towards the Soviet decision to send troops. In the 1980s, Afghanistan became central to the American efforts, launched with the help of Pakistan, Saudi Arabia, and Communist China, to drain the resources of the Soviet Union and ultimately defeat the mighty Soviet Empire (Bruno, 2008). As a result, powerful armies of the Soviet Union remained entangled in Afghanistan for years with no apparent end in sight, fighting the brutal, Islamist Mujahidin fighters supported by the US and its allies. In the course of time, the Soviet Union was humiliated; its armies were defeated and later, in the aftermath of the withdrawal from Afghanistan, the superpower itself broke up (in 1991). Thus, Afghanistan ended up becoming the Soviet Union's 'Vietnam' (Cohen, 1988). In the 1990s, Afghanistan was in the grips of the civil war and later became a hotbed of international terrorism under Taliban rule (1996–2001).

In the twenty-first century, as a response to the terrorist attacks launched by Al-Qaeda (primarily operating out of Afghanistan) in September 2001, the US invaded Afghanistan by launching 'Operation Enduring Freedom' (CNN, 2019). Since then, the US along with its North Atlantic Treaty Organization (NATO) partners were engaged in an effort to defeat terrorist organizations like Al-Qaeda and the Taliban, bring peace to the war-torn country, and build a modern, viable state with a capacity to defend itself. After the initial success in toppling the Taliban regime and installing a new Afghan state, the US and NATO forces have not been able to eliminate the Taliban completely from the body-politic of Afghanistan. In fact, within a few years of the invasion, the US was forced to fight the resurgent Taliban and was unable to bring peace to the large parts of the war-torn country. In fact, the US since 2014 attempted to find an 'honourable' exit from Afghanistan and make sure that the country does not become a hotbed of anti-US terrorists. However, the domestic wariness about long-running foreign wars and the changing geopolitical scenario – the rise of revisionist Russia and China in Eurasia and in the Indo-Pacific – resulted in the US's decision to leave Afghanistan in August 2021.

The common pattern between all three examples is the enduring interest of great powers and their humbling military defeats on the battlefields of Afghanistan. Consequently, Afghanistan is known as the 'graveyard of empires' and has proven extremely difficult for any foreign power to exert control (Pillalamarri, 2017). In the last 200 years, a great power rivalry has played out in Afghanistan often leaving Afghans at the mercy of the machinations of external powers and their strategic interests. It needs to be recognized that the interest of external players in Afghan affairs was not limited to great powers only. Afghanistan's neighbours and important regional powers such as Pakistan and Iran have also been active in influencing the politics of the country (Weinbaum, 2006). Afghanistan's complex ethnic composition and cross-border ethnic ties do influence policy of major regional powers and neighbours. For example, Pashtuns are found on both sides of the Durand Line, which separates Afghanistan from Pakistan, and thus, Pakistan becomes a key stakeholder in any future arrangement in Afghanistan. India and China, for their specific strategic reasons, are also demonstrating willingness in developments in Afghanistan. Both are *de jure* neighbours of Afghanistan and share a small boundary. India's boundary with Afghanistan falls in Pakistan-occupied Kashmir (PoK) and thus India does not enjoy direct land access to Afghanistan.

Despite the lessons of history, foreign powers continue to find reasons to demonstrate their strategic interest in the rugged, mountainous, and difficult terrain of Afghanistan. Afghanistan's pivotal geopolitical location at the crossroads of South, Central, and West Asia is the primary reason behind this obsession. Thus, from a great power's perspective, Afghanistan is too important a geopolitical prize to be left to any other power. Control over this crucial piece of territory would allow any of these great powers to secure and perhaps even expand their area of influence. For example, in the second half of the twentieth century, the US was worried that if the Soviet Union succeeded in controlling Afghanistan, it would be able to position itself within the striking distance of the Persian Gulf region, energy heartland of the world, and consequently would be able to threaten global oil supplies as well as America's national energy security. In response to this looming threat, in 1980, President Jimmy Carter announced the 'Carter Doctrine' which linked oil supplies from the Persian Gulf with the US's core national security interests (Carter, 1980). The US considered Afghanistan to be a crucial staging point in its strategy of exploiting the soft, Islamic underbelly of the Soviet Empire in Central Asia (Parenti, 2001). In the twenty-first century, the American presence in Afghanistan was seen as a move to serve twofold purposes apart from the counter-terror strategy: to deter hostile Iran and to acquire military bases on China's western periphery.

China's interest in Afghanistan has to be seen in this context of great power politics and the history of Afghanistan. Due to its rapid economic growth and military modernization program, China is emerging as a great power in the twenty-first century. Following the trend of the last 200 years, it seems quite natural for China to take an active interest in shaping the political future of Afghanistan. In the first decade of this century (2001–2010), China was genuinely concerned about the US's role in, and intentions behind, the presence in Afghanistan. It feared that the US, through its military presence in Afghanistan, might actually encircle China and would try to contain China's rise. China's engagement with Afghanistan is primarily aimed at limiting the growing spectre of Islamic extremism and its spillover effects in Xinjiang. China's domestic vulnerabilities and the need for a stable Afghanistan loom large in its Afghan policy. Preventing the flow of narcotics, limiting the influence of a foreign power, and extraction of resources such as copper as well as oil are other key Chinese interests in Afghanistan.

II. China-Afghanistan Relations: From the Cold War to the Fall of the Taliban

Since its inception, the PRC is obsessed with the security of the regime and has consistently made efforts to ensure a secure periphery. The PRC's leadership imagines the security of the state in four concentric circles. The first circle consists of the territory that China currently controls including, of course, Xinjiang and Tibet. The second circle includes areas that are on China's periphery and are, in fact, adjoining to China's borders. The third concentric circle comprises China's wider neighbourhood including the Asia-Pacific region and South, Central, and Southeast Asia. And lastly, the fourth circle includes the entire world (Scobell, 2015, p. 326). These four concentric circles define China's threat perceptions and its approach towards those threats. It is also relevant to note here that the Chinese state is as much concerned about internal security as it is about external security. Areas in the second and third concentric circles are crucial for ensuring the peace and stability within China. Afghanistan, owing to its geopolitical location, falls in the second and third circles and its importance is underscored by the fact that it borders the restive Xinjiang region. For China, Afghanistan is more significant because it blends China's internal and external security concerns.

Afghanistan is one of the 14 neighbours of China and shares a land boundary of about 76 km (Taneja, 2018). The Afghan region that borders China is known as the Wakhan Corridor. It is a tiny strip of land in the northwest part of Afghanistan. The corridor is a thinly populated, near-isolated part of Afghanistan and borders Tajikistan in the north and Pakistan and Kashmir in the south. The corridor was created as a buffer between the British Empire and Tsarist Russia to avoid their collision (Levi-Sanchez, 2018). The land border between China and Afghanistan remains closed despite several requests by Afghanistan to open it up for trade. In 2018, there were unconfirmed reports of an upcoming Chinese military base near the corridor (Chan, 2018). Given the huge scale of China's investments in the China-Pakistan Economic Corridor (CPEC) that passes through Gilgit-Baltistan, a territory which is part of the PoK and lies just south of the Wakhan Corridor, these reports cannot be dismissed out of hand. The security and stability of the Xinjiang region is a paramount concern for China. A military base in this region would be able to serve multiple purposes. In this context, it is relevant to consider China's overall engagement with, and concerns about, Afghanistan.

China-Afghanistan relations could be divided into three phases: the first phase began with the founding of the PRC in 1949 and lasted until the Soviet invasion of Afghanistan in 1979. The second phase began in 1979 and continued until the fall of the Taliban regime in 2001 (Scobell, 2015). This was a phase marked by continued violence, instability, and civil war. The third phase began with the American invasion of Afghanistan in 2001 and ended in 2021 when the American forces left Afghanistan and the Taliban took over. Amidst these three phases, China was never a major player in the politics of Afghanistan nor was it able to shape the course of action. It maintained a low profile and was in fact more interested in securing its interests by nullifying threats or by cutting off external support to these threats than the desire to project power.

Although Afghanistan recognized the PRC in 1950, formal diplomatic relations were established in 1955. Both countries signed a treaty of friendship and mutual non-aggression in 1960. In this phase, China's relations with Afghanistan were overshadowed by its ties with India, Pakistan, and the Soviet Union. After the 1962 war with India, China's interest in Afghanistan and Pakistan went up considerably. In 1963, China and Afghanistan resolved their border dispute and Afghanistan began to receive a modest level of financial assistance from China (Scobell, 2015, p. 327). It is interesting to note here that in 1963, Pakistan began to take steps to strengthen its relationship with China. Hostility to India was a common factor binding Sino-Pakistan ties (Small, 2015, pp. 9–25). By the mid-1960s, the Sino-Afghan relationship was important enough for China to even arrange a presidential visit to Afghanistan. The PRC's then-President Liu Shaoqi visited Afghanistan in 1966. So far, Shaoqi remains the highest-ranking Chinese leader ever to visit Afghanistan (Scobell, 2015, p. 327).

In the 1970s, Afghanistan and China, both, were undergoing their own domestic political upheavals. China was more concerned about the military and political threat posed by the Soviet Union after the Sino-Soviet schism and military clashes along the Ussuri River in 1969. In the shifting geopolitics of the Cold War, China and the US began to build ties in the 1970s to contain the Soviet Union. Domestically, the era of Mao Zedong ended in 1976 and China launched economic reforms in 1978 under the stewardship of Deng Xiaoping (Denmark, 2018). Meanwhile, in Afghanistan, in the 1970s, the rule of the monarchy ended and the Afghan Communists seized power. Throughout the decade, the country remained in the grips of instability and political turmoil (Jackson, 2017). In this situation, Soviet invasion of Afghanistan in 1979 was a turning point in the history of the Cold War and South Asian geopolitics.

In the 1980s, a loose coalition of unlikely partners, bound by their politico-military-ideological fears about the Soviet Union, emerged to repel the Soviet armies from Afghanistan. Due to the geographic location, Pakistan became a 'frontline state' in this fight. Frontline states are those states which share borders with a troubled region or state and serve as key entry and exit points to influence the trajectory of the conflict, often in the service of great powers. Afghan Mujahidin fighters were trained and armed in camps set up in Pakistan and were sent to fight on the Afghan battlefields. The anti-Soviet Mujahidin effort was financially supported by the US and Saudi Arabia. The PRC was an active participant in these efforts. It supplied weapons such as assault rifles and grenade launchers to the Mujahidin fighters and further strengthened its relationship with Pakistan (Hong, 2013, p. 2). The Afghan situation had brought attention back to the significance of Sino-Pakistan friendship in the context of South Asian geopolitics. In Afghanistan, meanwhile, China had downgraded its relationship with the

Soviet-installed regime and refused to recognize it. It was quite ironic that Communist China was supporting Afghan Mujahidin fighters in their 'Jihad' against Soviet power. China was deeply concerned about the Soviet military foothold in Afghanistan and its implications for China's security.

In fact, in the 1980s, in China's view, there were three major irritants in Sino-Soviet ties: firstly, the Soviet military build-up along China's border; secondly, the presence of Soviet forces in Afghanistan; and thirdly, the Vietnamese occupation of Cambodia (Scobell, 2015, p. 327). By the early 1990s, all three irritants had gone away. The Soviet Union withdrew from Afghanistan and Vietnam withdrew from Cambodia. The Soviet Union itself broke up and five new post-Soviet Central Asian states were born on China's periphery. For the purposes of internal and external security, China needed to stabilize its ties with these states and ensure stability in the Xinjiang (Ibid.). In the meantime, Afghanistan, after the Soviet withdrawal, plunged into the civil war and different parts of the country were ruled by warlords. In this chaotic situation, the Taliban, which enjoyed overt and covert support from China's closest friend in South Asia, Pakistan, emerged as a major force and subsequently went on to capture power in 1996. The Taliban, with its Islamic fundamentalist ideology, ruled Afghanistan for the next five years and under their watch, Afghanistan became a major hub for international terrorism with even Osama bin Laden setting up base in the country (Maizland and Laub, 2020). In this context of growing power of Islamist extremists and their strong base in next-door Afghanistan, China was concerned about the spillover of radicalization into the Muslim majority Xinjiang and the Central Asian neighbourhood as well as the likely training and arming of Uighur separatists in Afghanistan.

In the late 1990s, China quietly reached out to the Taliban leadership. For the Taliban, it was an opportunity to end their global isolation, while for China, a relationship with the Taliban would be useful to curb activities of the East Turkestan Islamic Movement (ETIM). The ETIM is a Uighur separatist organization active in the Xinjiang and had launched armed attacks against the Chinese state. Pakistan, the major patron of the Taliban, also encouraged the tentative outreach between the Taliban and China. In fact, during 1998–2001, China had established a limited working relationship with the Taliban. It announced the resumption of trade ties and direct flights between Kabul and Urumqi (in Xinjiang). It was also reported that China had agreed to provide some amount of military support to the Taliban in exchange for cutting ties with the ETIM. It was believed that Chinese telecom companies Huawei and ZTE had agreed to provide phone services in Afghanistan. According to the deal, ZTE was supposed to install 5,000 phone lines in Kabul whereas Huawei was going to install 12,000 lines in Kandahar. In return, the Taliban ordered ETIM fighters to cease attacks against the Chinese state and assured China that the Taliban would not support anti-China elements (Small, 2015, pp. 127–130). It was a deal that benefited both parties.

Despite reaching out to the Taliban, China remained cautious and did not provide diplomatic recognition which was eagerly sought by the Taliban. The Taliban's destruction of the Bamyan Buddha statues and the September 2001 terror attacks on the US changed the entire context of the China-Taliban relationship (Ibid.). In the next few months, the Taliban regime in Kabul fell and the US forces had firmly taken control of Afghanistan. Despite the fall of the Taliban, China remained wary about the stability of Xinjiang and the threat of Islamic extremism emanating from the bordering regions of Afghanistan and Pakistan.

III. The Xinjiang Question

The PRC, since the 1950s, has been paranoid about the security of its periphery, and Xinjiang and Tibet occupy a special place in the matrix of Chinese security concerns. Of these two, Xinjiang borders Afghanistan, is an integral part of the BRI, and is relevant for this discussion about the China-Afghanistan relationship. Xinjiang is a westernmost region of China and is considered to be Central Asia within the Chinese territorial confines (Kaplan, 2018, pp. 254–255). The vast region, officially known as the 'Xinjiang Uighur Autonomous Region' (XUAR), occupies one sixth of Chinese territory and shares borders with eight countries. It connects China with the Central Asian states of Kazakhstan, Tajikistan, and Kyrgyzstan as well as with Afghanistan and Pakistan (Maizland, 2020).

The CPEC is a key part of the BRI and connects Kashgar in Xinjiang to the port of Gwadar in Pakistan. Several other connectivity projects and energy pipelines that link Central Asia with China also pass through Xinjiang. These infrastructure projects and energy pipelines make Xinjiang one of the most important geopolitical hotspots in the wenty-first century (Kaplan, 2018, pp. 259–260). In fact, the future of Chinese power hinges on what happens in this region. If China succeeds in stabilizing its internal security situation, it would be able to project a considerable amount of power into the maritime reaches of the Western Pacific. The stability and security in Xinjiang are important not just for China's internal security but also for the success/failure of foreign and strategic policies of an upcoming superpower. In a way, China's practical and prestige-related issues link up in Xinjiang and hence it is central to the efforts of ensuring security.

It is interesting to note here that the XUAR is a Muslim-majority region within the PRC. The population of the XUAR is predominantly Turkish-speaking with affinities for Turkish culture. The separate identity of Uighurs based on the religion, culture, and ethnicity and the repressive policies of the PRC under the guise of assimilation has resulted in continued unrest (and demands for a separate state) in Xinjiang (Hastings, 2011). Besides, efforts of economic modernization and the rapid pace of change initiated by the Chinese state are also generating new anxieties about the loss of identity for Uighurs (Kaplan, 2018, pp. 25–26). In response to these trends, there have been incidents of armed attacks and riots in Xinjiang and Beijing believes that separatist tendencies in this geostrategically crucial region constitute a major threat to the survival of the Chinese state.

Exiled Uighurs like Rebiya Kadeer, one of the most well-known Uighur activists, is based in the US and China fears that the US, if not openly then tacitly, supports separatism in the XUAR (Scobell, 2015, p. 330). Western human rights organizations have been vocal about the abuse of rights and treatment of citizens in Xinjiang (Maizland, 2020). China harbours deep suspicions about the role of the US in fomenting unrest in Xinjiang. The PRC has sought to maintain a tight grip over Xinjiang by deploying ruthless methods. In fact, demonstrating paranoia about the threat of Islamic extremism and separatism that exist in the region, a Chinese official who was posted in the XUAR was quoted as saying, 'Ethnic Separatism is their goal, religious extremism is their garb, and terrorist acts are their means' (Scobell, 2015, pp. 327–328).

Over the years, the Chinese state has actively promoted Han immigration from the 'mainland' to this border region (AFP, 2015). It was also revealed that China is also running the so-called 're-education camps' in Xinjiang in which, reportedly, more than a million Uighurs have been detained and are being treated harshly (Maizland, 2020). Several human rights organizations (such as the Human Rights Watch) and media outlets (such as the *New York Times*) have extensively documented how Chinese authorities are systematically attempting to re-educate, subdue, and 'discipline' the Uighur population by erasing their identity. These camps have been operating since 2014 and have grown in numbers (Ibid.). As China intensified its efforts to operationalize the BRI, it also cracked down harder on the Uighurs. Xinjiang's demographic structure and location as a neighbouring region to another restive region of China, Tibet, and Muslim majority Central Asian states and Afghanistan increases China's anxieties about the security and stability of the XUAR. Xinjiang always remains a factor in the Chinese strategic calculations towards Central Asia and Afghanistan.

In the 1990s, as new, post-Soviet states emerged in Central Asia, China made deliberate efforts to build cordial relationships with these states, keeping the security concerns regarding Xinjiang in mind. China wanted to ensure that these new states would not extend any amount of support to the Uighur separatism or radical Islamism. Authoritarian rulers of these Central Asian states were also worried about the threat posed by political Islam. Hence, China, along with Russia, Kazakhstan, Tajikistan, and Kyrgyzstan, launched an initiative, known as the Shanghai Five, to curb the 'three evils' of separatism, extremism, and terrorism in 1996. Five years later, the Shanghai Five gave way to the Shanghai Co-operation Organization (SCO) (Scobell, 2015, p. 344). The formation of the SCO did not change the core focus of the organization on separatism, extremism, and terrorism. China has also made deliberate efforts to bring Afghanistan into the fold of SCO. In 2005, the SCO-Afghanistan contact group was established and in 2012, Afghanistan became an observer in the SCO (SCO, 2020).

Apart from the spillover effects of the radical Islamic agenda, Afghanistan features high in the list of concerns for China owing to its role in the global narcotics supply chain. Afghanistan is probably the largest producer of opium in the world and along with Pakistan and Iran forms the 'Golden Crescent'. The Golden Crescent is a major source of narcotics for Europe and supply routes pass through Central Asia and Russia. Xinjiang is considered a 'victim' of the drug trafficking and in fact, during 1991–2004, Xinjiang's police forces seized 127 kg of narcotics that was believed to have originated in the Golden Crescent. Xinjiang's geographic proximity to Afghanistan and Central Asia plays a crucial role in the relatively seamless flow of drugs into the region. Stopping the flow of drugs into Xinjiang is one of the key concerns for China. Besides, China has had a chequered history with opium trade dating back to the colonial era and therefore, opium remains a politically sensitive issue for the Chinese Communist Party (Scobell, 2015, pp. 334–335).

Throughout the 1990s, the unrest in Xinjiang continued to simmer and the ETIM also gathered strength. ETIM fighters received support and training in Afghanistan controlled by the Taliban and we saw how China sought to wean that support away. Even after the fall of the Taliban, ETIM fighters continued to operate in the bordering regions of Afghanistan and Pakistan. Inability and/or unwillingness of the Pakistan army to curb ETIM activities and hand over ETIM fighters had upset China. The ETIM had also developed close links with other Islamic terror organizations such as Al Qaeda; so much so that, in 2012, Al Qaeda's head of the Federally Administered Tribal Area (FATA), which is part of Pakistan, was also operating as Chief of the ETIM (Small, 2015, pp. 145–147). It was reported that 300 Uighurs have joined the Islamic State in Syria and that southern Xinjiang, which borders Afghanistan and Pakistan, had become a hotbed for terror-related incidents and radicalization (Godbole, 2019, p. 231).

Meanwhile, heightening Chinese security concerns, Xinjiang experienced bloody riots in 2009 and at least 200 people died in these riots. Subsequent years also witnessed violence from the radicalized Uighurs. In 2013, three Uighurs used a car to launch an attack in the heart of the Chinese capital, Beijing (Gohel, 2014). This attack shocked the Chinese leadership and, for them, underlined the need to take strict measures to 'control' Xinjiang and Uighurs. The year 2014 turned out to be the most violent year since more than 300 people died in violent incidents. The Islamic State had also declared Xinjiang as part of their caliphate and called on the Muslims in China to join the fight (Godbole, 2019, p. 231). The planned withdrawal of the US troops from Afghanistan, increasing violence in the XUAR, and concerns about the stability of Afghanistan prompted China in 2014–15 to diplomatically engage key players involved in Afghanistan, including India, to discuss the evolving security situation in Afghanistan. China's sudden diplomatic activism and willingness over Afghanistan surprised observers who have been watching China's detached and cautious approach since the fall of the Taliban regime in 2001.

IV. China-Afghanistan Relations Since 2001

Although China had sought to engage the Taliban in the late 1990s, it was not comfortable having a regime next door with a radical Islamist agenda. Even though China was not averse to engaging the Taliban on the question of the support to the ETIM, it was unwilling to grant diplomatic recognition to their regime. The US invasion of Afghanistan in the aftermath of the September 2001 terror attacks and the consequent fall of the Taliban regime put China in a dilemma. It was happy to see the Taliban go and yet was not comfortable having the US military bases in Afghanistan and Central Asia. China believed that the US military bases near its southwest borders were a threat and would be used in future to contain China. It also feared that the Afghan regime that would emerge under the US influence was most likely to be a pro-Western regime and Chinese interests regarding Afghanistan and Central Asia would not be respected.

As the post-Taliban reconstruction began in Afghanistan, China re-crafted its strategy. It engaged with the new Afghan regime under the leadership of Hamid Karzai and yet did not abandon the Taliban completely. It was a difficult balancing act and China successfully managed to do that. It also helped that China's closest friend, Pakistan, was a chief benefactor of the Taliban and while the US-led forces took control of Afghanistan, hundreds of Taliban fighters, with an active assistance from the Pakistani deep state, crossed over into Pakistan in 2001. China had always treated the Taliban as a legitimate political group in the hope that the ETIM would not receive any form of support from the Taliban. This understanding suited both parties. As the political power in Kabul shifted, China also reached out to the new regime. For China, the ideological preferences of the governing regime in Afghanistan did not seem to matter too much. As the new Afghan government was finding its feet, China, just like other many other international partners, began to provide some form of economic and developmental assistance.

In the 'new' Afghanistan, Chinese telecom companies ZTE and Huawei won a contract to build 200,000 subscriber lines to provide digital telephone services. ZTE also won a major contract to build a fibre-optic network in

Afghanistan. Chinese construction companies saw opportunities in the reconstruction of Afghanistan, and companies like the China Railway Shisiju Group began to rebuild the Kabul-Jalalabad Road. Chinese companies also built a hospital in Kabul and many Chinese 'restaurants' sprang up in the Afghan capital (Small, 2015, pp. 132–133). Although the Chinese presence was modest, it was steadily expanding its activities in Afghanistan. It was noteworthy that, nearly a decade after the fall of the Taliban, China was still not a major player in Afghan affairs. China had pledged to provide $197 million as official developmental assistance to Afghanistan for the period 2002–2013. This assistance was so low that China ranked twenty-third in the list of donors (Hong, 2013, p. 6). Given China's economic and diplomatic capabilities, these figures demonstrate low priority and purposeful disinterest.

In 2007, a Chinese state-owned firm, MCC, won the contract for the copper mine at Aynak. It is estimated that Aynak holds copper deposits worth $88 billion. MCC along with Jiangxi Copper prepared a package deal that included promises to build a power plant, a coal mine, a cement mill, and a railway line which would connect the Aynak mine to Uzbek and Pakistani borders (Small, 2015, pp. 119–120). Thirty thousand jobs were supposed to be generated through the mine and the local population was expected to receive handsome direct/indirect benefits from the project (Hong, 2013, p. 16). The mine and other promised investments made it a large, integrated project and in fact were considered to be a key to the success of the regime in Kabul. The entire package of investment would total about $10 billion and China would become the largest investor in Afghanistan. It was expected that the mine would generate $390 million in tax revenue for the Afghan government which was always short of cash and desperately needed domestic sources of revenue (Small, 2015, pp. 119–120). It was also hoped that owing to China's strong relationship with Pakistan, potential dangers and security threats to such a large investment would be minimum.

The Aynak mine project could not take off for a variety of reasons. There were allegations of bribery and corruption in awarding the contract. The Afghan government's main patron, the US, was unhappy with the contract being awarded to a Chinese consortium (Small, 2015, pp. 119–121). Despite the heavy lifting that the US did in Afghanistan, it seemed as if the real economic benefits of the US presence were reaped by China. Many US analysts pointed out that the real costs of securing Afghanistan were paid by the US (in terms of financial assistance, diplomatic engagements, and military commitments) and China was 'free-riding' on it (Ng, 2010). Meanwhile, China also took a cautious approach to these investments. By 2006, the Taliban had regrouped and started launching vicious attacks inside Afghanistan (Small, 2015, p. 133). The security situation in the country was worsening day by day and the regime in Kabul and US-led international forces were unable to contain the violence. In this context, China was wary of investing such a large sum in an insecure environment. Thus, China continued to drag its feet and never really delivered on its commitment.

Four years after the Aynak copper mine project, China won the contract to prospect for oil in the Sari-i-Pul and Faryab provinces in northwest Afghanistan (Hong, 2013, p. 17). China's excessive dependence on the Malacca Strait, known as the 'Malacca Dilemma', for its oil supplies and its security implications are well known. China has been making frantic efforts to ensure that the 'Malacca Dilemma' does not threaten China's energy security and hinder economic growth (Lanteigne, 2008). Therefore, any oil found in Afghanistan would be considered a contributing factor in lessening China's dependence on the Malacca Straits. The state-owned China National Petroleum Corporation (CNPC) won the contract along with a local Afghan partner in 2011 (Scobell, 2015, p. 334). It is estimated that Afghanistan holds 1,596 million barrels of oil and 15,687 trillion cubic feet of natural gas (Hong, 2013, p. 15). The fate of this project also remained unclear.

Meanwhile, the US presence in Central Asian states was becoming a matter of real security and political concern for Beijing. The US was dependent on Central Asian states for supply routes to Afghanistan. In the process, the US opened military bases in Central Asia and solidified its footprint in the region (Beehner, 2005). From these bases, the US could closely monitor activities of China, Russia, and Iran and could project its influence in the region. However, the US presence came under the scanner due to the occurrence of the 'Tulip Revolution' in Kyrgyzstan in 2005. It was feared that the US had supported and engineered the regime change in Kyrgyzstan through its bases in the country (Small, 2015, p. 134). In response to this, the SCO had issued a strong statement calling for the timetable to close bases in Central Asia (SCO, 2005). Uzbekistan was apprehensive that it would be the next target for the US attempts to change the regime. It was also unhappy with the US criticism of the Andijan massacre of 2005 and hence had ordered the closure of the US base at K-2 (Walsh, 2005). In early 2009, when the US requested China to open up land routes connecting Afghanistan, the suggestion was received with a great deal of apprehension. China was worried that associating with a US-led war effort would be received adversely in the Muslim world. It was also believed that the real intention behind this request was to get a chance to spy on and fuel unrest in Xinjiang (Hong, 2013, p. 7). The 2009 riots in Xinjiang ended the discussion on this subject and China continued to refuse to take up a larger role in Afghanistan.

The announcement of the planned US withdrawal from Afghanistan in 2014 and its implications for the region seemed to have generated concerns in Beijing. Initially, there was some apprehension in China about the actual possibility of the US withdrawal. The announcement of the US's strategy of rebalance to Asia and the assessment of the political mood in Washington convinced policymakers in Beijing that the prospects of the US withdrawal from Afghanistan were real and that China needed to position itself to secure its interests in the post-2014 Afghanistan (Small, 2015, pp. 159–160). In this context, China began to change its cautious and ambivalent approach towards Afghanistan. In 2011, the first US-China dialogue on Central Asia took place (Hong, 2013, p. 10). It was followed by a China-Pakistan dialogue on Afghanistan and the launch of the first trilateral meeting of China, Afghanistan, and Pakistan. China also began to discuss Afghanistan with India in a bilateral setting and also engaged Russia and India in a trilateral summit (Small, 2015, p. 160).

Apart from the willingness to discuss Afghanistan with the important players, in 2012, China also worked with members of the SCO to grant observer status to Afghanistan and to bring Afghanistan into the fold of the SCO. The year 2012 turned out to be a seminal year for China-Afghanistan ties when Zhou Yongkang, China's security chief and a member of the Politburo Standing Committee, visited Afghanistan. He was the highest-ranking official to visit Afghanistan in 46 years and his visit signalled the political importance that Beijing attaches to the situation in the war-torn country. In 2012, China and the US, jointly, began to train Afghan diplomats. China also signed an agreement with Afghanistan to 'train, fund and equip' Afghan national police (Hong, 2013, p. 11).

As the withdrawal date came closer, China found itself in an enviable position. China was the only power that had maintained cordial ties with the Afghan government and the Taliban. Even when the Taliban was on the defensive, China had not cut off ties with the insurgent group (Small, 2015, p. 161). Besides, it was also in a position to put pressure on Pakistan for changing its policy towards Afghanistan. When serious efforts were made to get the Taliban on board, China appeared supportive. In 2013, the US had met with Taliban representatives for exploratory meetings and in the same year, the Taliban opened its political office in Doha, Qatar (Reuters, 2013). China also openly reached out to the Taliban and sought to nudge the group towards political reconciliation. Plus, China signalled that it was willing to play a larger role in Afghan affairs.

In 2014, China hosted the first major multilateral conference on Afghanistan, the 'Heart of Asia' meeting. The new Afghan president, Ashraf Ghani, paid his first official overseas visit to China and sought to convince China to invest in the infrastructure and connectivity projects (AP, 2014). Before Ghani, during Hamid Karzai's tenure, the focus was to get China to invest in the mining sector of Afghanistan. Ghani seemed to demonstrate the change of approach (Small, 2015, p. 194). He also reached out to Pakistan, put breaks on military co-operation with India, and addressed Pakistani concerns in the hope that Pakistan would be able to prove helpful in peace talks with the Taliban. These efforts did not bring any tangible benefits. Ghani's outreach to Pakistan proved controversial at home whereas the Taliban also was unwilling to be seen as being forced into the peace talks. The spring offensive of 2015, launched by the Taliban, was bloodier than usual. Meanwhile, the news of the death of a key Taliban figure, Mullah Omar, was leaked and the prospect of peace talks as well as Afghan reconciliation appeared bleaker than usual (Ibid., pp. 195–98). Nevertheless, despite the uncertainty about the situation in Afghanistan, China had moved ahead and deepened its relationship with Pakistan through the CPEC (Houreld, 2015). The CPEC is a key part of China's ambitious foreign and economic policy project known as the 'Belt and Road Initiative' (BRI) and the success of the BRI, and by extension of China, depends on the ability of China and Pakistan to complete the CPEC. The CPEC links land and maritime dimensions of the BRI and also amalgamates China's economic and strategic interests (Kaplan, 2018, p. 28).

V. Belt and Road Initiative (BRI) and Afghanistan

In 2013, as the geopolitical situation in Afghanistan was beginning to enter a period of flux, China launched its ambitious project of the BRI. China sought to revive the ancient Silk Road and place itself at the centre of the emerging global geopolitical and economic order. The BRI seeks to connect China with Europe and Africa via land and maritime routes. The land component of the BRI is known as the Silk Road Economic Belt and the maritime component is known as the Twenty-First Century Maritime Silk Road (Macaes, 2019, pp. 23–24). The BRI is seen as China's 'Marshall Plan' and is considered a grand idea which has the potential to remake our world (Kuo and Kommenda, 2018). It is estimated that the BRI has a budget of $1 trillion and involves building connectivity projects, energy pipelines, and infrastructure (such as roads and ports) (Chatzky and McBride, 2020). The BRI has sparked global excitement as well as concerns about the debt trap for participating countries.

The CPEC is a key component of the BRI. The CPEC connects Kashgar in Xinjiang to the Gwadar port on the Arabian Sea. As part of the CPEC, China is developing the port of Gwadar as well as building connectivity and energy projects. The total planned investment of the CPEC stands at $46 billion and is expected to revive the struggling economy of Pakistan. The CPEC is expected to reduce China's dependence on the Malacca Strait for energy imports and partially allay concerns about the Malacca Dilemma. The CPEC passes through the PoK and has obvious geopolitical implications in the context of India-China-Pakistan triangular security dynamic. The CPEC passes through Baluchistan (in Pakistan) and ends in Xinjiang (Kaplan, 2018, pp. 28–30). Both of these are restive regions and need heavy security cover to ensure that militants do not attack CPEC projects. Instability in Afghanistan is likely to spill over into the prospects for the CPEC. As a result, the Pakistani army has created a separate force to protect the CPEC (Khan, 2016).

China has also proposed a long-term, $400 billion deal with Iran in the framework of the BRI. The deal is expected to cover key areas such as connectivity, industrial development, energy, and finance. According to the deal, China will invest in Iran and in return, Iran will supply energy resources to China for the duration of the deal (Shidore, 2020). China also sees Central Asia as a core component of the Silk Road Economic Belt and has launched a spate of infrastructure projects in the region. In fact, the China-Central Asia-West Asia Corridor is one of the six major corridors under the BRI and connects Xinjiang with the Arabian Peninsula via Iran. All five Central Asian states are part of this corridor (Sim and Aminjonov, 2020). Furthermore, China has built energy pipelines from Central Asian states and is now a major consumer of natural gas and oil exported from the region.

In this context, if we are to look at the map, it is clear that all states around Afghanistan are the recipient of significant Chinese investment. They are part of the BRI and are expected to garner handsome benefits from the enhanced connectivity and economic investments. Owing to the security situation in Afghanistan, China has not been enthusiastic to invest in Afghanistan. In 2016, it was estimated that China has invested $2.2 million in Afghanistan (Sun, 2020). China also signed a Memorandum of Understanding (MoU) with Afghan government pledging $100 million (Stone, 2019). How much of that money is actually invested remains unclear. What is clear is that, if there is any power that can bring massive economic investment to Afghanistan, it is China. It can draw Afghanistan into the regional connectivity projects and reshape the geo-economic map of the region. It seems that China is wary of the politico-security situation in Afghanistan and just like its political engagement has preferred to hedge its bets. For Afghanistan, to imagine a better future and attract foreign investments, political stability and security is a key factor.

VI. The American Exit and Post-American Afghanistan

The arrival of Donald Trump in 2017 as the US President signalled the change of the US's approach towards Afghanistan. President Trump was keen to end the war in Afghanistan and bring the US troops back home. He seemed impatient to finish the war before his re-election bid in November 2020. With the strong push from the US President, the pace of events picked up. The appointment of the veteran diplomat Zalmay Khalilzad as a Special Envoy in 2018 was an indication that the US was seriously thinking about a deal with the Taliban and leaving Afghanistan (Landay and Walcott, 2018).

Although the talks between the Taliban and the US were considered controversial, it did produce an agreement. The agreement basically sought guarantees from the Taliban to not allow Afghanistan to become a base of the anti-US terror activities. In return, the US agreed to leave Afghanistan.

This agreement was supposed to set the stage for the intra-Afghan talks and ultimately result in political reconciliation. However, the proposed deal was considered a 'humiliation' for the US and the outcry over it forced the US to postpone the signing of the deal in 2019 (Baker, Mashal, and Crowley, 2019). The deal was ultimately signed in February 2020 (BBC News, 2020). After the signing of the deal, the fighting between the Taliban and the US-supported Afghan government intensified. The US, demonstrating a clear lack of political will for an orderly transition, left the country in a hurry in August 2021. The US retreat was so chaotic and humiliating that it reminded many analysts of the US's exit from Vietnam in 1975.

Since August 2021, the Taliban has been in power and implementing 'conservative', Islamic vision in Afghanistan. The US-supported Afghan government led by Ashraf Ghani just melted away. The country is staring at an uncertain future including a humanitarian crisis. The future of cultural diversity, gender rights, and the prospects for democracy in Afghanistan has never been bleaker. When the Taliban took over power, only four countries kept their embassies in Kabul open – Pakistan, Iran, Russia, and China. These four countries, through their links with the Taliban, felt secure enough to operate their diplomatic staff in a normal fashion. In 2022, countries like India returned to Afghanistan to ensure the ground presence in Taliban-controlled Afghanistan.

China was never averse to the Taliban returning to the power in Kabul. However, it would like to ensure that any regime in Kabul would not support anti-China terrorists and deliver stability as far as possible. Stable Afghanistan, even if controlled by the Taliban, is in China's interest. Beijing believes that, being a neighbour of Afghanistan and an emerging great power with expansive economic and military interests, it has genuine stakes in the future of the country (Sun, 2020). In any situation, China has accumulated enough levers, on its own as well as through Pakistan, to influence Afghan affairs to respect Chinese interests.

The US's withdrawal from Afghanistan presented China with an interesting paradox: although apprehensive about the US bases on its southwest border, it still was happy to see the US playing a major role in Afghanistan. The US presence prevented the spillover of the radical Islamic elements into China. For a considerable amount of time, the US remained bogged down in Afghanistan (and Iraq) and was unable to concentrate on the rise of China. This situation allowed China to grow and expand its power relatively unhindered in the Asia-Pacific region (Small, 2015, pp. 162–164). As the US extricated itself from the Afghan quagmire, the focus of the US strategy shifted to the Indo-Pacific and, with the Russian invasion of the Ukraine, to Europe.

In Taliban-ruled Afghanistan, China has continued with its cautious approach. There were reports of China supplying advanced weaponry, including unmanned aerial vehicles, to the Taliban (ANI, 2023). China has continued its policy of providing humanitarian aid to Afghanistan. A Chinese company has also signed an energy deal with the Taliban worth $540 million (Hoskins, 2023). However, the history of resource extraction in Afghanistan has been complicated and fraught with uncertainty. Therefore, it remains to be seen if the Taliban-China deal actually materializes or not. Meanwhile, the internal security situation in Afghanistan, in the context of growing challenge from the Islamic State-Khorasan (IS-K), will continue to remain a cause of worry and focus of Chinese engagement with Afghanistan.

Concluding Remarks

China's role in Afghanistan has evolved over the years. Afghanistan was not a major priority for Chinese foreign policy until the 1970s. It changed with the Soviet invasion of Afghanistan in 1979. Along with the US, Pakistan, and Saudi Arabia, China supported Afghan mujahidin fighters. In the 1990s, China's concerns about Afghanistan were centred on the spillover of Islamic terrorism into Xinjiang and support for the ETIM in Afghanistan. Even when the whole world had isolated Afghanistan, China reached out to the Taliban to control the ETIM activities. China's contacts with the Taliban continued even after the American invasion in 2001. China was quick to extend support and recognition to the new Afghan regime. It had also undertaken a limited amount of developmental work in the war-torn country. China had won major contracts for extracting copper and oil in Afghanistan. Owing to security concerns, these projects have not taken off. China has displayed ambivalent and hesitant behaviour until about 2011–12. Since then, China has become very active in Afghan affairs.

Overall, China has been worried about the security and stability of Afghanistan. Unstable Afghanistan is not in China's interest in the context of Xinjiang as well as the success and security of the BRI. China has pledged to undertake massive investments in Pakistan and Iran. Central Asia plays a very crucial role in the Silk Road Economic Belt of the BRI. Unstable Afghanistan is likely to affect all these countries and their stability. China's economic and infrastructure investments in the region would also be threatened if Afghanistan descends back into a chaotic, unstable situation as it existed in the 1990s.

As of now, Afghanistan, as well as the broader region, stands at an uncertain juncture. A lot depends on the ability of the Taliban to ensure internal security. In the context of growing challenge from the IS-K, how will China engage with the Taliban? Will China also open lines of communication with the IS-K? How will the growing instability in Pakistan affect China's interests, especially the CPEC? What are the implications of the fraying of ties between Pakistan and the Taliban for China's security interests in the region? These are some of the questions that will shape the Chinese strategy towards Afghanistan.

References

AFP. (2015). *China's Drive to Settle New Wave of Migrants in Restive Xinjiang*. Retrieved July 31, 2020, from www.scmp.com/news/china/society/article/1789160/chinas-drive-settle-new-wave-migrants-restive-xinjiang

ANI. (2023, January 22). China Providing Modern Weaponry to Taliban: Report. *Times of India*. Retrieved February 28, 2022, from https://timesofindia.indiatimes.com/world/us/china-providing-modern-weaponry-to-taliban-report/articleshow/97222160.cms

AP. (2014, October 28). Ghani Seeks Chinese Investment in First Foreign Trip. *Dawn*. Retrieved August 1, 2020, from www.dawn.com/news/1140938/ghani-seeks-chinese-investment-in-first-foreign-trip

Baker, P., Mashal, M., and Crowley, M. (2019, September 8). How Trump's Plan to Secretly Meet with the Taliban Came Together, and Fell Apart. *The New York Times*.

BBC News. (2020, February 29). Afghan Conflict: US and Taliban Sign Deal to End 18-Year War. *BBC*. Retrieved August 1, 2020, from www.bbc.com/news/world-asia-51689443

Beehner, L. (2005, July 26). ASIA: U.S. Military Bases in Central Asia. *Council on Foreign Relations*. Retrieved August 1, 2020, from www.cfr.org/backgrounder/asia-us-military-bases-central-asia

Bruno, G. (2008). Saudi Arabia and the Future of Afghanistan. *Council on Foreign Relations*. Retrieved July 30, 2020, from www.cfr.org/backgrounder/saudi-arabia-and-future-afghanistan

Carter, J. (1980). *The state of the union address delivered before a joint session of the congress*. Retrieved February 5, 2019, from www.presidency.ucsb.edu/documents/the-state-the-union-address-delivered-before-joint-session-the-congress

Chan, M. (2018). China Is Helping Afghanistan Set Up Mountain Brigade to Fight Terrorism. *South China Morning Post*. Retrieved July 31, 2020, from www.scmp.com/news/china/diplomacy-defence/article/2161745/china-building-training-camp-afghanistan-fight

Chatzky, A., and McBride, J. (2020, January 28). China's Massive Belt and Road Initiative. *Council on Foreign Relations*. Retrieved August 1, 2020, from www.cfr.org/backgrounder/chinas-massive-belt-and-road-initiative

CNN. (2019). Operation Enduring Freedom Fast Facts. *CNN*. Retrieved July 30, 2020, from https://edition.cnn.com/2013/10/28/world/operation-enduring-freedom-fast-facts/index.html

Cohen, R. (1988, April 22). The Soviets' Vietnam. *The Washington Post*. Retrieved July 30, 2020, from www.washingtonpost.com/archive/opinions/1988/04/22/the-soviets-vietnam/5e7fde43-6a0c-46fb-b678-dbb89bcb720b/

Denmark, A. (2018). 40 Years Ago, Deng Xiaoping Changed China—and the World. *Monkey Cage*. Retrieved July 31, 2020, from www.washingtonpost.com/news/monkey-cage/wp/2018/12/19/40-years-ago-deng-xiaoping-changed-china-and-the-world/

Garrity, P. J. (2013). Kim's Great Game. *Claremont Review of Books*. Retrieved July 30, 2020, from https://claremontreviewofbooks.com/digital/kims-great-game/

Godbole, A. (2019). Stability in the Xi Era: Trends in Ethnic Policy in Xinjiang and Tibet Since 2012. *India Quarterly*, 75(2), 228–244.

Gohel, S. M. (2014). The "Seventh Stage" of Terrorism in China. *CTC Sentinel*, 7(11), 16–20.

Hastings, J. V. (2011). Charting the Course of Uyghur Unrest. *The China Quarterly*, (208), 893–912.

Hong, Z. (2013). China's Afghan Policy: The Forming of the "March West" Strategy? *The Journal of East Asian Affairs*, 27(2), 1–29.

Hoskins, P. (2023, January 6). Taliban and China firm Agree Afghanistan Oil Extraction Deal. *BBC News*. Retrieved February 28, 2023, from www.bbc.com/news/business-64183083

Houreld, K. (2015, April 20). China and Pakistan Launch Economic Corridor Plan Worth $46 Billion. *Reuters*. Retrieved August 1, 2020, from www.reuters.com/article/us-pakistan-china/china-and-pakistan-launch-economic-corridor-plan-worth-46-billion-idUSKBN0NA12T20150420

Jackson, N. (2017). *The Great Game Revisited: Afghanistan in the 1970s*. Retrieved July 31, 2020, from www.amdigital.co.uk/about/blog/item/the-great-game-revisited-afghanistan-in-the-1970s

Kaplan, R. D. (2018). *The Return of Marco Polo's World: War, Strategy and American Interests in the Twenty-First Century*. New York: Random House.

Khan, R. (2016, Augus 12). 15,000 Troops of Special Security Division to Protect CPEC Projects, Chinese Nationals. *Dawn*. Retrieved August 21, 2020, from www.dawn.com/news/1277182

Kuo, L., and Kommenda, N. (2018). What Is China's Belt and Road Initiative? *The Guardian*. Retrieved August 1, 2020, from www.theguardian.com/cities/ng-interactive/2018/jul/30/what-china-belt-road-initiative-silk-road-explainer

Landay, J., and Walcott, J. (2018, August 22). *U.S. to Bring Back Khalilzad as Special Afghanistan Envoy: Sources. Reuters*. Retrieved August 1, 2020, from www.reuters.com/article/us-usa-afghanistan/u-s-to-bring-back-khalilzad-as-special-afghanistan-envoy-sources-idUSKCN1L71Z3

Lanteigne, M. (2008). China's Maritime Security and the "Malacca Dilemma". *Asian Security*, 4(2), 143–161.

Levi-Sanchez, S. (2018). *The Corridor of Power*. Retrieved July 31, 2020, from www.lowyinstitute.org/the-interpreter/corridor-power

Macaes, B. (2019). *Belt and Road: A Chinese World Order*. Gurgaon: Penguin.

Maizland, L. (2020). *China's Repression of Uighurs in Xinjiang*. Retrieved July 31, 2020, from www.cfr.org/backgrounder/chinas-repression-uighurs-xinjiang

Maizland, L., and Laub, Z. (2020). The Taliban in Afghanistan. *Council on Foreign Relations*. Retrieved July 31, 2020, from www.cfr.org/backgrounder/taliban-afghanistan

Ng, T. P. (2010). *China's Role in Shaping the Future of Afghanistan*. Washington, DC: Carnegie Endowment for International Peace.

Parenti, C. (2001). America's Jihad: A History of Origins. *Social Justice*, 28(3), 31–38.

Pillalamarri, A. (2017). Why Is Afghanistan the "Graveyard of Empires"? *The Diplomat*. Retrieved July 30, 2020, from https://thediplomat.com/2017/06/why-is-afghanistan-the-graveyard-of-empires/

Reuters. (2013, June 12). *Afghan Taliban Opens Qatar Office, Says Seeks Political Solution*. Retrieved August 1, 2020, from www.reuters.com/article/us-afghanistan-taliban-opening/afghan-taliban-opens-qatar-office-says-seeks-political-solution-idUSBRE95H0NU20130618

Reuveny, R., and Prakash, A. (1999). The Afghanistan War and the Breakdown of the Soviet Union. *Review of International Studies*, 25(4), 693–708.

SCO. (2005). *Declaration by the Heads of the Member States of the Shanghai Cooperation Organization*. Astana: SCO. Retrieved August 1, 2020.

SCO. (2020). *SCO Secretariat Holds Roundtable Discussion on Afghanistan*. Retrieved July 31, 2020, from http://eng.sectsco.org/news/20200109/621306.html

Scobell, A. (2015). China Ponders Post-2014 Afghanistan: Neither "All in" Nor Bystander. *Asian Survey*, 55(2), 325–345.

Shidore, S. (2020, July 18). The Iran-China Deal Deepens India's Strategic Bind in an Increasingly Hostile Neighbourhood. *Scroll*. Retrieved August 1, 2020, from https://scroll.in/article/967781/the-iran-china-deal-deepens-indias-strategic-bind-in-an-increasingly-hostile-neighbourhood

Sim, L.-C., and Aminjonov, F. (2020, February 1). Potholes and Bumps Along the Silk Road Economic Belt in Central Asia. *The Diplomat*. Retrieved August 1, 2020, from https://thediplomat.com/2020/02/potholes-and-bumps-along-the-silk-road-economic-belt-in-central-asia/

Small, A. (2015). *The China-Pakistan Axis: Asia's New Geopolitics*. Gurgaon: Penguin.

Stone, R. (2019, February 18). Slowly But Surely, China Is Moving into Afghanistan. *TRT World*. Retrieved August 1, 2020, from www.trtworld.com/magazine/slowly-but-surely-china-is-moving-into-afghanistan-24276

Sun, Y. (2020, April 8). China's Strategic Assessment of Afghanistan. *War on the Rocks*. Retrieved August 1, 2020, from https://warontherocks.com/2020/04/chinas-strategic-assessment-of-afghanistan/

Taneja, K. (2018). China in Afghanistan: A Military Base in the Offing? *ORF*. Retrieved July 31, 2020, from www.orfonline.org/expert-speak/china-in-afghanistan-a-military-base-in-the-offing/

Tripodi, C. (2010). Grand Strategy and the Graveyard of Assumptions: Britain and Afghanistan, 1839–1919. *The Journal of Strategic Studies*, 33(5), 701–725.

Walsh, N. P. (2005, August 1). Uzbekistan Kicks US Out of Military Base. *The Guardian*. Retrieved August 1, 202, from www.theguardian.com/world/2005/aug/01/usa.nickpatonwalsh

Weinbaum, M. G. (2006). *Afghanistan and Its Neighbors: An Ever Dangerous Neighborhood*. Special Report, United States Institute of Peace, Washington, DC.

9

IS THE PAST A PROLOGUE? DECIPHERING INDIA'S NORTH-WEST ENGAGEMENT

Raghav Sharma

Introduction

> How can a small Power like Afghanistan, which is like a goat between these lions [Britain and Tsarist Russia], or a grain of wheat between two strong millstones of the grinding mill, stand in the midway of the stones without being ground to dust?[1]

> But Afghanistan's difficulties are larger than those of Pakistan. Pakistan only smokes one side's opium, whereas Afghanistan smokes the opium of two sides. If Afghanistan were not a tool, the United States and the Soviet Union would not invest in it.[2]

These caustic appraisals concerning Afghanistan's status in the regional and international order encapsulate the changing geo-political dynamics that have underpinned the trajectory of its engagement with the contemporary world. Nineteenth-century colonial geo-politics in particular left an indelible imprint in shaping the contours of the modern Afghan nation-state in its present *avatar*. Chronicles of history offer us a sound empirical basis to dispel the oft invoked historical misnomer of Afghanistan being "the grave-yard of empires". Prior to 1747, the year regarded as marking the foundation of the modern Afghan state,[3] the political geography of the region known as Afghanistan was dominated by three monumental empires: namely, the Mughals projecting their power from Peshawar into Eastern Afghanistan and Kabul; the Safavids holding sway over Herat and lower Helmand; and the Uzbeks controlling Maimana, Balkh and Kunduz. The vacuum created by the near simultaneous decline of these empires, in particular the assassination

DOI: 10.4324/9780429281631-12

of Nadir Shah of Iran, provided the Abdali Pushtuns under Ahmad Shah, himself a military commander for the army of Nadir Shah, an opportunity to carve out an independent Afghan kingdom.[4]

Raids into the plains of India, often justified by resorting to religious lexicon, provided the Durrani Kingdom an important and politically expedient source of revenue without generating conflict with its own people. However, the efficacy of this strategy was put to the test in light of a dramatic reconfiguration of the geo-political landscape following the expansion of Russian imperial power into Central Asia and their encouragement to Persia in laying claim to Herat. While the ebbing power of the Mughal dynasty in the Indian subcontinent provided an opportunity to the British as well as the Sikhs in Punjab under Ranjit Singh (1801–39) to attempt to fill in the void. However, following Ranjit Singh's death, the Sikh empire unravelled briskly and for the first time, the frontiers of British India were geographically contiguous to those of Afghanistan.[5] This marked a watershed, for these developments would set the stage for animating the strategic landscape for the Afghans, British and the Russian empires and subsequently for the modern nation states that succeeded them, most notably Pakistan.

Strategies of Imperial Control

The Russian and British imperial behemoths expanded briskly, shrinking the geographical span between the two from 4,000 miles in 1759 to 400 miles by 1885.[6] This provided the overarching template against which the British scripted their strategies of imperial control vis-à-vis Afghanistan which would continue to animate South Asia's geo-strategic landscape long after the retreat of the Raj.

Apprehensive of the threat posed by Russian expansionism and in particular the fear of the potential to use Afghanistan as a springboard for launching expansionist designs on the Indian subcontinent, London oscillated between an aggressive 'forward policy'[7] and a relatively passive 'closed border' policy.[8] The three Anglo Afghan Wars (1839–1842; 1878–1880; and May–August 1919) were a manifestation of these contrasting policy positions adopted by London at different points in time.

Although not new to dealing with the ebb and flow of empires, it was Afghanistan's interaction with imperial Britain and Russia that shaped in the most profound manner its contours as a nation-state and a geo-political entity. The brief period of direct control exercised by Britain after the First Anglo-Afghan War laid the foundations for the Afghan state to develop a professional infantry commanded by the central government. The British whittled down the autonomy of the chiefs who provided the state with irregular troops to fight wars in return for generous grants, estimated to have consumed nearly half the state's revenues. The British war effort costing about

8 million pounds led to a large-scale influx of money in Afghanistan and aided the process of undermining the power of those whose standing rested on feudal obligations to the state while bolstering the socio-economic standing of those engaged in trade and services.[9]

However, a disastrous conclusion to the war effort saw the British take recourse to a reliance on indirect means of control. Taking a leaf out of the Mughal practice of granting subsidies to tribal chiefs in exchange for peace and right of passage from the Khyber Pass, the British periodically employed the practice. For instance in 1857, Dost Muhammad was provided with 4,000 muskets and 500,000 rupees to thwart the Persian threat to Herat. Notably British aid to the tune of 2.6 million rupees flowed into the *amir's* coffers after the Persian threat to Herat disappeared after their defeat at the hands of the British, rewarding him for his refusal to assist the Indian mutiny against the British the same year.

Russian penetration deep into Central Asia forced London to engage Moscow and by 1873 the two agreed to fixing the Afghan frontier at the Amu Darya. However, Russian diplomatic manoeuvres eventually propelled Britain to embark on the Second Anglo-Afghan War which was brought to a conclusion through the Treaty of Gandamak signed in 1879. It cast the die for trajectory of future engagement, with the Raj successively chipping away at Afghan territory, including the Khyber Pass along with the Afghan kingdom ceding control over foreign policy to the British. In return Kabul was rewarded an annual subsidy of 600,000 rupees, subsequently climbing to 1.2 million rupees in 1883. From the following year, beginning in 1884 in the northwest the British and Russian empires sought to de-limit frontiers of what today constitutes Afghanistan. It was in this period that the most significant border de-limitation exercise was undertaken in 1893 – the Durand Line, drawn in absolute disregard of topographical and ethnographic realities. This cartographic transformation effectively split up Pushtun tribes who inhabited the area. This development left an indelible impression in shaping contemporary regional geo-politics.[10]

Abdur Rehman's reluctance to accede to the Durand agreement was negotiated through a 'carrot and stick' approach. On the one hand British subsidies to Abdur Rehman Khan swelled to 1.8 million rupees, supplementing his drive towards supplanting internal political autonomy by putting in place a centralized state apparatus whose strength rested on a powerful army equipped with modernized weaponry. Notably landlocked Afghanistan depended on British India for import of arms and raw materials to produce them. London leveraged this dependency to the hilt, responding to the *amir's* recalcitrance on the Durand award by imposing an economic embargo in 1893, at a time when the former was waging a military campaign to subdue the Hazaras.[11]

The desire to secure frontiers of British India which were frequently plagued by raids from Pushtuns into the Indus valley plains without resorting

to a 'forward policy' in the aftermath of the Second Anglo-Afghan War cul-
minated in the Durand Line. The agreement delineated 'respective spheres
of the two governments' and the *amir* insisted it did not constitute a permanent international boundary – a position subscribed to by governments
of all ideological hues in Kabul. However, contrary to its professed aim of
bringing stability to the frontier, "the line Durand Line proved politically,
geographically, and strategically untenable. British and Indian troops fought
many bloody engagements with the fiercely independent border mountain-
eers. Much of the fighting was the direct result of British attempts to demarcate the hated Durand Line".[12]

Inability to stabilize the frontier in the years to follow and mounting military costs of confronting rebellion led the British to embark on a "modified
closed border policy that involved creation of the North West Frontier Province (NWFP) in 1901 and re-deployment of military resources". The NWFP
was so crafted as to serve not merely as boundary with Afghanistan but
also as a buffer between the settled and tribal districts, protecting the latter
against any potential threats of encroachment.[13] The latter were deliberately
left out of the regular governance framework of the empire, and were instead
regulated by the notorious Frontier Crimes Regulation (FCR). Attempts
at canvassing for extension of governance reforms were severely punished
under the FCR which imposed collective punishments. Hasan Kakar lucidly
lays bare the profundity of the implications of the British inability to exercise
effective control over areas it removed from the authority of Amir Abdur
Rehman Khan in 1893, arguing that it "created a no-man's land. By intro-
ducing the Durand Line, the British caused the region to remain isolated,
with its inhabitants more divided and economically underdeveloped, resulting in the retention of a medieval way of life".[14]

These developments in the nineteenth century shaped by colonial
geo-politics that decisively cast the mould for Pakistan's Afghan Policy following the retreat of the Raj from the Indian subcontinent in 1947.

Partition and Its Aftermath[15]

The retreat of the British Raj and ensuing bloody partition of the Indian subcontinent in 1947 along religious lines dramatically altered the geopolitical
landscape, giving rise to new nation-states: India and Pakistan. The latter,
founded on a religious principle, found large portions of its borders contested
with both India – pre-dominantly over Jammu and Kashmir – and Afghanistan.
Ironically with the latter, religious affiliation notwithstanding, the dispute was
ethno-political in nature. Pakistan's difficulties were confounded by the fact
that its limited resources were further strained given that prior to partition 80
per cent of the Indian army was stationed in the NWFP; however, after 1947,
the bulk of its forces had to be stationed along the Indo-Pakistan border.[16]

Afghanistan became the only member to object to Pakistan's entry into the United Nations, only to retreat a month later and become one of the first countries to establish diplomatic relations with Pakistan. However, following an air bombing raid by the Pakistan Air Force on villages on the Afghan side of the Durand Line Kabul upped the ante early on, convening a *Loya Jirga* and asserting that it "recognized neither imaginary Durand nor any similar line". Afghanistan claimed an area of 180,000 square miles from Pakistan, much of which ceded to British India under the Durand Line agreement of 1893, inhabited predominantly by Pushtuns. Pakistan was convinced of Indian abetment for the Afghan position which otherwise only found sympathy in the Communist world.[17] Pakistan's difficulties were confounded by the fact that the Muslim League (ML) had no presence in the Pashtun-dominated North West Frontier Province (NWFP), where the Indian National Congress (INC) had established a presence with the active support of Khan Abdul Ghaffar Khan's *Khudai Khidmatgar's* (Servants of God) winning 15 of the 36 seats in the 1937 elections, whereas the ML has no representation. Prior to the creation of Pakistan, the *KKs* actively advocated for integration with India or creation of an independent Pushtunistan. These developments cast a shadow on their relationship, with the Pakistani state regarding the Pushtuns as the "most potent internal security threat to the state".[18]

Kabul's belligerence was ratcheted up through vociferous propaganda by the state machinery in support of Pushtunistan coupled with localized military offenses along the Durand Line in September and October 1960 and then in May 1961 that would precipitate a crisis culminating in the closure of the border and a severing of diplomatic ties between Pakistan and Afghanistan. Kabul also sought to curry favour with Baloch separatists, providing sanctuary and training to them in Afghanistan over various phases beginning in 1948, then in the mid-1950s and finally between 1973 and 1977.[19] The secession of Pakistan's eastern wing with Indian help in 1971, inking of the Indo-Soviet Friendship treaty the same year, followed by the Soviet Union's military invasion of Afghanistan in December 1979, only served to heighten Pakistani anxieties.

Pakistan responded by seeking to harness Afghan state's weakness vis-á-vis its '*national minorities*', reaching out to them under the government of Zulfikar Ali Bhutto. Ethno-centric movements amongst the Hazaras found refuge in Quetta, Balochistan and cadres from the *Sittam-i-Milli* received arms training in Peshawar as did the Islamist opposition to Daoud Khan which he had attempted to purge by jailing or liquidating several of their leaders and sympathizers and severely limiting the number of Afghan students pursuing religious studies. In 1975 the Islamists armed and trained in Pakistan staged simultaneous uprisings in Panjshir, Herat and Laghman while the *Sittamis* opened the front in Baharak, Badakshan, all of which were crushed; but they forced Kabul to take note of the forces Islamabad could potentially wield against it.[20]

Internally Pakistan attempted to dampen the impact of irredentist propaganda emanating from Kabul, by imprisoning Bacha Khan in June 1948 and clamping down on his *KKs*. Secondly, it strove for a closer integration of its large Pashtun minority, principally by providing greater representation and visibility of Pashtuns in its army and civil services. Pashtuns composed 15.42 per cent of the population but as early as 1948 they made up 19.5 per cent of the Pakistani army – owing to the British policy of recruiting from amongst the "martial races" – and by the 1960s, 19 out of 48 senior-most military officers were Pathans. This was significant, for the army has governed Pakistan for much of its history, exemplified above all by the ascendance of Ayub Khan, a Pashtun, to the post of Commander in Chief in 1951 and subsequently as President of Pakistan in a coup in 1958. He was succeeded by yet another Pashtun General Aga Mohammad Yahya Khan (1969–1971).[21]

However, it was the Soviet military invasion of 1979 that qualitatively transformed Pakistan's Afghan engagement. Securing a US $3.2 billion package by the Reagan administration, the government of military dictator Zia-ul-Haq sought to give traction to Pakistan's strategic objectives in Afghanistan. Pakistan's notorious intelligence agency the Inter-Services Intelligence (ISI) funelled the money to seven Sunni resistance parties (five of whom were Pushtun-dominated) it recognized in Peshawar, among whom Gulbuddin Hikmatyar's *Hizb-i-Islami* had been the disproportionate benificiary of military aid and political support. This, Pakistan liked to believe, would provide it immense leverage in realzing its three key objectives: firstly, to preempt Afghan irredentia by installing a Pushtun-dominated government with an Islamist orientation that would help counter ethno-centric irredentia and bestow recognition on the Durand Line as the international border between the two countries[22]; secondly, facilitate direct access to energy-rich Central Asia; and finally, decisively pull Kabul away from New Delhi's influence and finally obtain 'strategic depth' against India.

However, Hekmatyar's failure to capture the state would frustrate these ambitions and eventually lead Rawalpindi to pivot towards the Taliban. By March 1995 the Taliban had emerged as a significant force outside its strongholds in southern Afghanistan, capturing Herat in September 1995 and Kabul in September 1996, with massive covert assistance from Pakistan – a development aptly described by William Maley as a "creeping invasion".[23] Pakistan sought to replicate the Raj's policy of manipulating internal affairs of Afghanistan, albiet in a changed geo-political environment, leading to debilitating consequences for Pakistan and the region. Foremost, Pakistan's conscious policy choices to this end helped entrench reactionary Islam in the region; an exercise begun on a monumental scale following the Soviet invasion of Afghanistan and facilitated by the legacy of British colonial rule. In 1901 the British created the NWFP which comprised the five settled districts of Peshawar, Bannu, Kohat, Hazara and Dera Ismail Khan, and five tribal districts of the Khyber agency, Kurram, Malakand agency and South and North Waziristan. The latter were governed by *riwaj* or customary practice and administered via the notorious FCR, these arrangements being retained by the Pakistani state as law of the land after 1947, coupled with the withdrawal army units from the tribal areas by late 1947. Retention of this legal and administrative vacuum of colonial vintage in a rapidly changing geo-political landscape would facilitate the transformation of the Pushtun-dominated tribal belt, as a sanctuary for spawning sectarianism within Pakistan and global *jihad* funded by the US and its allies in response to Soviet military adventurism in Afghanistan.[24]

Consider in this context of the mushrooming of Deobandi *Deeni Madrasahs* (religious seminaries) supported by state funds and *Zakat* funds from the 1980s to counter growing Shi'ii activism. By 1985 with the setting up of militant Sunni sectarian groups like the Sipah-i-Sabah Pakistan, endorsed by Zia-ul-Haq, set the stage for intensifying sectarian violence and an enmeshing of Sunni sectarian and *jihadi* groups.[25]

Secondly, Rawalpindi's policy choices, far from securing its strategic objectives, further soured relations with governments of all hues in Kabul, none of whom have recognized the Durand Line. The deep hesitation of Pakistan to recognize Afghanistan as a sovereign political entity has reinforced Kabul's drive for cultivating close relations with New Delhi, which is its fifth largest international donor and one of first capitals with whom Kabul inked a Strategic Partnership Agreement in 2011. Anxieties pertaining to the growing Indian footprint in Afghanistan continue to deeply animate the security landscape for Rawalpindi. Consider for instance rhetoric published in Pakistan military's mouthpiece:

> Since 2001, India's "influence" in Afghanistan has derived from the U.S. presence and the installation in power of its old friends in the Northern Alliance. This era will end with the U.S. withdrawal. New Delhi's next aim will be to prevent a political settlement and Taliban dominance in Kabul. While Pakistan promotes a negotiated settlement in Afghanistan, one of its urgent goals must be to eliminate – diplomatically or otherwise – the TTP and BLA terrorism sponsored by Indian intelligence from Afghanistan.[26]

Furthermore, Rawalpindi continues to seek to impinge on Kabul's political sovereignty by manipulating and seeking to inextricably link its dispute with India over Jammu and Kashmir to the outcome of political settlement to the ongoing conflict in Afghanistan. Consider for instance the brazen statement by the Pakistani ambassador to Kabul in light of an attack on Indian security forces in Kashmir, responsibility for which was claimed by the Bhawalpur based *Jaish-i-Mohammad*, one among an assortment of non-state actors cultivated by the Pakistani state: "Afghanistan peace talks would be affected if India resorts to violence against Pakistan in response to last week's attack in Kashmir", prompting a strong démarche from Kabul.[27] However these regional alignments were dramatically reconfigured with the fall of the Islamic Republic of Afghanistan to the Taliban on 15 August 2021.

These reconfigurations notwithstanding, there have been few signs of Pakistan's willingness to eschew its past policies underpinned by its strategic imperatives rooted in its somewhat dystopian past. Prime Minister Imran Khan defiantly declared the Taliban's ascent symbolizing the "breaking of the shackles of slavery" by Afghans. His Climate Minister, Zartaj Gul Wazir, went a step further, delightfully proclaiming in a now deleted tweet, "India gets an appropriate gift on its independence day . . . the Kabul regime it used to wreak terrorism in Pakistan across many years has fallen and people are rejoicing all across Afghanistan".[28] Such gleeful political rhetoric sits uncomfortably with the grim reality of reactionary Islamist groups like the *Tehrik-i-Taliban Pakistan* (TTP) seemingly poised to acquire 'reverse strategic depth' in Pakistan. As the Taliban swept through Afghanistan, one of the first acts was to free thousands of Islamist fighters and ideologues – notable among them being Faqir Mohammed, a former TTP deputy *emir* – held in high security prisons. In fact, Noor Wali Mehsud, the *emir* of the TTP, renewed his oath of allegiance to the Taliban's Islamic Emirate of Afghanistan and celebrated their "historic and blessed victory". Given the close ties between the two groups it came as little surprise that a Taliban "victory" in Afghanistan has been accompanied by a spike in violence in in Pakistan's frontier regions. For instance in the period between July and September 2021 alone, a total of 44 attacks were recorded (directed primarily at Pakistani security forces) that resulted in 73 casualties. Notably the establishment in Pakistan continues to adopt a benign approach to groups such as the TTP, manifested for instance in a month-long ceasefire inked with the proscribed organization with the help of the Taliban leadership in Afghanistan. This stands in stark contrast to the bellicose attitude adopted by the establishment in Pakistan towards the non-violent *Pushtun Tahffuz Movement*[29] (PTM, also known as the Pushtun Protection Movement). The magnitude of the challenge posed by the PTM to the Pakistani state is amplified by depth of its social reach and mobilization, penetrating the tribal areas unlike the *Khudai Khidmatgars* and thereby challenging the reactionary Islamists and their backers head on.[30] These developments underscore the "pyrrhic" nature of the Taliban's purported "victory" which as in the past will be accompanied by a spectre of growing instability and violence within Pakistan. In fact Pakistan's long-elusive goal of securing recognition of the Durand Line too is unlikely to fructify. The Taliban's spokesperson, Zabihullah Mujahid, criticized the fencing of the line, stating, "The Afghans are unhappy and are opposing the fencing". The movement's foot soldiers have been more blunt in expressing their sentiments to the press, claiming it's only a matter of time before they uproot the fence and sell it as scrap.[31]

Arguably these developments will impact the larger regional landscape and underscore some of the profound challenges India will encounter in its northwestern neighbourhood. A deep and critical engagement with the past history in New Delhi will help it in contextualizing the contemporary landscape while also providing it with dexterity as it seeks to navigate the complex geo-political tapestry.

Notes

1 Amir Abdur Rahman Khan (1900), quoted in (Dupree 1980, p. 415).
2 Summary of Conversation between Premier Zhou EnLai and Pakistan Ambassador to the PRC, Rashidi (Declassified Document 1962).
3 Prior to this the only briefly successful attempt at setting up an independent Afghan kingdom was in April 1709 by Ghilzai Pushtuns led by Mirwais Hottak who encroached upon the waning Safavid power and expanded into Persia. However by 1729 Hottak rule was in decline before being entirely vanquished by Nadir Shah Afshar by 1738.
4 (Barfield 2010, pp. 92, 97).
5 (Barfield 2010, p. 128).
6 (Fair 2014, p. 105).
7 It envisioned protection of British imperial interests by "confronting and defeating external threats before they could threaten the British Indian territory. This policy entailed pushing the boundaries of the empire as far North and North west as possible" (Fair 2014, p. 106). Thus, this policy pushed Britain to strive for tighter control over Afghanistan.
8 It called for consolidation of British rule up to the Sutlej River and exercising indirect control over Afghanistan by funneling financial and military subsidies to the Afghan rulers (Olesen 1995, p. 23).
9 (Barfield 2010, pp. 118–120).
10 (Barfield 2010, pp. 126–128, 141).
11 (Barfield 2010, pp. 138, 153–154; Olesen 1995, p. 28).
12 (Dupree 1980, pp. 426–428; Lambah 2011, p. 8).
13 NWFP comprised five settled districts: Peshawar, Banu, Kohat, Dera Ismail Khan and Hazara; and five tribal agencies: Khyber, Kurram, North and South Waziristan and Malakand.
14 (Fair 2014, pp. 109–110; Kakkar 2006, p. 188).
15 Parts of this section have been re-produced from the author's earlier publication (Sharma R., Nation, Ethnicity and the Conflict in Afghanistan: Political Islam and the Rise of Ethno-Politics, 2016).
16 (Fair 2014, p. 113) The same would hold true in the case of predominantly Bengali East Pakistan which would secede and become Bangladesh in 1971, making Pakistan the first country to break up after the Second World War.
17 Notable in this regard was the support of Afghanistan to a Soviet-sponsored resolution at the 1958 Geneva Conference for the Law of the Sea which demanded an "absolute right of transit across other countries for coastless countries". Additionally the Soviet Union came to the aid of the Afghans each time it faced an economic blockade by Pakistan on the question of Pushtunistan (Sharma 2016, p. 109).
18 (Sharma 2016, pp. 56, 86; Dupree 1980, p. 488; Fair 2014, p. 113; Siddique 2014, p. 38).
19 (Sharma 2016, p. 86); (Dupree, "Pushtunistan": The Problem and Its Larger Implications 1961, p. 4).

20 (Sharma 2016, p. 107).
21 (Sharma 2016, p. 107).
22 The then leader of opposition Benazir Bhutto had called on the Government of Pakistan to move expeditiously for a "formalization" of the Durand Line between Afghanistan and Pakistan now that "a friendly *mujahideen* government was in power in Kabul" (Frontier Post 1992).
23 (Maley 2002, p. 221).
24 (Fair 2014, pp. 109–110; Siddique 2014, pp. 35–37).
25 (Sharma 2010, pp. 41–43, 59–60).
26 (Akram n.d.). Also see (Rizvi n.d.).
27 (Tolo News 2019; Ministry of Foreign Affairs 2019). Also see (Khattak 2019).
28 (Wazir 2021; Sharma 2021).
29 Several leaders and activists of the PTM such as Ali Wazir, Mohsin Dawar and Gulalai Ismail to name a few have been incarcerated by the Pakistani state on trumped up charges. In contrast not only has the establishment in Pakistan courted groups like the TTP but more recently has also embraced others like the *Tehrik-i-Labaik Pakistan* (TLP) widely seen as a reactionary Islamist party that has engaged in violent street protests and has killed Pakistani policemen on duty (Gul 2021; International, Amnesty 2019).
30 (Hussain 2021; Johnson 2021; Ahmad 2021; Taqi 2019).
31 (Khan 2021).

Works Cited

Ahmad, M. (2021, November 09). *Pakistan Announces 1 Month Ceasefire with Pakistani Taliban*. Retrieved November 2021, from The Diplomat: https://thediplomat.com/2021/11/pakistan-announces-1-month-cease-fire-with-pakistani-taliban/

Akram, M. (n.d.). *Afghanistan's Rocky Road to Peace*. Retrieved February 2019, from Hilal: The Pakistan Armed Forces Magazine: www.hilal.gov.pk/eng-article/afghanistan's-rocky-road-to-peace/MjQ5OQ==.html

Barfield, T. (2010). *Afghanistan: A Cultural and Political History*. Princeton, NJ: Princeton University Press.

Declassified Document. (1962, March 06). *Wilson Centre, Digital Archive: International History Declassified*. Retrieved January 2019, from Wilson Centre: https://digitalarchive.wilsoncenter.org/document/121570.pdf?v=770f07ac805899ceceb28538d937210c

Dupree, L. (1961). *"Pushtunistan": The Problem and Its Larger Implications*. Kabul: American Universities Field Staff.

Dupree, L. (1980). *Afganistan*. Princeton, NJ: Princeton University Press.

Fair, C. C. (2014). *Fighting to the End: The Pakistan Army's Way of War*. Delhi, India: Oxford University Press.

Gul, A. (2021, November 08). *Pakistan – TTP Militants Agree on "Complete Ceasefire"*. Retrieved November 2021, from Voice of America: www.voanews.com/a/pakistan-ttp-militants-agree-on-complete-cease-fire-/6304928.html

Hussain, A. (2021, October 13). *Violence Surges in Pakistan's Tribal Belt as Taliban, IS-K Go on Attack*. Retrieved November 2021, from BBC News: www.bbc.com/news/world-asia-58891613

International, Amnesty. (2019, February 06). *Pakistan: End Crackdown on PTM and Release Protestors*. Retrieved November 2021, from Amnesty International: www.amnesty.org/en/latest/news/2019/02/pakistan-end-crackdown-on-ptm-and-release-protestors/

Johnson, T. (2021, August 19). *Pakistani Taliban's Emir Renews Oath of Allegiance to Afghan Taliban*. Retrieved November 2021, from The Long War Journal: www.

longwarjournal.org/archives/2021/08/pakistani-talibans-emir-renews-allegiance-to-afghan-taliban.php

Kakkar, M. H. (2006). *A Political and Diplomatic History of Afghanistan: 1863–1901.* Leiden: Brill's Inner Asian Library.

Khan, O. F. (2021, August 31). *Taliban Consider Governance Models, Oppose Pakistan Fence on: Read More at: http://timesofindia.indiatimes.com/articleshow/85779590.cms?utm_source=contentofinterest&utm_medium=text&utm_campaign=cppst.* Retrieved November 2021, from The Times of India: https://timesofindia.indiatimes.com/world/south-asia/taliban-consider-governance-models-oppose-pakistan-fence-on-durand-line/articleshow/85779590.cms

Khattak, T. M. (2019). *Changing Kaleidoscope in Afghanistan.* Retrieved February 2019, from Hilal: The Pakistan Armed Forces Magazine: www.hilal.gov.pk/eng-article/changing-kaleidoscope-in-afghanistan/Mjc2Nw==.html

Lambah, S. K. (2011). *The Durand Line.* New Delhi: Aspen Institute India.

Maley, W. (2002). *The Afghanistan Wars.* New York: Palgrave MacMillan.

Ministry of Foreign Affairs. (2019, February 20). *Foreign Ministry Statement Regarding Pakistani Ambassador's Recent Remarks.* Retrieved February 2019, from Ministry of Foreign Affairs, Islamic Republic of Afghanistan: www.mfa.gov.af/press-releases/745-foreign-ministry-statement-regarding-pakistani-ambassador-s-recent-remarks.html

Olesen, A. (1995). *Islam and Politics in Afghanistan.* Great Britain: Curzon Press.

Rizvi, H. A. (n.d.). *Pakistan's Security Challenges in the Next Decade (2015–2025).* Retrieved February 2019, from Hilal: The Pakistan Armed Forces Magazine: www.hilal.gov.pk/eng-article/pakistan's-security-challenges-in-the-next-dec-ade-(2015-2025)/MTU0NA==.html

Saljouki, M. S. (1992). *Pakhtoonistan Now a Tale of Past.* Islamabad, Pakistan: Frontier Post, 09 May 1992.

Sharma, K. (2021, August 16). *Taliban Has "Broken Shackles of Slavery", Says Pak PM Imran Khan.* Retrieved November 2021, from NDTV: www.ndtv.com/world-news/taliban-has-broken-shackles-of-slavery-says-pak-pm-imran-khan-2511573

Sharma, R. (2010). Secterian Violence in Pakistan. In D. S. Chari (ed.), *Armed Conflicts in South Asia 2009: Continuing Violence, Failing Peace Processes.* New Delhi: Routledge.

Sharma, R. (2016). *Nation, Ethnicity and the Conflict in Afghanistan: Political Islam and the Rise of Ethno-Politics.* London, UK: Routledge.

Siddique, A. B. (2014). *The Pushtun Question: The Unresolved Key to the Future of Pakistan and Afghanistan.* London, UK: Hurst and Company.

Taqi, M. (2019, June 02). *What's Next for Pakistan's Pashtun Movement after a Brutal Army Crackdown.* Retrieved November 2021, from The Wire: https://thewire.in/south-asia/pakistan-army-pashtun-tahaffuz-movement-fata

Tolo News. (2019, February 20). *Kabul Asks Pakistan to Act on Its Committments.* Retrieved 2019 February, from Tolo News: www.tolonews.com/index.php/afghanistan/kabul-asks-pakistan-act-its-commitments

Wazir, Z. G. (2021, August 15). Retrieved October 2021, from Twitter: Pakistan's Minister for Climate: https://twitter.com/zartajgulwazir?ref_src=twsrc%5Etfw@zartajgulwazir, having a normal one – celebrating the fall of Kabul. And she's not the on.

INDEX

Abdullah, Abdullah 64
Acharya, Amitav 120
adaptive peace 41
Afghanistan: after 9/11 terrorist attack
    18–19; attention and interest of great
    powers 125–127; borders 15; as a
    buffer state 11; China's policy toward
    9; conflict in 66; developments in 24;
    economy of 20; ethnic composition
    and cross-border ethnic ties 126;
    ethnic groups 15; geopolitical location
    127; Ghani regime 21, 24, 70, 75;
    under globalisation 7; globalisation of
    12–14; as graveyard of empires 126;
    Hussein regime 19; invasion by Red
    Army 102; issues related to ethnicity,
    nationality, tribalism, and borders
    14; Jihad against communist presence
    in 17; Karzai regime 19; multi-scalar
    disputes in 64; nation-building in
    66; official languages 15; opium
    industry and poppy cultivation
    20, 25; political instability and
    violence in 24; political Islam 102;
    political transition 16; reconstruction
    project 21; relations with major
    powers 7; sharing of power in 21;
    as Soviet Union's 'Vietnam' 114,
    126; state-building in 8; strategies
    of imperial control 146–148; USA's
    policy in 8; see also peace processes in
    Afghanistan

Afghan National Defense and Security
    Forces (ANDSF) 4
Afghan National Security Forces
    (ANSF) 19
Afghan refugees 18, 24, 25n1
Ahl-e Hal-o Aqd Council 95
Akhundzada, Hibatullah 55, 61
Akhundzada, Muhammad
    Habaitullah 72
alliance hubs 30
Al-Qaeda 5, 12, 13, 17, 18, 22, 53, 59,
    65, 115, 118, 119; alliances 18
Al-Qaeda in the Indian Subcontinent
    (AQIS) 66
Al Samood 57
Al Shabaab 13, 48
Ameerul Mu'mineen 54, 58,
    60–61, 61n2
Amin, Hafizullah 16, 98
Amir of Muslims 101
Anglo-Afghan wars (1838 and 1878)
    15, 146, 147
anti-immigration policy 14
apartheid regimes 17
asabiyya 34
Atatürk, Kemal 96
aterritorial and non-state phenomenon 66

Bacon, T. 30
Baradar, Mullah 40
Belt Road Initiative (BRI) 22, 124,
    138–139

Bhutto, Zulfikar Ali 149
Bonn conference of December 2001 4
Brexit of 2016 14
Brzezinski, Zbigniew 114
Bush, George W 18, 117

Camp David 74
capitalism 12, 13; movements against 13
Central Asian Republics 13–14
Central Asia Petroleum and Gas
    Company (CAPEIC) 22
Cheney, Dick 117
China–Afghanistan relations 9,
    124–125, 127–131; Belt Road
    Initiative (BRI) 22, 124, 138–139; in
    context of great power politics 127;
    humanitarian aid 141; Marshall Plan
    138; Memorandum of Understanding
    (MoU) 139; post September 2001
    terror attacks 134–138; post US exit
    139–141; resource extraction 141; in
    Xinjiang 124–125, 131–134
China Pakistan Economic Corridor
    (CPEC) 22, 72, 128, 131, 138
Chinese National Petroleum Company
    (CNPC) 22
closed border policy 146
Cold War 11, 13
Cold War phase (1945-90) 16
9/11 Commission Report 113, 117
Costs of War Project 118
Cyrus the Great 15

Dadullah, Mansur 36
Daesh 32, 41n2
Daoud, Mohammad 16
Darul Uloom Haqqaniyyah 103
Defensive Jihad 36
Democratic Republic of Afghanistan
    (DRC) 16
Deobandi *Deeni Madrasahs* (religious
    seminaries) 151
dictatorial regimes 16–17
Doha Agreement 59, 65, 74–76, 76n1
Doha dialogue, 2020 21
drug industry in Afghanistan 20
Durand, Mortimer 15
Durand Line 15–16, 126, 148, 149, 150

Eastern Europe: ethno-nationalism in 14
East Turkestan Independence Movement
    (ETIM) 22
emerging governscapes 40
ethno-nationalism 14

external powers, role in Afghanistan
    21–24; China 22–23; India 23–24; Iran
    24; Pakistan 22–23; Russia 24; Saudi
    Arabia 24; Turkey 24; USA 21–22

Farrell, T. 54
Fasihuddin, Qari 96
first absolute states 82
fixed and rigid borders 34–35
fluid frontiers 34–35
forward policy 146
France 14
Frontier Crimes Regulation (FCR) 148
Fukuyama, Francis 109

Germany 14
Ghani, Ashraf 4, 12, 20, 68, 69, 70, 73,
    75, 124, 140
Gilpin, Robert 115–116
Giustozzi, A. 54
globalisation: forms of capitalism
    and 12–13; relevance to
    Afghanistan 12–14
global jihadism 38
global war on terror (GWOT) 66
Gopal, A. 60
gray zone 34
Great Game 15
Guistozzi, A. 38, 39

Hanafi, Qari Abdul Salam 96
Hanafis 34
Hanif, Qari Din Mohammad 96
Hanifa, Abu 34, 41n4
Haqqani, Abdul Hakim 48, 55, 57
Haqqani, Sirajuddin 40, 103
Haqqanis 39
Harakat-ul-Mujahideen (HuM) 115
Hazaras 41
Heart of Asia Conference-Istanbul
    Process (HoA) 24, 69
Hekmatyar, Gulbuddin 70, 95
High Council of Islamic Emirate 36
Hikmatyar, Gulbuddin 150
Hintze, Otto 83
Horowitz, M.C. 30
Human Terrain Teams 39
Huntington, Samuel P. 117
Hussain, Zahid 73
Hussein, Saddam 19

ideology, idea of 52
imperial control in Afghanistan
    146–148

India: "influence" in Afghanistan 23–24, 151–153; partition and aftermath 148–153
Indian Council of World Affairs (ICWA) 9
Indo-Soviet Friendship treaty 149
in-progress intra-Afghan dialogue 65, 74, 140
International Security Assistance Forces (ISAF) 19
intra-Afghan dialogue 64
Iran 24
Iraq war 118–119, 120
Ishaqzais 36
ISIS 56
Islamic Brotherhood 59
Islamic Emirate of Afghanistan (IEA) 47, 55, 58, 59, 61n1
Islamic Movement of Uzbekistan 115
Islamic radicalism 17
Islamic revolution 17
Islamic Revolutionary Guard Corps (IRGC) 39
Islamic State (IS) 66
Islamic State-Khorasan (IS-K): central and regional affiliate 33; Kabul cell 37; resurgence 36–37; Salafi-jihadist interpretation of Islam 34; strategies of 37; strength of advisors and trainers 38–39; survivability 38–39, utilization of historicity of Hijrah 39
Islamic State-Khorasan (IS-K)–Taliban conflict-cooperation continuum 7, 29; clashes 35; cooperation 36; counteroffensives 35; fluid frontiers *vs* fixed and rigid borders 34–35; high-end and low-end relationships 30; impact on dynamics of various rebel groups 30; nationalism and Salafism 34; for organizational needs 30; for sense of empowerment 30; shared identity characteristics 30; shared ideological goals 29; survival as a fundamental motivator 29; for tactical or strategic purposes 30–31; transnational affiliates 30–31; trust 30
Islamic State's conception of territoriality 34–35
Islamophobia 14

Jabhat al-Nusra 35
Jadoon, A. 30, 38
Jaish-e Mohammed (JeM) 18, 23, 115, 151
Jalalabad prison break, 2020 37

Jamad-Ul Dawa (JuD) 18
Jamat-e Islami 22
Jamat-ul-Dawa 22
Jamiat-e-Islami 95
Jamia Uloom Islamic School 103
jihadist groups 28–29; Provincial Reconstruction Teams (PRT) 28
Juergensmeyer, M. 56–57
Juergensmeyer, Mark 47

Kadercan, B. 34–35
Kalakani, Habibullah 97, 101
Kant, Immanuel 52
Karmel, Babrak 98–99
Karzai, Hamid 4, 19, 20, 124
Kashmir issue 15–16, 17
Khalilzad, Zalmay 74, 100, 139
Khan, Abdul Ghaffar Khan 149
Khan, Abdur Rehman 147
Khan, Amanullah 96, 101
Khan, Amir Abdur Rehaman 15
Khan, Ayub 150
Khan, Bacha 150
Khan, Imran 152
Khan, Nadir 97
Khan, Sardar Dawood 97–98
'Khorasan' movement 32–33
Khudai Khidmatgars 152
Khyber Pakhtunkhwa 15
Kipling, Rudyard 125
Kuehn, F. 53

Laden, Osama bin 5, 12, 17, 58
Lashkar e-Taiba (LeT) 18, 115
Lehman Brothers collapse 119
Lewis, Bernard 117
Loya Jirga 75
Ludhianvi, Mufti 60
Lugo, L. 56

Maley, William 150
Malkasian, C. 54
Mansour, Mullah Akhtar 70
Marshall Plan 66
Massoud, Ahmad Shah 115
Maududi 102
Moghadam, A. 30
Mojaddedi, Sibghatullah 95
Moscow-Format 71–73
Moscow-Format (2016–18) 64
Muhammad, Dost 147
Mujahid, Zabihullah 100, 152
Mujahidin (Ahl-e Hal-o Aqd) Council 95

Murree Process (2015) 64, 65, 67–69, 76; Chinese involvement in 68–69; regional and international state actors 68; rift between Quetta and Doha offices 68
Muslim League (ML) 149
Mutawakkil, Mullah Wakil Ahmad 60
Muttaqi, Amir Khan 57

nationalism 34
NATO 22, 24–25
negotiations 64–65
New Cold War 17
North Atlantic Treaty Organization (NATO) 12, 126
Northern Alliance 19, 115
North West Frontier Province (NWFP) 148, 149

Omar, Mullah 20, 68, 115
Operation Enduring Freedom 118, 126
Osman, B. 37, 60

Pakistan 16, 71, 149, 151; Inter-Services Intelligence (ISI) 5, 17, 40, 68, 150; poppy cultivation 18; problem of refugees 18; support for Taliban regime 18; Zia regime (1978-1986) 17
Pashtuns 95, 121; Durand Line and 15–16
peace concept 28
peace processes in Afghanistan 64; Doha Agreement 65, 74–76, 76n1; in-progress intra-Afghan dialogue 65, 74, 76; Moscow-Format 71–73; Murree Process (2015) 64, 67–69, 76; Quadrilateral Coordination Group on Afghanistan (QCG 2017) 64, 69–70
Pearl Harbor attack, 1945 65
People's Democratic Party 98–99, 102
People's Democratic Party of Afghanistan (PDPA) 16
Phillips, B.J. 30
Plichka, Viktor Petrovich 99
Podder, S. 40
political Islam movement 102
Potter, B.K. 30
pragmatic peace 40; advocacy of 40
Pulwama attack, 2019 23
Pushtuns 146, 150
Pushtun Tahffuz Movement29 (PTM) 152

Quadrilateral Coordination Group on Afghanistan (QCG 2017) 8, 64, 69–70; HoA-Istanbul Process 69–70; objective 69; state actors 69

Rabbani, Burhanuddin 95
Rafi, Habibullah 96
Rawalpindi Treaty of 1919 15
religious worldview of Taliban 47–48; concept of Ummah 58–59; emphasis on the Ulema 55; epistemic worldview 51–53; in the field of international relations 48–51; for goal attainment 55; obeying the Amir 60–61; principles of Shariah law 57–58, 59; religious justification and divine ordainment 59–60; sociotheological approach 51–52; theme of divine sovereignty 57–58
Riedel, Bruce 76
Russia-China-Pakistan trilateral discussions 71
Russia-Ukraine war 110
Ruttig, Thomas 70

Safavids 145
Salafi Jihadism 56
Salafism 34, 38
Saudi Arabia 24
Second World War 85
Seyyed Qutb 102
Shah, Mohammad Zahir 16
Shah, Nadir 15, 146
Shamali Khilafat 35
Shanghai Cooperation Organization 58
Sheikh, M. K. 56
Sheikh, Mona Kanwal 47
Silk Road Economic Belt 138, 139
Singh, Ranjit 146
Sino-Afghan relations 9
Sirat, Abdul Sattar 4
South Asian Association for Regional Cooperation (SAARC) 13
Soviet intervention in Afghanistan 16–17
Soviet military intervention in Afghanistan 4, 11
Soviet Union 109; ideas associated with *glasnost* and *perestroika* 17; withdrawal of troops from Afghanistan 17
Soviet Union, disintegration of 21
state building in Europe: as an offspring of economic and social changes 84;

church and clergy 84–85; in creating boundaries 85; stage of evolution 85; war as driving indicator 83
state building process in Afghanistan 81–82; as an offspring of economic and social changes 84; creation of legislative institutions, executive institutions and judicial affairs 82; Doha Agreement and 93; external or international factor 82, 96–99; feudalism and 84; history 86–89; important indicators 82; issue of ethnicity 95–96; Mujahidin government 90; under Najib's Presidency 99–100; for regulation of tax affairs 84; role of clergy 84–85; rule of order 82; rules and cause of state collapse 94; as a social and political concept 82; stage of evolution 85; under Taliban government 90–91, 100–104; 9/11 terrorist attack 91–92; war as driving indicator 83
Stenersen, A. 57
Stepanova, Ekaterina 71
Stepputat, F. 40
Strategic Partnership Agreement, 2011 151

Takfir 38, 41n5
Taliban 41, 65, 115; association with Al Qaeda 5; attitude towards women 3, 6, 39–40, 121; ban on women's education 39–40; capture of Kabul 100–101; closeness with terrorist groups 6; counteroffensive 35; criticisms of 95–96; dealing with Iran and IRGC 39, 41n6; diplomatic skills 8; distinction between 'conciliatory' and 'irreconcilable' 70; on Ghani regime 4; identity 53–54; internal schisms 36; interpretation of Sharia 6; *modus operandi* of 3; networking with Islamic radicals 5; notion of state 8; policies and engagement with world 8; post-2021 3; primacy of the 'political' 39–40; retreat in 2015 35; support from Pakistan 6; 9/11 terrorist attack 5; title of martyrdom or "suicide" 103; understanding 55–61; violent actions 56; *see also* religious worldview of Taliban
Taliban 2.0 6 120
Taliban-China deal 141

Taraki, Nur Mahammad 16, 98
Tehrik-i-Taliban Pakistan (TTP) 152
Terpstra, N. 54
9/11 terrorist attack 5, 11–12, 65, 81, 120
9/11 terrorist attacks 117
Third World 14
Tilly (1990) 83
Trans-Pacific Partnership 14
Treaty of Gandamak, 1879 147
Trump, Donald 14, 71, 74, 100, 139
Turkey, role in Afghanistan 24
Turkmenistan, Afghanistan, Pakistan, and India (TAPI) 24

Ummah (Muslim community) 58–59
United Nations Security Council Resolution No. 1386 19
US-Iraq war of 1991 17
US/USA, role in Afghanistan 3–4, 17, 109–110, 140; Bilateral Security Agreement (BSA) 21–22; cost of military and economic engagement in Afghanistan 5; elimination of Osama bin Laden 5; international military operation 4–5, 65–67; neo-conservative position 117; peace deal agreement with Taliban 4; post-Cold War 110–113; President Obama's Afghanistan policy 119–120; support to Afghan Mujahedeen 4–5; terrorist attacks 4–5; withdrawal from Afghanistan 28, 101, 120–121
Uyghurs 22

Van Linschoten, A. S. 53

Wallerstein, Immanuel 84
war on terror 117–119
weapons of mass destruction (WMD) 118, 119
World Islamic Front, 1998 18
World Trade Organization (WTO) 13

Yaqub, Mullah Mohammad 40, 103

Zabihullah 57
Zain, F. Omar 116
Zakaria, Fareed 119
Zaraj-Delaram Highway 23
Zawahiri 58
Zia-ul-Haq 150, 151